P9-AFJ-435

3

MATH Trailblazers®

A BALANCED MATHEMATICS PROGRAM INTEGRATING SCIENCE AND LANGUAGE ARTS

Facts Resource Guide

×	0	1	2	3	4	5	6	7	8	9	10
0	0	0	0	0	0	0	0	0	0	0	0
1	0	1	2	3	4	5	6	7	8	9	10
2	0	2	4	6	8	10	12	14	16	18	20
3	0	3	6	9	12	15	18	21	24	27	30
4	0	4	8	12	16	20	24	28	32	36	40
5	0	5	10	15	20	25	30	35	40	45	50
6	0	6	12	18	24	30	36	42	48	54	60
7	0	7	14	21	28	35	42	49	56	63	70
8	0	8	16	24	32	40	48	56	64	72	80
9	0	9	18	27	36	45	54	63	72	81	90
10	0	10	20	30	40	50	60	70	80	90	100

THIRD EDITION

KENDALL/HUNT PUBLISHING COMPANY
4050 Westmark Drive   Dubuque, Iowa 52002

A TIMS® Curriculum
University of Illinois at Chicago

UIC The University of Illinois
at Chicago

The original edition was based on work supported by the National Science Foundation under grant No. MDR 9050226 and the University of Illinois at Chicago. Any opinions, findings, and conclusions or recommendations expressed in this publication are those of the author(s) and do not necessarily reflect the views of the granting agencies.

Copyright © 2004, 2008 by Kendall/Hunt Publishing Company

ISBN 978-0-7575-3515-4

All rights reserved. No part of this publication may be reproduced, stored in a retrieval system, or transmitted, in any form or by any means, electronic, mechanical, photocopying, recording, or otherwise, without the prior written permission of the copyright owner. Permission is granted to the purchaser to reproduce each blackline master in quantities suitable for non-commercial classroom use.

Printed in the United States of America

1 2 3 4 5 6 7 8 9 10   11 10 09 08 07

Grade 3 Acknowledgments

Teaching Integrated Mathematics and Science (TIMS) Project Directors
Philip Wagreich, Principal Investigator
Joan L. Bieler
Howard Goldberg (emeritus)
Catherine Randall Kelso

Director
Third Edition   Joan L. Bieler

Curriculum Developers
Third Edition   Lindy M. Chambers-Boucher   Philip Wagreich
                               Janet Simpson Beissinger

Contributors
Third Edition   Eileen Wynn Ball   Sandy Niemiera
                               Jenny Bay-Williams   Christina Nugent
                               Ava Chatterjee-Belisle   Janet M. Parsons
                               Elizabeth Colligan   Leona Peters
                               Marty Gartzman   Catherine Reed
                               Carol Inzerillo

Editorial and Production Staff
Third Edition   Kathleen R. Anderson   Christina Clemons
                               Lindy M. Chambers-Boucher   Anne Roby

TIMS Professional Developers
                               Barbara Crum   Cheryl Kneubuhler
                               Catherine Ditto   Lisa Mackey
                               Pamela Guyton   Linda Miceli

TIMS Director of Media Services
                               Henrique Cirne-Lima

TIMS Research Staff
                               Stacy Brown   Catherine Ditto
                               Reality Canty   Kathleen Pitvorec
                               Alison Castro   Catherine Randall Kelso

TIMS Administrative Staff
                               Eve Ali Boles   Enrique Puente
                               Kathleen R. Anderson   Alice VanSlyke
                               Nida Khan

Director
Second Edition   Catherine Randall Kelso

Curriculum Developers

Second Edition

Lindy M. Chambers-Boucher   Jennifer Mundt Leimberer
Elizabeth Colligan   Georganne E. Marsh
Marty Gartzman   Leona Peters
Carol Inzerillo   Philip Wagreich
Catherine Randall Kelso

Editorial and Production Staff

Second Edition

Kathleen R. Anderson   Georganne E. Marsh
Ai-Ai C. Cojuangco   Cosmina Menghes
Andrada Costoiu   Anne Roby
Erika Larsen

Principal Investigators

First Edition   Philip Wagreich   Howard Goldberg

Senior Curriculum Developers

First Edition

Janet Simpson Beissinger   Carol Inzerillo
Joan L. Bieler   Andy Isaacs
Astrida Cirulis   Catherine Randall Kelso
Marty Gartzman   Leona Peters
Howard Goldberg   Philip Wagreich

Curriculum Developers

First Edition

Janice C. Banasiak   Jenny Knight
Lynne Beauprez   Sandy Niemiera
Andy Carter   Janice Ozima
Lindy M. Chambers-Boucher   Polly Tangora
Kathryn Chval   Paul Trafton
Diane Czerwinski

Illustrator

First Edition   Kris Dresen

Editorial and Production Staff

First Edition

Glenda L. Genio-Terrado   Sarah Nelson
Mini Joseph   Birute Petrauskas
Lynette Morgenthaler   Anne Roby

Research Consultant

First Edition   Andy Isaacs

Mathematics Education Consultant

First Edition   Paul Trafton

National Advisory Committee

First Edition

Carl Berger   Mary Lindquist
Tom Berger   Eugene Maier
Hugh Burkhart   Lourdes Monteagudo
Donald Chambers   Elizabeth Phillips
Naomi Fisher   Thomas Post
Glenda Lappan

Grade 3 | # Table of Contents

Math Trailblazers® includes a comprehensive, research-based program for teaching basic math facts. This program is carefully integrated into the lessons and Daily Practice and Problems (DPP) of each grade and the Home Practice in Grades 3–5. The *Grade 3 Facts Resource Guide* is a compilation of much of the math facts materials for third grade. These include math facts lessons, relevant DPP items, Home Practice parts, flash cards, *Facts I Know* charts, the TIMS Tutor: *Math Facts,* and information for parents about *Math Trailblazers* math facts philosophy.

Classrooms that stay close to the suggested pacing schedule for teaching lessons will have little difficulty implementing the complete math facts program without the use of this guide. In those classrooms, teachers can simply use the math facts materials that are built into the lessons, Daily Practice and Problems, and Home Practice. However, because the math facts program is closely linked to the recommended schedule for teaching lessons, classrooms that differ significantly from the suggested pacing of units will need to make special accommodations to ensure that students receive a consistent program of math facts practice and assessment throughout the year. This manual will assist teachers with that process. (A pacing schedule can be found in the Grade 3 Overview section in the *Teacher Implementation Guide.*

All materials included in the *Grade 3 Facts Resource Guide* are located elsewhere in *Math Trailblazers.* Wherever appropriate, we will include a reference to an item's location in other *Math Trailblazers* components.

A major goal of *Math Trailblazers* is to prepare students to compute accurately, flexibly, and appropriately in all situations. Standard topics in arithmetic—acquisition of basic math facts and fluency with whole-number operations—are covered extensively.

In developing our program for the math facts, we sought a careful balance between strategies and drill. This approach is based on a large body of research and advocated by the National Council of Teachers of Mathematics (NCTM) *Principles and Standards for School Mathematics* and by the National Research Council in *Adding It Up: Helping Children Learn Mathematics.* The research indicates that the methods used in the *Math Trailblazers* math facts program lead to more effective learning and better retention of the math facts and also help develop essential math skills.

For a detailed discussion of the math facts program in *Math Trailblazers,* see Section 3 TIMS Tutor: *Math Facts.* See also Section 2 *Information for Parents: Math Facts Philosophy.*

What Is the *Math Trailblazers Facts Resource Guide?*

Introduction to the Math Facts in *Math Trailblazers*

The following table describes the development of math facts and whole number operations in *Math Trailblazers*. The shaded portions of the table highlight development of the math facts program in each grade. Expectations for fluency with math facts are indicated in bold. The white portions of the table highlight development of the whole-number operations.

Grade	Addition	Subtraction	Multiplication	Division
K	Introduce concepts through problem solving and use of manipulatives.			
1	Develop strategies for addition facts.	Develop strategies for subtraction facts.	Develop concepts through problem solving and use of manipulatives.	
	Solve addition problems in context.	Solve subtraction problems in context.		
2	Continue use of addition facts in problems. Continue use of strategies for addition facts. **Assess for fluency with addition facts.**	Continue use of subtraction facts in problems. Continue use of strategies for subtraction facts. **Assess for fluency with subtraction facts.**	Continue concept development through problem solving and use of manipulatives.	
	Continue solving addition problems in context. Introduce procedures for multidigit addition using manipulatives and paper and pencil.	Continue solving subtraction problems in context. Introduce procedures for multidigit subtraction using manipulatives and paper and pencil.		
3	Diagnose and remediate with addition facts as needed.	Maintain fluency with subtraction facts through review and assessment.	Continue use of multiplication facts in problems. Develop strategies for multiplication facts. **Assess for fluency with multiplication facts.**	Continue use of division facts in problems. Develop strategies for division facts.
	Develop procedures for multidigit addition using manipulatives and paper and pencil. Practice and apply multidigit addition in varied contexts.	Develop procedures for multidigit subtraction using manipulatives and paper and pencil. Practice and apply multidigit subtraction in varied contexts.	Solve multiplication problems in context. Introduce paper-and-pencil multiplication (1-digit × 2-digits).	Continue concept development. Solve division problems in context.
4	Diagnose and remediate with addition facts as needed.	Diagnose and remediate with subtraction facts as needed.	Maintain fluency with multiplication facts through review and assessment.	Continue use of division facts in problems. Continue development of strategies for division facts. **Assess for fluency with division facts.**
	Practice and apply multidigit addition in varied contexts. Review paper-and-pencil procedures for multidigit addition.	Practice and apply multidigit subtraction in varied contexts. Review paper-and-pencil procedures for multidigit subtraction.	Develop procedures for multiplication using manipulatives and paper and pencil (1-digit and 2-digit multipliers). Practice and apply multiplication in varied contexts.	Solve division problems in context. Develop procedures for division using manipulatives and paper and pencil (1-digit divisors).
5	Diagnose and remediate with addition facts as needed.	Diagnose and remediate with subtraction facts as needed.	Maintain fluency with multiplication facts through review and assessment.	Maintain fluency with division facts through review and assessment.
	Practice and apply multidigit addition in varied contexts.	Practice and apply multidigit subtraction in varied contexts.	Review paper-and-pencil procedures. Practice and apply multiplication in varied contexts.	Develop paper-and-pencil procedures (1-digit and 2-digit divisors). Practice and apply division in varied contexts.

Table 1: *Math Facts and Whole-Number Operations Overview*

Most work with math facts in Grade 3 focuses on reviewing, practicing, and assessing the subtraction and multiplication facts. The Addition Math Facts Review in Section 8 provides practice for students who require further work with the addition math facts. Students can use the suggested activities, games, and flash cards at home with family members. Distribute this work over time, rather than giving it all at once. While using the supplemental material in the Addition Math Facts Review, students should continue with the rest of the class reviewing and practicing the subtraction and multiplication facts in the DPP, Home Practice, and other lessons. They can use strategies and manipulatives as they solve problems in class or at home.

Practice and Assessment of the Subtraction and Multiplication Facts

A systematic, strategies-based review of the subtraction facts begins in Unit 2 and continues through Unit 10. Students develop strategies for the multiplication facts in Units 3–10. In Units 11–20, students concentrate on the practice and assessment of the multiplication facts. See Table 2 for the sequence in which the facts will be reviewed and assessed. For a detailed explanation of our approach to learning and assessing the facts, see the TIMS Tutor: *Math Facts* in Section 3 of this book or in the *Teacher Implementation Guide*.

Unit	Review and Assessment of the Math Facts Groups
1	Review addition facts
2	Review subtraction facts in Groups 1 and 2 (12 − 9, 12 − 10, 13 − 9, 13 − 10, 13 − 4, 15 − 9, 15 − 10, 15 − 6, 19 − 10, 14 − 10, 14 − 9, 14 − 5, 17 − 10, 17 − 9, 11 − 9, 16 − 9, 16 − 7, 16 − 10)
3	Review subtraction facts in Groups 3 and 4 (10 − 4, 9 − 4, 11 − 4, 10 − 8, 11 − 8, 9 − 5, 10 − 6, 11 − 6, 11 − 5, 10 − 7, 9 − 7, 11 − 7, 10 − 2, 9 − 2, 9 − 3, 10 − 3, 11 − 3, 9 − 6) Develop strategies for the multiplication facts for the 5s and 10s
4	Review subtraction facts in Groups 5 and 6 (7 − 3, 7 − 5, 7 − 2, 11 − 2, 8 − 6, 5 − 3, 8 − 2, 4 − 2, 5 − 2, 6 − 4, 6 − 2, 13 − 5, 8 − 5, 8 − 3, 13 − 8, 12 − 8, 12 − 4, 12 − 3) Develop strategies for the multiplication facts for the 2s and 3s
5	Review subtraction facts in Groups 7 and 8 (14 − 7, 14 − 6, 14 − 8, 12 − 6, 12 − 7, 12 − 5, 10 − 5, 13 − 7, 13 − 6, 15 − 7, 16 − 8, 17 − 8, 18 − 9, 18 − 10, 8 − 4, 7 − 4, 6 − 3, 15 − 8) Develop strategies for the multiplication facts for the square numbers
6	Develop strategies for the multiplication facts for the 9s
7	Review and assess the subtraction facts in Groups 1 and 2 Develop strategies for the last six multiplication facts (4 × 6, 4 × 7, 4 × 8, 6 × 7, 6 × 8, 7 × 8)
8	Review and assess the subtraction facts in Groups 3 and 4 Develop strategies for the multiplication facts for the 2s, 5s, and 10s
9	Review and assess the subtraction facts in Groups 5 and 6 Develop strategies for the multiplication facts for the 3s, 9s, and square numbers

(continued next page)

Table 2: *Math Facts Groups*

Unit	Review and Assessment of the Math Facts Groups *(continued)*
10	Review and assess the subtraction facts in Groups 7 and 8 Subtraction Facts Inventory Develop strategies for the last six multiplication facts (4×6, 4×7, 4×8, 6×7, 6×8, 7×8)
11	Practice and assess the multiplication facts for the 5s and 10s
12	Practice and assess the multiplication facts for the 2s and 3s
13	Practice and assess the multiplication facts for the square numbers
14	Practice and assess the multiplication facts for the 9s
15	Practice and assess the last six multiplication facts (4×6, 4×7, 4×8, 6×7, 6×8, 7×8)
16	Practice and assess the multiplication facts for the 2s, 5s, and 10s
17	Practice and assess the multiplication facts for the 3s and 9s
18	Practice and assess the multiplication facts for the square numbers
19	Practice and assess the last six multiplication facts (4×6, 4×7, 4×8, 6×7, 6×8, 7×8)
20	Multiplication Facts Inventory

(continued from previous page)

Table 2: *Math Facts Groups*

Launching the Study of the Subtraction and Multiplication Facts. Unit 2 Lesson 5 *Subtraction Facts Strategies* sets up the subtraction math facts strand in Grade 3. Students learn to use the flash cards to study and self-assess the subtraction facts in Unit 2 Lesson 7 *Assessing the Subtraction Facts.* Students continue to practice the subtraction facts in small groups in Units 2–10 by completing various DPP items.

Students begin their study of the multiplication facts in Units 3–10. They use strategies to solve multiplication facts in lessons, DPP items, and Home Practice parts. Beginning in Unit 11 Lesson 4 *Completing the Table* students concentrate on studying the multiplication facts. Students use *Triangle Flash Cards* and DPP items to practice the multiplication facts in small groups in Units 11–20.

Sorting Flash Cards. When each fact group is introduced in the DPP, students are asked to practice the facts with a partner using flash cards. Students sort the cards into three piles: those they know and can answer quickly, those they can figure out with a strategy, and those they need to learn. After sorting the flash cards, students should discuss the strategies they used to find the differences or products. Students circle those facts they know quickly on their *Subtraction* or *Multiplication Facts I Know* charts.

Quizzes and Inventory Tests. To assess students on each group of facts, short quizzes are offered regularly in the DPP. The short quizzes are less threatening to students and are as effective as longer tests, so we strongly recommend against weekly testing of 60 to 100 facts. Unit 10 includes an inventory test for the subtraction facts while Unit 20 includes an inventory test for the multiplication facts.

As indicated above, the *Math Trailblazers* program for teaching math facts in Grade 3 is based on a distributed study of the facts, located largely in the DPP and Home Practice for each unit. The orderly distribution of the facts will be disrupted if the pacing of the program is altered from the recommended schedule. The *Grade 3 Facts Resource Guide* provides an alternative schedule for the study and assessment of math facts for teachers who fall significantly behind the estimated number of class sessions assigned per unit. (If you do not fall behind the recommended schedule, you do not need the *Grade 3 Facts Resource Guide*—simply follow the math facts program in the units.)

The *Grade 3 Facts Resource Guide* translates the math facts program into a week-by-week calendar that roughly approximates the schedule for studying the math facts that a class would follow if they remain close to the designated schedule for *Math Trailblazers* lessons. (See the Math Facts Calendar in Section 4.) In this manner, students will review all the math facts for their particular grade even if they do not complete all the units for the year.

This program is based on research that shows that students learn the facts better using a strategies-based approach accompanied by distributed practice of small groups of facts. Therefore, we strongly recommend against using the math facts program in a shorter amount of time. The program can be tailored to the needs of individual students using the *Subtraction* and *Multiplication Facts I Know* charts. Those students who know the facts based on the *Triangle Flash Cards* self-assessment will not need much practice. Other students will find that they only need to study one or two facts in a group. Still others will need to work on more facts, using the flash cards and games at home.

It is important to note that in *Math Trailblazers* much of the work for gaining fluency with math facts arises naturally in the problem-solving activities completed in class and in the homework. Thus, the math facts items included in the *Grade 3 Facts Resource Guide* do not reflect the full scope of the math facts program in the *Math Trailblazers* curriculum.

Fuson, K.C. "Developing Mathematical Power in Whole Number Operations." In *A Research Companion to Principles and Standards for School Mathematics.* National Council of Teachers of Mathematics, Reston, VA, 2003.

Isaacs, A.C., and W.M. Carroll. "Strategies for Basic Facts Instruction." *Teaching Children Mathematics,* 5 May, pp 508–15, 1999.

National Research Council. "Developing Proficiency with Whole Numbers." In *Adding It Up: Helping Children Learn Mathematics,* J. Kilpatrick, J. Swafford, and B. Findell, eds. National Academy Press, Washington, DC, 2001.

Principles and Standards for School Mathematics. National Council of Teachers of Mathematics, Reston, VA, 2000.

Thornton, C.A. "Strategies for the Basic Facts." In J.N. Payne (ed.), *Mathematics for the Young Child.* National Council of Teachers of Mathematics, Reston, VA, 1990.

To inform parents about the curriculum's goals and philosophy of learning and assessing the math facts, send home a copy of the *Grade 3 Math Facts Philosophy* that immediately follows. This document is also available in the Unit 2 *Unit Resource Guide* immediately following the Background and on the *Teacher Resource CD*.

Information for Parents

Grade 3 Math Facts Philosophy

The goal of the math facts strand in *Math Trailblazers* is for students to learn the basic facts efficiently, gain fluency with their use, and retain that fluency over time.

A large body of research supports an approach in which students develop strategies for figuring out the facts rather than relying on rote memorization. This not only leads to more effective learning and better retention, but also to the development of mental math skills. In fact, too much drill before conceptual understanding may interfere with a child's ability to understand concepts at a later date. Therefore, the teaching of the basic facts in *Math Trailblazers* is characterized by the following elements:

Use of Strategies. In all grades we encourage students to use strategies to find facts, so they become confident they can find answers to facts problems they do not immediately recall. In this way, students learn that math is more than memorizing facts and rules which "you either get or you don't."

Distributed Facts Practice. Students study small groups of facts that can be found using similar strategies. In Units 1–10 of third grade, they review the subtraction facts and develop strategies for the multiplication facts. Students focus on developing fluency with the multiplication facts in Units 11–20. They use flash cards at home to study each group of facts.

Practice in Context. Students continue to practice all the facts as they use them to solve problems in the labs, activities, and games.

Appropriate Assessment. Students are regularly assessed to see if they can find answers to facts problems quickly and accurately and retain this skill over time. They take a short quiz on each group of facts. Students record their progress on *Facts I Know* charts and determine which facts they need to study. They take an inventory test of all the subtraction facts at the end of Unit 10 and all the multiplication facts at the end of the year.

A Multiyear Approach. In Grades 1 and 2, the curriculum emphasizes the use of strategies that enable students to develop fluency with the addition and subtraction facts by the end of second grade. In Grade 3, students review the subtraction facts and develop fluency with the multiplication facts. In Grade 4, the addition and subtraction facts are checked, the multiplication facts are reviewed, and students develop fluency with the division facts. In Grade 5, students review the multiplication and division facts.

Facts Will Not Act as Gatekeepers. Use of strategies and calculators allows students to continue to work on interesting problems and experiments while learning the facts. They are not prevented from learning more complex mathematics because they do not have quick recall of the facts.

Copyright © Kendall/Hunt Publishing Company

Información para los padres

La filosofía de los conceptos matemáticos básicos en 3er grado

El objetivo de la enseñanza de los conceptos matemáticos básicos en *Math Trailblazers* es que los estudiantes aprendan los conceptos básicos eficazmente, logren el dominio del uso de estos conceptos y mantengan ese dominio con el paso del tiempo.

Las extensas investigaciones realizadas respaldan la aplicación de un enfoque en el que los estudiantes desarrollan estrategias para resolver las operaciones en lugar de hacerlo de memoria. Esto no sólo permite un aprendizaje más eficaz y una mejor retención, sino que también promueve el desarrollo de habilidades matemáticas mentales. De hecho, el exceso de repetición antes de comprender los conceptos puede interferir con la habilidad de los niños para entender conceptos más adelante. Por lo tanto, la enseñanza y la evaluación de los conceptos básicos en *Math Trailblazers* se caracteriza por los siguientes elementos:

El uso de estrategias. En todos los grados, alentamos el uso de estrategias para resolver operaciones básicas, de modo que los estudiantes tengan la confianza de que pueden hallar soluciones a problemas que no recuerdan inmediatamente. De esta manera, los estudiantes aprenden que las matemáticas son más que tablas y reglas memorizadas que un estudiante "sabe o no sabe".

Práctica gradual de los conceptos básicos. Los estudiantes estudian pequeños grupos de conceptos básicos que pueden hallarse usando estrategias similares. En las unidades 1 a 10 de tercer grado, repasan las restas básicas y desarrollan estrategias para aprender las tablas de multiplicación. Los estudiantes se concentran en desarrollar el dominio de las tablas de multiplicación en las unidades 11 a 20. Usan tarjetas para estudiar cada grupo pequeño en casa.

Práctica en contexto. Los estudiantes continúan practicando todos los conceptos básicos a medida que los usan para resolver problemas en las investigaciones, las actividades y los juegos.

Evaluación apropiada. Se evalúa con frecuencia a los estudiantes para determinar si pueden hallar la respuesta a problemas relacionados con los conceptos básicos en forma rápida y precisa y si pueden retener esta habilidad con el paso del tiempo. Los estudiantes tomarán una prueba breve sobre cada grupo de conceptos básicos. Los estudiantes registrarán su avance en las tablas tituladas *"Las tablas que conozco"* y determinan qué conceptos básicos necesitan estudiar. Al final de la unidad 10 tomarán una prueba sobre todas las restas básicas y al final del año tomarán una sobre todas las tablas de multiplicación.

Un enfoque que abarca varios años. En primer y segundo grado, el programa da énfasis en el uso de estrategias que permiten a los estudiantes adquirir el dominio de las sumas y restas básicas para fines de segundo grado. En tercer grado, los estudiantes repasan las restas básicas y desarrollan el dominio de las tablas de multiplicación. En cuarto grado, se verifica el aprendizaje de las sumas y restas básicas, se repasan las tablas de multiplicación, y se desarrolla el dominio de las tablas de división. En quinto grado, los estudiantes repasan las tablas de multiplicación y las división.

El nivel de dominio de los conceptos básicos no impedirá el aprendizaje. El uso de estrategias y calculadoras permite a los estudiantes continuar trabajando con problemas y experimentos interesantes mientras aprenden los conceptos básicos. Si los estudiantes no recuerdan fácilmente los conceptos básicos, podrán igualmente aprender conceptos matemáticos más complejos.

Copyright © Kendall/Hunt Publishing Company

The TIMS Tutor: _Math Facts_ provides an in-depth exploration of the math facts concepts and ideas behind the math facts strand in _Math Trailblazers_. This document also appears in the _Teacher Implementation Guide_.

Students need to learn the math facts. Estimation, mental arithmetic, checking the reasonableness of results, and paper-and-pencil calculations require the ability to give quick, accurate responses when using basic facts. The question is not if students should learn the math facts, but how. Which teaching methods are most efficient and effective? To answer this question, we as authors of *Math Trailblazers* drew upon educational research and our own classroom experiences to develop a comprehensive plan for teaching the math facts.

Philosophy

The goal of the *Math Trailblazers* math facts strand is for students to learn the basic facts efficiently, gain fluency with their use, and retain that fluency over time. A large body of research supports an approach that is built on a foundation of work with strategies and concepts. This not only leads to more effective learning and better retention, but also to development of mental math skills. Therefore, the teaching and assessment of the basic facts in *Math Trailblazers* is characterized by the following elements:

- *Early emphasis on problem solving.* Students first approach the basic facts as problems to solve rather than as facts to memorize. Students invent their own strategies to solve these problems or learn appropriate strategies from others through class discussion. Students' natural strategies, especially counting strategies, are explicitly encouraged. In this way, students learn that math is more than memorizing facts and rules that "you either get or you don't."

- *De-emphasis of rote work.* Fluency with the math facts is an important component of any student's mathematical learning. Research shows that overemphasizing memorization and frequent administration of timed tests are counterproductive. Both can produce undesirable results (Isaacs and Carroll, 1999; Van de Walle, 2001; National Research Council, 2001). We encourage the use of strategies to find facts, so students become confident they can find answers to fact problems they do not immediately recall.

- *Gradual and systematic introduction of facts.* Students study the facts in small groups they solve using similar strategies. Students first work on simple strategies for easy facts and then progress to more sophisticated strategies and harder facts. By the end of the process, they gain fluency with all required facts.

- *Ongoing practice.* Work on the math facts is distributed throughout the curriculum, especially in the Daily Practice and Problems (DPP), Home Practice, and games. This practice for fluency, however, takes place only after students have a conceptual understanding of the operations and have achieved proficiency with strategies for solving basic fact problems. Delaying practice in this way means that less practice is required to achieve fluency.

- *Appropriate assessment.* Teachers assess students' knowledge of the facts through observations as they work on activities, labs, and games as well as through the appropriate use of written tests and quizzes. Beginning in first grade, periodic, short quizzes in the DPP naturally follow the study of small groups of facts organized around specific strategies. As self-assessment in Grades 3–5, students record their progress on *Facts I Know* charts and determine which facts they need to study. Inventory tests of all facts for each operation are used sparingly in Grades 2–5 (no more than twice per year) to assess students' progress with fact fluency. The goal of the math facts assessment program is to determine the degree to which students can find answers to fact problems quickly and accurately and whether they can retain this skill over time.
- *Multiyear approach.* In Grades 1 and 2, *Math Trailblazers* emphasizes strategies that lead to fluency with the addition and subtraction facts. In Grade 3, students gain fluency with the multiplication facts while reviewing the addition and subtraction facts. In Grade 4, students achieve fluency with the division facts and verify fluency with the multiplication facts. In Grade 5, the multiplication and division facts are systematically reviewed and assessed.
- *Facts are not gatekeepers.* Students are not prevented from learning more complex mathematics because they do not perform well on fact tests. Use of strategies, calculators, and other math tools (e.g., manipulatives, hundred charts, printed multiplication tables) allows students to continue to work on interesting problems while still learning the facts.

The following goals for the math facts are consistent with the recommendations in the National Council of Teachers of Mathematics *Principles and Standards for School Mathematics:*

- In kindergarten, students use manipulatives and invent their own strategies to solve addition and subtraction problems.
- By the end of first grade, all students can solve all basic addition and subtraction problems using some strategy. Fluency is not emphasized; strategies are. Some work with beginning concepts of multiplication takes place.
- In second grade, learning efficient strategies for addition and especially subtraction continues to be emphasized. Work with multiplication concepts continues. By the end of the year, students are expected to demonstrate fluency with all the addition and subtraction facts.
- In third grade, students review the subtraction facts. They develop efficient strategies for learning the multiplication facts and demonstrate fluency with the multiplication facts.
- In fourth grade, students review the multiplication facts and develop strategies for the division facts. By the end of year, we expect fluency with all the division facts.
- In fifth grade, students review the multiplication and division facts and are expected to maintain fluency with all the facts.

Expectations by Grade Level

This is summarized in the following chart:

Grade	Addition	Subtraction	Multiplication	Division
K	• invented strategies	• invented strategies		
1	• strategies	• strategies		
2	• strategies • practice leading to fluency	• strategies • practice leading to fluency		
3	• review and practice	• review and practice	• strategies • practice leading to fluency	
4	• assessment and remediation as required	• assessment and remediation as required	• review and practice	• strategies • practice leading to fluency
5	• assessment and remediation as required	• assessment and remediation as required	• review and practice	• review and practice

Table 1: *Math Facts Scope and Sequence*

Strategies for Learning the Facts

Students are encouraged to learn the math facts by first employing a variety of strategies. Concepts and skills are learned more easily and are retained longer if they are meaningful. By first concentrating on concepts and strategies, we increase retention and reduce the amount of time necessary for rote memorization. Researchers note that over time, students develop techniques that are increasingly sophisticated and efficient. Experience with the strategies provides a basis for understanding the operation involved and for gaining fluency with the facts. In this section, we describe possible strategies for learning the addition, subtraction, multiplication, and division facts. The strategies for each operation are listed roughly in order of increasing sophistication.

Strategies for Addition Facts

Common strategies include counting all, counting on, doubles, making or using 10, and reasoning from known facts.

Counting All

This is a particularly straightforward strategy. For example, to solve $7 + 8$, the student gets 7 of something and 8 of something and counts how many there are altogether. The "something" could be beans or chips or marks on paper. In any case, the student counts all the objects to find the sum. This is perhaps not a very efficient method, but it is effective, especially for small numbers, and is usually well understood by the student.

Counting On

This is a natural strategy, particularly for adding 1, 2, or 3. Counters such as beans or chips may or may not be used. As an example, consider $8 + 3$. The student gets 8 beans, and then 3 more, but instead of counting the first 8 again, she simply counts the 3 added beans: "9, 10, 11."

Even if counters are not used, finger gestures can help keep track of how many more have been counted on. For example, to solve $8 + 3$, the student counts "9, 10, 11," holding up a finger each time a number word is said; when three fingers are up, the last word said is the answer.

Doubles

Facts such as $4 + 4 = 8$ are easier to remember than facts with two different addends. Some visual imagery can help, too: two hands for $5 + 5$, a carton of eggs for $6 + 6$, a calendar for $7 + 7$, and so on.

Making a 10

Facts with a sum of 10, such as $7 + 3$ and $6 + 4$, are also easier to remember than other facts. Ten frames can create visual images of making a 10. For example, 8 is shown in a ten frame like the one in Figure 1:

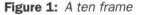

Figure 1: *A ten frame*

This visual imagery helps students remember, for example, that $8 + 2 = 10$.

Using a 10

Students who are comfortable partitioning and combining small numbers can use that knowledge to find the sums of larger numbers. In particular, there are many strategies that involve using the number 10. For example, to find $9 + 7$, we can decompose 7 into $1 + 6$ and then $9 + 7 = 9 + 1 + 6 = 10 + 6 = 16$. Similarly, $8 + 7 = 8 + 2 + 5 = 10 + 5 = 15$.

Reasoning from Known Facts

If you know what $7 + 7$ is, then $7 + 8$ is not much harder: it's just 1 more. So, the "near doubles" can be derived from knowing the doubles.

Strategies for Subtraction Facts

Common strategies for subtraction include using counters, counting up, counting back, using 10, and reasoning from related addition and subtraction facts.

Using Counters

This method models the problem with counters like beans or chips. For example, to solve $8 - 3$, the student gets 8 beans, removes 3 beans, and counts the remaining beans to find the difference. As with using the addition strategy "counting all," this relatively straightforward strategy may not be efficient but it has the great advantage that students usually understand it well.

Counting Up

The student starts at the lower number and counts on to the higher number, perhaps using fingers to keep track of how many numbers are counted. For example, to solve $8 - 5$, the student wants to know how to get from 5 to 8 and counts up 3 numbers: 6, 7, 8. So, $8 - 5 = 3$.

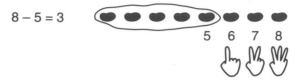

Figure 2: *Counting up*

Counting Back

Counting back works best for subtracting 1, 2, or 3. For larger numbers, it is probably best to count up. For example, to solve $9 - 2$, the student counts back 2 numbers: 8, 7. So, $9 - 2 = 7$.

Figure 3: *Counting back*

Using a 10

Students follow the pattern they find when subtracting 10, e.g., $17 - 10 = 7$ and $13 - 10 = 3$, to learn close facts, e.g., $17 - 9 = 8$ and $13 - 9 = 4$. Since $17 - 9$ will be 1 more than $17 - 10$, they can reason that the answer will be 8, or $7 + 1$.

Making a 10

Knowing the addition facts that have a sum of 10, e.g., $6 + 4 = 10$, can be helpful in finding differences from 10, e.g., $10 - 6 = 4$ and $10 - 4 = 6$. Students can use ten frames to visualize these problems as in Figure 4. These facts can then also be used to find close facts, such as $11 - 4 = 7$.

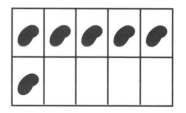

$10 - 4 = 6$

Figure 4: *Using a ten frame*

Using Doubles

Students can use the addition doubles, e.g., $8 + 8 = 16$ and $6 + 6 = 12$, to learn the subtraction "half-doubles" as well: $16 - 8 = 8$ and $12 - 6 = 6$. They can then use these facts to figure out close facts, such as $13 - 6 = 7$ and $15 - 8 = 7$.

Reasoning from Related Addition and Subtraction Facts

Knowing that $8 + 7 = 15$ would seem to be of some help in solving $15 - 7$. Unfortunately, however, knowing related addition facts may not be so helpful to younger or less mathematically mature students. Nevertheless, reasoning from known facts is a powerful strategy for those who can apply it and should be encouraged.

Strategies for Multiplication Facts

Common strategies for multiplication include skip counting, counting up or down from a known fact, doubling, breaking a product into the sum of known products, and using patterns.

Skip Counting

Students begin skip counting and solving problems informally that involve multiplicative situations in first grade. By the time they begin formal work with the multiplication facts in third grade, they should be fairly proficient with skip counting. This strategy is particularly useful for facts such as the 2s, 3s, 5s, and 10s, for which skip counting is easy.

Counting Up or Down from a Known Fact

This strategy involves skip counting forwards once or twice from a known fact. For example, if children know that 5×5 is 25, then they can use this to solve 6×5 (5 more) or 4×5 (5 less). Some children use this for harder facts. For 7×6, they can use the fact that $5 \times 6 = 30$ as a starting point and then count on by sixes to 42.

Doubling

Some children use doubling relationships to help them with multiplication facts involving 4, 6, and 8. For example, 4×7 is twice as much as 2×7. Since $2 \times 7 = 14$, it follows that 4×7 is 28. Since 3×8 is 24, it follows that 6×8 is 48.

Breaking a Product into the Sum of Known Products

A fact like 7×8 can be broken into the sum $5 \times 8 + 2 \times 8$ since $7 = 5 + 2$. See Figure 5. The previous two strategies are special cases of this more general strategy.

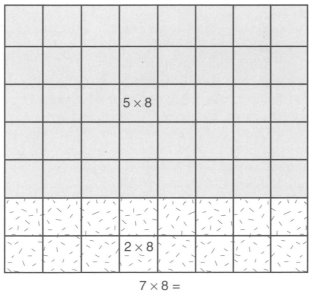

$$7 \times 8 =$$
$$5 \times 8 + 2 \times 8 =$$
$$40 + 16 = 56$$

Figure 5: *Breaking up 7×8*

Patterns

A. Perhaps the best-known examples of patterns are the nines patterns:
    1. When the nines products are listed in a column, as shown below, it is easy to see that the digits in the tens place count up by one (0, 1, 2, 3, . . .) and that the digits in the ones place count down by one (9, 8, 7, . . .).

    9
    18
    27
    36
    45
    54
    63
    72
    81

    2. The sums of the two digits in each of the nines products above are all equal to nine. For example, the sum of the digits in 36 is $3 + 6 = 9$; the sum of the digits in 72 is $7 + 2 = 9$. Adding the digits of a number to see whether they add up to nine can be a strategy in remembering a nines fact. For example, a student might think, "Let me see, does 9×6 equal 54 or 56? It must be 54 since $5 + 4$ is 9, but $5 + 6$ is not 9."

    3. The digit in the tens place in a nines fact is one less than the number being multiplied. For example, $4 \times 9 = 36$, and 3 is one less than 4. This can be combined with the previous pattern to derive nines facts. For example, 3×9 is in the twenties. Since $2 + 7$ is 9, 3×9 must be 27.

    4. Nines can easily be computed using the counting down strategy. Nine times a digit is the same as 10 times the digit, minus the digit. For example, 9×6 is $10 \times 6 - 6 = 54$.

B. Other patterns.
    Other patterns that are useful in remembering other special facts:
    1. 0 times a number equals 0.
    2. 1 times a number equals the number.
    3. 2 times a number is double the number.
    4. 5 times a number ends in 0 or 5; even numbers times 5 end in 0 and odd numbers times five end in 5.
    5. 10 times a number is the same number with a 0 on the end.

Sequencing the Study of Multiplication Facts

In kindergarten, children solve word problems involving multiplication situations. Beginning in first grade, the curriculum develops a conceptual foundation for multiplication through a variety of multiplication models, including repeated addition, the array model, and the number-line model. Fluency with the multiplication facts is expected by the end of third grade. Strategies are often introduced in specific, third-grade lessons. Practice is continued in subsequent lessons and especially in the Daily Practice and Problems and Home Practice. We do not introduce the multiplication facts in the order in which they are traditionally taught (first learning the 2s, then the

3s, then the 4s, etc.). Rather, we emphasize thinking strategies for the facts, introducing fact-groups in the following order:

2s, 3s, 5s, and 10s. The 2s, 3s, 5s, and 10s are easily solved using skip counting.

Square numbers such as $3 \times 3 = 9$, $4 \times 4 = 16$, and $5 \times 5 = 25$. These are introduced by arranging tiles into square arrays.

Nines. Students explore patterns for nines.

Last six facts. After students have learned the facts listed above and their turn-around facts ($9 \times 6 = 6 \times 9$), there are only six more facts to learn: 4×6, 4×7, 4×8, 6×7, 6×8, and 7×8.

Strategies for the Division Facts

The main strategy for learning the division facts is to think of the related multiplication fact. Therefore, students review the multiplication facts and develop fluency with the division facts by working with fact families. (Fact families are groups of related facts. An example of a fact family is $3 \times 4 = 12$, $4 \times 3 = 12$, $12 \div 3 = 4$, and $12 \div 4 = 3$.)

Using the Right Strategy

Different strategies appeal to different students. Students should not feel overburdened with the need to determine which is the "correct" strategy for a given fact. We do not intend to give them a new layer of things to learn. For example, when asked to explain a strategy for a fact, a student may say, "I've used it so much that now I just remember it." "Just remembering" is obviously an efficient strategy. The purpose of suggesting and discussing various strategies is to give students other, perhaps helpful, ways of learning the facts and to give them the confidence to think problems through when necessary. Students should have the opportunity to choose the strategies that work best for them or to invent their own.

The *Math Trailblazers* math facts program pervades most of the curriculum's components. Work with math facts are in different kinds of lessons. These are described in this section.

Math Facts Lessons

Figure 6: *Discussing fact strategies*

Everyday Work

As students work on problems in the labs and activities, encourage them to use and discuss various strategies for solving math facts problems. A number of important goals can best be reached through such discussions.

One goal is to legitimize all valid strategies, even those that may be less efficient. When students see their intuitive methods recognized and validated, they tend to perceive mathematical knowledge as continuous with everyday knowledge and common sense. We thus hope to avoid the unfortunate tendency of many students to separate their knowledge of mathematics from their knowledge of the real world.

By discussing strategies as they arise in context, students and teachers can explore how the strategies work and can verify that they are being used properly. Students should come to realize that a fact strategy that gives wrong answers is not very useful.

A second goal of our approach is to encourage students to communicate mathematical ideas. There are several reasons to stress communication: Students can learn from one another; communicating a method requires higher orders of thinking than simply applying that method; and skill at communicating is important in itself. We are social creatures. Mathematics and science are social endeavors in which communication is crucial.

A third goal of encouraging discussions of various methods is to give the teacher opportunities to learn about how students think. Knowing more about students' thinking helps the teacher ask better questions and plan more effective lessons.

Strategy Lessons

We feel that occasionally it is appropriate for lessons to focus on certain strategies that are developmentally appropriate for most students. Our plan is to begin with simple strategies that should be accessible to all students and to progress gradually to more complex forms of reasoning. For example, in the fall of first grade, we have several lessons that stress counting on to solve certain addition problems. Later, we explicitly introduce making a 10 and other, more sophisticated, strategies.

In general, you should expect your students to come up with effective strategies on their own. Our strategy lessons are intended to explore how and why various strategies work and also to codify and organize the strategies the students invent. They are not meant to dictate the only appropriate strategy for a given problem or to discourage students from using strategies they understand and like. They should be seen as opportunities to discuss strategies that may be appropriate for many students and to encourage their wider use.

> As students work on problems in the labs and activities, they should be encouraged to use and to discuss various strategies for solving math facts problems.

Our ultimate goal is to produce students who can think mathematically, who can solve problems and deal easily with quantified information, and who enjoy mathematics and are not afraid of it. It is easier to do all of the above if one has fluency with the basic math facts. Practice strengthens students' abilities to use strategies and moves students towards fluency with the facts. Practice that follows instruction that stresses the use of strategies has been shown to improve students' fluency with the math facts. We recommend, and have incorporated into the curriculum, the following practice to gain this fluency.

Practice in Context

The primary practice of math facts will arise naturally for the students as they participate in the labs and other activities in the curriculum. These labs and activities offer many opportunities to practice addition, subtraction, multiplication, and division in a meaningful way. The lessons involve the student visually with drawings and patterns, auditorily through discussion, and tactilely through the use of many tools such as manipulatives and calculators.

Pages of problems on the basic facts are not only unnecessary, they can be counterproductive. Students may come to regard mathematics as mostly memorization and may perceive it as meaningless and unconnected to their everyday lives.

Structured Practice

Student-friendly, structured practice is built into the curriculum, especially in the DPP, Home Practice, and games. One small group of related math facts is presented to the students at a time. The practice of groups of facts is carefully distributed throughout the year. A small set of facts grouped in a meaningful way leads students to develop strategies such as adding doubles, counting back, or using a 10 for dealing with a particular situation. Furthermore, a small set of facts is a manageable amount to learn and remember.

Beginning in the second half of first grade and continuing through fifth grade, a small group of facts to be studied in a unit is introduced in the DPP. Through DPP items, students practice the facts and take a short assessment. Beginning in second grade, students use flash cards for additional practice with specific groups of facts. Facts are also practiced in many word problems in the DPP, Home Practice, and individual lessons. These problems allow students to focus on other interesting mathematical ideas as they also gain more fact practice.

Games

A variety of games are included in the curriculum, both in the lessons and in the DPP items of many units. A summary of the games used in a particular grade can be found in the Games section. Once students learn the rules of the games, they should play them periodically in class and at home for homework. Games provide an opportunity to encourage family involvement in the math program. When a game is assigned for homework, a note can be sent home with a place for the family members to sign, affirming that they played the game with their student.

Figure 7: *Playing a game*

> *Our ultimate goal is to produce students who can think mathematically, who can solve problems and deal easily with quantified information, and who enjoy mathematics and are not afraid of it. It is easier to do all of the above if one has fluency with the basic math facts.*

Use of Calculators

The relationship between knowing the math facts and the use of calculators is an interesting one. Using a multiplication table or a calculator when necessary to find a fact helps promote familiarity and reinforces the math facts. Students soon figure out that it is quicker and more efficient to know the basic facts than to have to use these tools. The use of calculators also requires excellent estimation skills so that one can easily check for errors in calculator computations. Rather than eliminating the need for fluency with the facts, successful calculator use for solving complex problems depends on fact knowledge.

When to Practice

Practicing small groups of facts often for short periods of time is more effective than practicing many facts less often for long periods of time. For example, practicing 8 to 10 subtraction facts for 5 minutes several times a week is better than practicing all the subtraction facts for half an hour once a week. Good times for practicing the facts for 5 or 10 minutes during the school day include the beginning of the day, the beginning of math class, when students have completed an assignment, when an impending activity is delayed, or when an activity ends earlier than expected. Practicing small groups of facts at home involves parents in the process and frees class time for more interesting mathematics.

> *Practicing small groups of facts often for short periods of time is more effective than practicing many facts less often for long periods of time.*

Assessment

Throughout the curriculum, teachers assess students' knowledge of the facts through observations as they work on activities, labs, and games. In Grades 3–5, students can use their *Facts I Know* charts to record their own progress in learning the facts. This type of self-assessment is very important in helping each student to become responsible for his or her own learning. Students are able to personalize their study of facts and not waste valuable time studying facts they already know.

In the second half of first grade, a sequence of facts assessments is provided in the Daily Practice and Problems. A more comprehensive facts assessment program begins in second grade. This program assesses students' progress in learning the facts, as outlined in the Expectations by Grade Level section of this tutor. As students develop strategies for a given group of facts, short quizzes accompany the practice. Students know which facts will be tested, focus practice in class and at home on those facts, then take the quiz. As they take the quiz, they use one color pencil to write answers before a given time limit, then use another color to complete the problems they need more time to answer. Students then use their *Facts I Know* charts to make a record of those facts they answered quickly, those facts they answered correctly but with less efficient strategies, and those facts they did not know at all. Using this information, students can concentrate their efforts on gaining fluency with those facts they answered correctly, but not quickly. They also know to develop strategies for those facts they could not answer at all. In this way, the number of facts studied at any one time becomes more manageable, practice becomes more meaningful, and the process less intimidating.

Tests of all the facts for any operation have a very limited role. They are used no more than two times a year to show growth over time and should not be given daily or weekly. Since we rarely, if ever, need to recall 100 facts at one time in everyday life, overemphasizing tests of all the facts reinforces the notion that math is nothing more than rote memorization and has no connection to the real world. Quizzes of small numbers of facts are as effective and not as threatening. They give students, parents, and teachers the information needed to continue learning and practicing efficiently. With an assessment approach based on strategies and the use of small groups of facts, students can see mathematics as connected to their own thinking and gain confidence in their mathematical abilities.

Conclusion

Research provides clear indications for curriculum developers and teachers about the design of effective math facts instruction. These recommendations formed the foundation of the *Math Trailblazers* math facts program. Developing strategies for learning the facts (rather than relying on rote memorization), distributing practice of small groups of facts, applying math facts in interesting problems, and using an appropriate assessment program— all are consistent with recommendations from current research. It is an instructional approach that encourages students to make sense of the mathematics they are learning. The resulting program will add efficiency and effectiveness to your students' learning of the math facts.

References

Ashlock, R.B., and C.A. Washbon. "Games: Practice Activities for the Basic Facts." In M.N. Suydam and R.E. Reys (eds.), *Developing Computational Skills: 1978 Yearbook.* National Council of Teachers of Mathematics, Reston, VA, 1978.

Beattie, L.D. "Children's Strategies for Solving Subtraction-Fact Combinations." *Arithmetic Teacher,* 27 (1), pp. 14–15, 1979.

Brownell, W.A., and C.B. Chazal. "The Effects of Premature Drill in Third-Grade Arithmetic." *Journal of Educational Research,* 29 (1), 1935.

Carpenter, T.P., and J.M. Moser. "The Acquisition of Addition and Subtraction Concepts in Grades One through Three." *Journal for Research in Mathematics Education,* 15 (3), pp. 179–202, 1984.

Cook, C.J., and J.A. Dossey. "Basic Fact Thinking Strategies for Multiplication—Revisited." *Journal for Research in Mathematics Education,* 13 (3), pp. 163–171, 1982.

Davis, E.J. "Suggestions for Teaching the Basic Facts of Arithmetic." In M.N. Suydam and R.E. Reys (eds.), *Developing Computational Skills: 1978 Yearbook.* National Council of Teachers of Mathematics, Reston, VA, 1978.

Fuson, K.C. "Teaching Addition, Subtraction, and Place-Value Concepts." In L. Wirszup and R. Streit (eds.), *Proceedings of the UCSMP International Conference on Mathematics Education: Developments in School Mathematics Education Around the World: Applications-Oriented Curricula and Technology-Supported Learning for All Students.* National Council of Teachers of Mathematics, Reston, VA, 1987.

Fuson, K.C., and G.B. Willis. "Subtracting by Counting Up: More Evidence." *Journal for Research in Mathematics Education,* 19 (5), pp. 402–420, 1988.

Fuson, K.C., J.W. Stigler, and K. Bartsch. "Grade Placement of Addition and Subtraction Topics in Japan, Mainland China, the Soviet Union, Taiwan, and the United States." *Journal for Research in Mathematics Education,* 19 (5), pp. 449–456, 1988.

Greer, B. "Multiplication and Division as Models of Situations." In D.A. Grouws (ed.), *Handbook of Research on Mathematics Teaching and Learning: A Project of the National Council of Teachers of Mathematics* (Chapter 13). Macmillan, New York, 1992.

Hiebert, James. "Relationships between Research and the NCTM Standards." *Journal for Research in Mathematics Education,* 30 January, pp. 3–19, 1999.

Isaacs, A.C., and W.M. Carroll. "Strategies for Basic Facts Instruction." *Teaching Children Mathematics,* 5 May, pp. 508–515, 1999.

Kouba, V.L., C.A. Brown, T.P. Carpenter, M.M. Lindquist, E.A. Silver, and J.O. Swafford. "Results of the Fourth NAEP Assessment of Mathematics: Number, Operations, and Word Problems." *Arithmetic Teacher,* 35 (8), pp. 14–19, 1988.

Myers, A.C., and C.A. Thornton. "The Learning-Disabled Child—Learning the Basic Facts." *Arithmetic Teacher,* 25 (3), pp. 46–50, 1977.

National Research Council. *Adding It Up: Helping Children Learn Mathematics.* National Academy Press, Washington, DC, 2001.

Principles and Standards for School Mathematics. National Council of Teachers of Mathematics, Reston, VA, 2000.

Rathmell, E.C. "Using Thinking Strategies to Teach the Basic Facts." In M.N. Suydam and R.E. Reys (eds.), *Developing Computational Skills: 1978 Yearbook.* National Council of Teachers of Mathematics, Reston, VA, 1978.

Rathmell, E.C., and P.R. Trafton. "Whole Number Computation." In J.N. Payne (ed.), *Mathematics for the Young Child.* National Council of Teachers of Mathematics, Reston, VA, 1990.

Swart, W.L. "Some Findings on Conceptual Development of Computational Skills." *Arithmetic Teacher,* 32 (5), pp. 36–38, 1985.

Thornton, C.A. "Doubles Up—Easy!" *Arithmetic Teacher,* 29 (8), p. 20, 1982.

Thornton, C.A. "Emphasizing Thinking Strategies in Basic Fact Instruction." *Journal for Research in Mathematics Education,* 9 (3), pp. 214–227, 1978.

Thornton, C.A. "Solution Strategies: Subtraction Number Facts." *Educational Studies in Mathematics,* 21 (1), pp. 241–263, 1990.

Thornton, C.A. "Strategies for the Basic Facts." In J.N. Payne (ed.), *Mathematics for the Young Child.* National Council of Teachers of Mathematics, Reston, VA, 1990.

Thornton, C.A., and P.J. Smith. "Action Research: Strategies for Learning Subtraction Facts." *Arithmetic Teacher,* 35 (8), pp. 8–12, 1988.

Van de Walle, J. *Elementary and Middle School Mathematics: Teaching Developmentally.* Addison Wesley, New York, 2001.

Section 4

Math Facts Calendar
Grade 3

The Grade 3 Math Facts Calendar outlines a schedule for math facts practice, review, and assessment that roughly follows the schedule in the Unit Outlines in the *Unit Resource Guides* and in the Overview section of the *Teacher Implementation Guide.* Classrooms that are moving significantly more slowly through the units than is recommended in the Unit Outlines can use this schedule for study of the math facts to ensure that students receive the complete math facts program.

All of the materials referenced in the Math Facts Calendar are located elsewhere in *Math Trailblazers* as well as the *Grade 3 Facts Resource Guide.*

The elements included in the Math Facts Calendar are described below.

① Math Facts Groups	② Weeks	③ Daily Practice and Problems	④ Home Practice	⑤ Flash Cards	⑥ Facts Quizzes and Tests
Subtraction: Groups 1 & 2 Multiplication: Last Six Facts	15–16	Unit 7: items 7A, 7B, 7C, 7F, 7G, 7I, 7P, 7Q & 7U	Unit 7 Parts 1 & 2	Subtraction Flash Cards: Groups 1 & 2	DPP item 7U is a quiz on the subtraction facts in Groups 1 & 2. The *Subtraction Facts I Know* chart is updated.
Subtraction: Groups 3 & 4 Multiplication: 2s, 5s & 10s	17–18	Unit 8: items 8A, 8B, 8C, 8D, 8G, 8H, 8I, 8L & 8M		Subtraction Flash Cards: Groups 3 & 4	DPP item 8M is a quiz on the subtraction facts in Groups 3 & 4. The *Subtraction Facts I Know* chart is updated.

Math Facts
Groups

①

This column describes the *Math Trailblazers* program for reviewing, practicing, and assessing the subtraction and multiplication facts. The subtraction facts are organized into 8 groups (Groups 1–8) while the multiplication facts are organized into five groups (2s and 3s, 5s and 10s, 9s, square numbers, and the last six facts).

Weeks

②

Week 1 in the alternative schedule refers to the first week of school. Week 2 refers to the second week of school, and so on.

Daily Practice and Problems

③

The DPP items from each unit that focus on the math facts are listed in this column.

The Daily Practice and Problems (DPP) is a series of short exercises that:

- provide distributed practice in computation and a structure for systematic review of the basic math facts;
- develop concepts and skills such as number sense, mental math, telling time, and working with money throughout the year; and
- review topics, presenting concepts in new contexts and linking ideas from unit to unit.

There are three types of items: Bits, Tasks, and Challenges. Most are written so that they can be quickly copied onto the blackboard.

- Bits are short and should take no more than five or ten minutes to complete. They often provide practice with a skill or the basic math facts.
- Tasks take ten to fifteen minutes to complete.
- Challenges usually take longer than fifteen minutes to complete and the problems are more thought-provoking. They stretch students' problem-solving skills.

The DPP may be used in class for practice and review, as assessment, or for homework. Notes for teachers provide answers as well as suggestions for using the items. Only those DPP items that focus on the math facts are listed here.

For more information on the Daily Practice and Problems, see the Daily Practice and Problems and Home Practice Guide in the *Teacher Implementation Guide.*

Home Practice

The Home Practice is a series of problems, located in the *Discovery Assignment Book,* that are designed to be sent home with students to supplement homework assignments. Each Home Practice is divided into several parts that can be assigned separately. For more information on the Home Practice, see the Daily Practice and Problems and Home Practice Guide in the *Teacher Implementation Guide.*

⑤ ## Flash Cards

As part of the DPP in Units 2–10 of third grade, students use flash cards to practice and assess their knowledge of specific groups of subtraction facts. In Units 11–20, students use *Triangle Flash Cards* to practice and assess the multiplication facts. Students categorize facts into three groups (facts I know quickly, facts I know using a strategy, facts I need to learn). They record this information on a chart, that is updated regularly.

The subtraction flash cards are distributed in Units 2–5 in the *Discovery Assignment Book.* Copies of the flash cards are also included in Section 7 and in the corresponding lessons in the *Unit Resource Guide.* The *Subtraction Facts I Know* chart is distributed as part of the *Assessing the Subtraction Facts* lesson (Unit 2 Lesson 7), which is reproduced in Section 5.

The *Triangle Flash Cards* are distributed in Units 11–15 in the *Discovery Assignment Book.* Copies of the flash cards are also included in Section 7 and in the corresponding lessons in the *Unit Resource Guide.* The *Multiplication Facts I Know* chart is distributed as part of the *Completing the Table* lesson (Unit 11 Lesson 4), which is reproduced in Section 5.

⑥ ## Facts Quizzes and Tests

Periodic quizzes of small groups of math facts are given as part of the DPP. Facts are grouped to encourage the use of strategies in learning facts. In third grade, an inventory test of the subtraction facts is given in Unit 10. A test on all the multiplication facts is given in Unit 20.

Grade 3 Math Facts Calendar

Math Facts Groups	Weeks	Daily Practice and Problems	Home Practice	Flash Cards	Facts Quizzes and Tests
Addition Review	1–2	Unit 1: items 1D, 1K, 1M, 1O, 1Q, 1R & 1S The lesson *Addition Facts Strategies* (Unit 2 Lesson 1) reviews partitioning numbers, rearranging addends, and addition facts strategies. Complete this lesson as a review of the addition facts.	Unit 1 Parts 1, 2 & 3		DPP items 1Q and 1S can serve as addition facts inventory tests.
Subtraction: Groups 1 & 2	3–5	The lessons *Subtraction Facts Strategies* (Unit 2 Lesson 5) and *Assessing the Subtraction Facts* (Unit 2 Lesson 7) launch the practice and assessment of the subtraction facts in Grade 3. *Assessing the Subtraction Facts* introduces the flash cards and the *Subtraction Facts I Know* chart. Unit 2: items 2A, 2E, 2L, 2N, 2O, 2Q, 2R, 2T & 2U	Unit 2 Parts 1 & 2	Subtraction Flash Cards: Groups 1 & 2	The *Subtraction Facts I Know* chart is updated.
Subtraction: Groups 3 & 4 Multiplication: 5s & 10s	6–7	Unit 3: items 3A, 3C, 3E, 3F, 3G, 3I, 3K, 3M, 3N & 3O	Unit 3 Part 1	Subtraction Flash Cards: Groups 3 & 4	The *Subtraction Facts I Know* chart is updated.
Subtraction: Groups 5 & 6 Multiplication: 2s & 3s	8–9	Unit 4: items 4B, 4C, 4D, 4E, 4F, 4G, 4H, 4K, 4M, 4S & 4T	Unit 4 Parts 1 & 2	Subtraction Flash Cards: Groups 5 & 6	The *Subtraction Facts I Know* chart is updated.
Subtraction: Groups 7 & 8 Multiplication: Square Numbers	10–11	Unit 5: items 5A, 5C, 5H, 5I, 5J, 5K, 5O & 5P	Unit 5 Part 1	Subtraction Flash Cards: Groups 7 & 8	The *Subtraction Facts I Know* chart is updated.
Multiplication: 9s	12–14	Unit 6: items 6B, 6C, 6D, 6F, 6H, 6V & 6DD	Unit 6 Part 1		
Subtraction: Groups 1 & 2 Multiplication: Last Six Facts	15–16	Unit 7: items 7A, 7B, 7C, 7F, 7G, 7I, 7P, 7Q & 7U	Unit 7 Parts 1 & 2	Subtraction Flash Cards: Groups 1 & 2	DPP item 7U is a quiz on the subtraction facts in Groups 1 & 2. The *Subtraction Facts I Know* chart is updated.
Subtraction: Groups 3 & 4 Multiplication: 2s, 5s & 10s	17–18	Unit 8: items 8A, 8B, 8C, 8D, 8G, 8H, 8I, 8L & 8M		Subtraction Flash Cards: Groups 3 & 4	DPP item 8M is a quiz on the subtraction facts in Groups 3 & 4. The *Subtraction Facts I Know* chart is updated.
Subtraction: Groups 5 & 6 Multiplication: 3s, 9s & Square Numbers	19–20	Unit 9: items 9A, 9B, 9C, 9E, 9G, 9I, 9J, 9K, 9L & 9M	Unit 9 Part 2	Subtraction Flash Cards: Groups 5 & 6	DPP item 9M is a quiz on the subtraction facts in Groups 5 & 6. The *Subtraction Facts I Know* chart is updated.
Subtraction: Groups 7 & 8 Multiplication: Last Six Facts	21–22	Unit 10: items 10A, 10C, 10E, 10F, 10G, 10I, 10J, 10K & 10L	Unit 10 Part 1	Subtraction Flash Cards: Groups 7 & 8	DPP item 10I is a quiz on the subtraction facts in Groups 7 & 8. Item 10K is an inventory test on all the subtraction facts. The *Subtraction Facts I Know* chart is updated.

Math Facts Groups	Weeks	Daily Practice and Problems	Home Practice	Flash Cards	Facts Quizzes and Tests
Multiplication: 5s & 10s	23–24	Part 2 of the lesson *Completing the Table* (Unit 11 Lesson 4) launches the assessment of the multiplication facts in Grade 3. This lesson also introduces the *Multiplication Facts I Know* chart. Unit 11: items 11B, 11C, 11D, 11E, 11F, 11J, 11L, 11N, 11O, 11P, 11Q, 11R, 11S & 11T	Unit 11 Parts 1 & 2	*Triangle Flash Cards: 5s & 10s*	DPP item 11S is a quiz on the multiplication facts for the 5s and 10s. The *Multiplication Facts I Know* chart is updated.
Multiplication: 2s & 3s	25–26	Unit 12: items 12A, 12C, 12J, 12K & 12M		*Triangle Flash Cards: 2s & 3s*	DPP item 12M is a quiz on the multiplication facts for the 2s and 3s. The *Multiplication Facts I Know* chart is updated.
Multiplication: Square Numbers	27	Unit 13: items 13A, 13D, 13E, 13F & 13K		*Triangle Flash Cards: Square Numbers*	DPP item 13K is a quiz on the multiplication facts for the square numbers. The *Multiplication Facts I Know* chart is updated.
Multiplication: 9s	28	Unit 14: items 14A, 14C, 14D, 14E, 14G & 14J		*Triangle Flash Cards: 9s*	DPP item 14G is a quiz on the multiplication facts for the 9s. The *Multiplication Facts I Know* chart is updated.
Multiplication: Last Six Facts	29–30	Unit 15: items 15A, 15B, 15I, 15J, 15K & 15M		*Triangle Flash Cards: Last Six Facts*	DPP item 15M is a quiz on the multiplication facts for the last six facts. The *Multiplication Facts I Know* chart is updated.
Multiplication: 2s, 5s & 10s	31	Unit 16: items 16C, 16E, 16G, 16J & 16K		*Triangle Flash Cards: 2s, 5s & 10s*	DPP item 16K is a quiz on the multiplication facts for the 2s, 5s, and 10s. The *Multiplication Facts I Know* chart is updated.
Multiplication: 3s & 9s	32	Unit 17: items 17A, 17I, 17J & 17K		*Triangle Flash Cards: 3s & 9s*	DPP item 17K is a quiz on the multiplication facts for the 3s and 9s. The *Multiplication Facts I Know* chart is updated.
Multiplication: Square Numbers	33	Unit 18: items 18A, 18B, 18E, 18G, 18I & 18K		*Triangle Flash Cards: Square Numbers*	DPP item 18K is a quiz on the multiplication facts for the square numbers. The *Multiplication Facts I Know* chart is updated.
Multiplication: Last Six Facts	34	Unit 19: items 19A, 19E, 19H, 19K, 19P & 19Q		*Triangle Flash Cards: Last Six Facts*	DPP item 19Q is a quiz on the multiplication facts for the last six facts. The *Multiplication Facts I Know* chart is updated.
Multiplication: All Facts Groups	35–36	Unit 20: items 20E, 20J & 20K		*Triangle Flash Cards: 2s, 3s, 5s, 9s, 10s, Square Numbers & Last Six Facts*	DPP item 20K is an inventory test on all the multiplication facts. The *Multiplication Facts I Know* chart is updated.

Math Facts Groups	Weeks	Daily Practice and Problems	Home Practice	Flash Cards	Facts Quizzes and Tests
Addition Review	1–2	Unit 1: items 1D, 1K, 1M, 1O, 1Q, 1R & 1S The lesson *Addition Facts Strategies* (Unit 2 Lesson 1) reviews partitioning numbers, rearranging addends, and addition facts strategies. Complete this lesson as a review of the addition facts.	Unit 1 Parts 1, 2 & 3		DPP items 1Q and 1S can serve as addition facts inventory tests.

Students may solve the items individually, in groups, or as a class. The items may also be assigned for homework. The DPPs are also available on the Teacher Resource CD.

Student Questions	Teacher Notes
1D Mike and Terrence Smart	**TIMS Task**
Mike Smart is helping his brother, Terrence, with his homework. Terrence says that $17 - 9$ is 9. Mike is trying to show Terrence that he is wrong. How do you think Mike should show Terrence his mistake?	Asking students to disprove an incorrect answer is a good technique for eliciting explanations and not just answers. Students can use manipulatives or draw pictures to show that $17 - 9 = 8$ or use the fact that $9 + 8 = 17$.
1K Mental Arithmetic	**TIMS Bit**
Solve these problems in your head. Write down the answers. Explain how you found your answers. 1. $7 + 5 =$ 2. $7 + 15 =$ 3. $7 + 75 =$ 4. $10 - 8 =$ 5. $100 - 8 =$ 6. $100 - 18 =$	Students can describe and compare strategies for solving the problems "in their heads." 1. 12 2. 22 3. 82 4. 2 5. 92 6. 82
1M More Mental Arithmetic	**TIMS Bit**
Solve these problems in your head. Write down the answers. Explain how you found your answers. 1. $8 + 100 =$ 2. $8 + 99 =$ 3. $8 + 499 =$ 4. $7 + 8 =$ 5. $7 + 18 =$ 6. $7 + 48 =$	Students can describe and compare strategies for solving the problems "in their heads." 1. 108 2. 107 3. 507 4. 15 5. 25 6. 55

10 Paper Dolls

Marla can make a paper doll in five minutes. How long does it take her to make six paper dolls?

TIMS Bit

Marla can make six paper dolls in 30 minutes. Students can skip count, use repeated addition, multiply on a calculator, or use a clock to help solve the problem.

1Q Addition Facts Quiz: Doubles, 2s, and 3s

A. $5 + 3 =$ _____   B. $8 + 8 =$ _____

C. $7 + 7 =$ _____   D. $2 + 4 =$ _____

E. $6 + 3 =$ _____   F. $6 + 6 =$ _____

G. $3 + 8 =$ _____   H. $3 + 3 =$ _____

I. $9 + 9 =$ _____   J. $3 + 4 =$ _____

K. $6 + 2 =$ _____   L. $7 + 3 =$ _____

M. $2 + 7 =$ _____   N. $2 + 8 =$ _____

O. $5 + 5 =$ _____   P. $4 + 4 =$ _____

TIMS Bit

Students need two pens or pencils of different colors. During the two minutes recommended for this quiz, they should write their answers using one color pen or pencil. After two minutes, they should write their answers with the other color pen or pencil. Have students check their work after a reasonable amount of time.

If students demonstrate difficulty with these addition facts, practice activities are provided in Section 8.

A. 8	B. 16
C. 14	D. 6
E. 9	F. 12
G. 11	H. 6
I. 18	J. 7
K. 8	L. 10
M. 9	N. 10
O. 10	P. 8

1R   Sample of Beans

Sun Feng took samples of beans. He pulled twenty-seven beans.

1. A. How many navy beans should he record?

   B. Explain your strategy for solving 1A.

K Kind	B Number of Beans
pinto	3
navy	
kidney	13
lima	3

2. Which bean was the most common?

3. Which bean was the least common?

4. How many more kidney beans than lima beans did Sun Feng pull?

TIMS Task

1. A. 8 navy beans

   B. Strategies may vary. Students may find the total of beans in the table (19) and then count up to find the missing portion (8).

2. kidney beans

3. pinto and lima

4. ten

1S   Addition Facts Quiz: More Addition Facts

A. 7 + 9 = _____   B. 6 + 8 = _____

C. 4 + 7 = _____   D. 9 + 5 = _____

E. 7 + 6 = _____   F. 8 + 9 = _____

G. 5 + 7 = _____   H. 4 + 6 = _____

I. 7 + 8 = _____   J. 9 + 4 = _____

K. 4 + 5 = _____   L. 8 + 5 = _____

M. 9 + 6 = _____   N. 4 + 8 = _____

O. 6 + 5 = _____   P. 9 + 3 = _____

Q. 10 + 4 = _____   R. 9 + 10 = _____

TIMS Bit

Students need two pens or pencils of different colors. During the two minutes recommended for this quiz, they should write their answers using one color pen or pencil. After two minutes, they should write their answers with the other color pen or pencil. Have students check their work after a reasonable amount of time.

If students demonstrate difficulty with these addition facts, practice activities are provided in Section 8.

A.	16	B.	14
C.	11	D.	14
E.	13	F.	17
G.	12	H.	10
I.	15	J.	13
K.	9	L.	13
M.	15	N.	12
O.	11	P.	12
Q.	14	R.	19

Unit 1 Home Practice

PART 1

1. **A.** 4 + 7 = _____   2. **A.** 10 − 4 = _____

   B. 5 + 9 = _____   **B.** 15 − 10 = _____

   C. 8 + 2 + 4 = _____   **C.** 15 − 9 = _____

3. Carl dropped thirty-three pennies. A bunch rolled under the refrigerator. He picked up seventeen pennies. How many pennies rolled under the refrigerator? Explain how you decided.

   _____

   _____

   _____

   _____

PART 2

1. **A.** 12 − 6 = _____   2. **A.** 4 + 6 + 8 = _____

   B. 14 − 10 = _____   **B.** 9 + 1 + 8 = _____

   C. 14 − 5 = _____   **C.** 17 + 3 + 5 = _____

3. Tina bought a folder for 67¢. She gave the clerk one dollar.

   A. How much change should she get back? Explain how you decided.

   _____

   _____

   _____

   B. What coins might the cashier give her?

   _____

   _____

   _____

Copyright © Kendall/Hunt Publishing Company

PART 3

1. Janelle's aunt just turned 34 years old. Janelle wrote the following number sentences to show how 34 can be broken into parts.

   30 + 4 = 34

   10 + 7 + 7 + 10 = 34

   Write five more number sentences that show 34 broken into parts.

   _____   _____   _____

   _____   _____

2. Thirty-four is...
   A. 10 more than _____   B. 20 + _____
   C. 10 less than _____   D. 100 less than _____
   E. about half of _____   F. about twice _____
   G. 5 less than _____   H. 9 more than _____

Copyright © Kendall/Hunt Publishing Company

Lesson 1

Addition Facts Strategies

Lesson Overview

Estimated Class Sessions

2

Students review addition strategies and use them to solve problems with more than two addends.

Key Content

- Using strategies to add.
- Using turn-around facts (commutativity) to add.
- Using grouping strategies (associativity) to add.
- Developing calculator skills.
- Developing mental math skills.

Key Vocabulary

- addend
- keystrokes
- sum

Math Facts

DPP Bit A provides practice with math facts.

Homework

1. Assign the *Switch It!* Homework Page in the *Discovery Assignment Book.*
2. Assign the *Calculator Explorations* Homework Page.

Assessment

Students complete the *Calculator Challenges* Assessment Page.

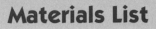

Supplies and Copies

Student	Teacher
Supplies for Each Student Pair • 40 connecting cubes • calculator	**Supplies**
Copies • 1 copy of *Calculator Challenges* per student (*Unit Resource Guide* Page 36)	**Copies/Transparencies** • 1 transparency of *Calculator Explorations*, optional (*Discovery Assignment Book* Page 27)

All blackline masters including assessment, transparency, and DPP masters are also on the Teacher Resource CD.

Student Books

Addition Facts Strategies (*Student Guide* Pages 14–15)
Switch It! (*Discovery Assignment Book* Page 25)
Calculator Explorations (*Discovery Assignment Book* Page 27)

Daily Practice and Problems and Home Practice

DPP items A–D (*Unit Resource Guide* Pages 19–20)

Note: Classrooms whose pacing differs significantly from the suggested pacing of the units should use the Math Facts Calendar in Section 4 of the *Facts Resource Guide* to ensure students receive the complete math facts program.

Daily Practice and Problems

Suggestions for using the DPPs are on page 34.

A. Bit: Quick Addition (URG p. 19)

Do these problems in your head. Write only the answers.

1. $4 + 9 =$
2. $40 + 90 =$
3. $20 + 90 =$
4. $20 + 30 =$
5. $30 + 50 =$
6. $40 + 60 =$
7. $10 + 90 =$
8. $60 + 80 =$
9. $80 + 70 =$
10. Explain your strategy for Question 9.

B. Task: Change (URG p. 19)

1. You go to the store with $1.00. You buy a pen that costs 73¢. The tax is 6¢. How much change will you get?
2. What coins could you get in change? How many different ways can you answer this question?

C. Bit: Calculator Counting (URG p. 20)

Work with a partner to find how long it will take to count to 100. One partner will count. The other will time how long the counting takes. Take turns.

A. Use a calculator to count by ones to 100. How long did it take?
B. Predict how long it would take to count by twos to 100. Use a calculator to count by twos to 100. How long did it take?

D. Challenge: Piano Practice (URG p. 20)

Abbey practices piano every day. Here are the songs she plays and the time it takes to play them:

"Evening Bells"	2 minutes
"Scottish Dance"	1 minute
"Air" by Mozart	$\frac{1}{2}$ minute

A. Can she play each song ten times in half an hour?
B. How long will she play if she warms up for five minutes and then plays each song six times?

Part 1 Using a Ten

Give each pair forty connecting cubes. Ask students to build a train with seven blue cubes and another train with eight red cubes. Ask:

- *What can you do with the cubes to make a train of ten?* (Move two blue cubes to the train of eight or move three red cubes to the train of seven.)

- *You now have a train of ten cubes and a train of five cubes. What is the sum?* (15)

- *Why is this problem (10 + 5) easier to solve than the first one (7 + 8)?*

Ask students to repeat this procedure and find groups of ten to do problems such as 6 + 7, 8 + 8, and 8 + 9.

Discuss how using a ten can help students remember some addition facts.

Part 2 Switch It!

Ask students to solve 14 + 7 + 6 with connecting cubes. They can use a different color to represent each addend. Ask students to group the cubes in as many tens as possible to achieve the sum. One way to find the sum:

- Break apart the fourteen into ten and four;

- Group the six cubes with the four cubes to make a ten;

- Represent the sum with two trains of ten cubes and a train of seven cubes.

Ask students to share their methods. Challenge them to complete 14 + 7 + 6 using mental arithmetic. It is easier to solve if the addends are first rearranged to find groups or multiples of ten. (14 + 6 = 20, then 20 + 7 = 27)

Give students other problems:

- 8 + 7 + 12
- 6 + 8 + 14
- 11 + 3 + 9

Encourage them to find groups of tens with the cubes and then do the arithmetic mentally. Note that other strategies can be equally efficient. For example, students may choose to use doubles to add 6 + 8 + 14 = 14 + 14 = 28.

Students should then read the dialog on the *Addition Facts Strategies* Activity Pages and do the Switching problems. Ask students to explain how they did the problems. Assign the *Switch It!* Homework Page.

Addition Facts Strategies

What strategies can you use to solve 6 + 10 + 4?

"There are many different ways to solve addition problems," said Miriam.

"I can think of at least two ways," said Eric. "You can count up using your fingers and toes, or you can use blocks or cubes."

"I like to find groups of ten, then add up what's left over," said Miriam.

Miriam and Eric used counters to help Tisha and Peter solve 6 + 10 + 4.

You can put together the four and six to make a ten.

14   SG • Grade 3 • Unit 2 • Lesson 1   Addition Facts Strategies

Student Guide - page 14

Content Note

The concepts introduced in this unit are formally known as the commutative and associative properties of addition. The **commutative property,** sometimes called the order property, means that when adding a series of numbers, the order in which they are added makes no difference. For example, when adding 5 + 6 + 5 the same answer is reached whether the numbers are added in the order given or not (5 + 6 + 5 = 5 + 5 + 6).

The **associative property** means that numbers may be grouped in different configurations when adding. An example is 4 + 8 + 2. The numbers may be added by grouping the 4 + 8 first and then adding the 2:

(4 + 8) + 2 = 12 + 2 = 14. In the alternative, the 8 + 2 can be grouped before the 4 is added:

4 + (8 + 2) = 4 + 10 = 14.

Students need not know the formal names for these properties, but they should develop the ability to use them when adding.

Part 3 Breaking Addends into Parts

Sometimes addends can be easily grouped into tens; however, this may not always be obvious. A worthwhile strategy for adding mentally is partitioning addends before finding groups of ten. For example, in the problem here the second addend, 5, can be rewritten as 3 + 2.

$$7 + \mathbf{5} + 2$$

$$7 + \mathbf{3} + \mathbf{2} + 2$$

Students can now group 7 + 3, and find the sum 10 + 2 + 2 = 14.

Give students similar problems to solve:

- 6 + 8 + 3
- 9 + 7 + 2
- 4 + 9 + 3

Students should discuss and compare solutions.

As students become adept at partitioning single-digit numbers, introduce two-digit addends in problems such as 11 + 5 + 3; 2 + 19 + 5; and 12 + 9 + 15. Ask students to explain how they did the problems. As students share their solutions, ask:

- *Did anyone find another way to solve that problem?*

Ask students to complete the problems in the Breaking Addends into Parts section in the *Student Guide*.

TIMS Tip

To help students quickly recognize the length of trains, they can use a train of ten connecting cubes as a benchmark. This will assist counting and building of trains for each problem.

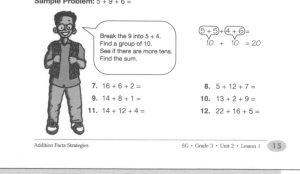

Switching

Do the following problems in your head. Make as many groups of ten as possible. There may be more than one way to solve each problem. A sample has been done for you.

Sample Problem: 4 + 9 + 6 =

> Make a ten with the 4 and 6. Then, add the 9. The answer is 19.

1. 5 + 6 + 5 =   **2.** 12 + 7 + 8 =

3. 5 + 9 + 11 =   **4.** 3 + 17 + 7 =

5. 16 + 4 + 11 =   **6.** 14 + 16 + 6 =

Breaking Addends into Parts

The numbers that are added in an addition problem are called the **addends.** The answer is called the **sum.**

Find groups of ten in the following number sentences by breaking an addend into two parts. Then find the sum. There may be more than one way to solve each problem. Be ready to explain your thinking to the class.

Sample Problem: 5 + 9 + 6 =

> Break the 9 into 5 + 4. Find a group of 10. See if there are more tens. Find the sum.

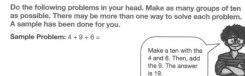

(5 + 5) + (4 + 6) =
10 + 10 = 20

7. 16 + 6 + 2 =   **8.** 5 + 12 + 7 =

9. 14 + 8 + 1 =   **10.** 13 + 2 + 9 =

11. 14 + 12 + 4 =   **12.** 22 + 16 + 5 =

Addition Facts Strategies   SG • Grade 3 • Unit 2 • Lesson 1   15

Student Guide - page 15 *(Answers on p. 37)*

Part 4 My Calculator Is Broken!

In this part, students partition addends using calculators. Begin by saying:

- *Today, we are going to imagine that some of the keys on the calculator are broken. That means that you cannot use those keys. First, let's imagine the five is broken. What keys would you press to do the problem 9 + 5 + 2?*

There are a number of ways to key this problem without using the five key. Encourage students to partition five so that a group of ten can be formed. For example, students might enter the following keystrokes:

Some students might skip a step on the calculator and press:

Provide additional problems that include addends such as 5, 15, or 25. For example:

- 8 + 5
- 5 + 7 + 6
- 15 + 6 + 3
- 9 + 25

Encourage students to predict the calculator's answer before they key it into the calculator. Ask students to list their keystrokes on the board or overhead. Encourage students to compare different keystroke sequences.

Assign the *Calculator Explorations* Homework Page.

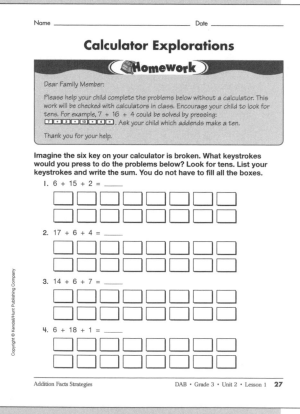

Discovery Assignment Book - page 25 *(Answers on p. 37)*

Name _____ **Date** _____

Switch It!

Homework

1. Complete the following problems in your head. Try to use a ten whenever possible. Choose two problems and tell how you solved each one. You can use pictures, words, or number sentences.

   A. 3 + 16 + 7 = _____

   B. 9 + 17 + 1 = _____

   C. 2 + 11 + 8 = _____

   D. 5 + 15 + 6 = _____

   E. 7 + 12 + 8 = _____

2. Write and solve your own addition problem.

Name _____ **Date** _____

Calculator Explorations

Homework

Dear Family Member:

Please help your child complete the problems below without a calculator. This work will be checked with calculators in class. Encourage your child to look for tens. For example, 7 + 16 + 4 could be solved by pressing: 7 + 3 + 13 + 4 =. Ask your child which addends make a ten.

Thank you for your help.

Imagine the six key on your calculator is broken. What keystrokes would you press to do the problems below? Look for tens. List your keystrokes and write the sum. You do not have to fill all the boxes.

1. 6 + 15 + 2 = _____

2. 17 + 6 + 4 = _____

3. 14 + 6 + 7 = _____

4. 6 + 18 + 1 = _____

Discovery Assignment Book - page 27 *(Answers on p. 38)*

Math Facts

DPP Bit A provides practice with math facts and adding numbers with ending zeros.

Homework and Practice

- Students switch the order of addends to make groups of ten on the *Switch It!* Homework Page in the *Discovery Assignment Book.*

- On the *Calculator Explorations* Homework Page in the *Discovery Assignment Book,* the six key is broken. Students complete this page at home without using a calculator and then check their work in class. You may want to make a transparency and model an example.

- DPP Task B provides practice with money and calculating change. Bit C develops number sense through skip counting on a calculator. For Challenge D, students make calculations involving elapsed time.

Assessment

Use the *Calculator Challenges* Assessment Blackline Master to measure students' abilities to partition and rearrange addends.

Extension

Challenge students to group three or more addends to make a group of ten. For example:

- 3 + 4 + 5 + 3
- 2 + 5 + 6 + 2 + 1
- 17 + 5 + 2 + 1

Estimated Class Sessions

2

At a Glance

Math Facts and Daily Practice and Problems

DPP Bit A provides practice with math facts. Task B provides practice with money. Bit C is skip counting on a calculator. Challenge D involves elapsed time.

Part 1. Using a Ten

1. Students build a train with seven blue cubes and another train with eight red cubes.
2. Review the using-ten strategy and have students model it with their cubes.
3. Students utilize the using-ten strategy and their cubes to solve more problems.
4. Students discuss how using a ten can help them add.

Part 2. Switch It!

1. Students solve 14 + 7 + 6 with connecting cubes and share their methods with the class.
2. Students complete 14 + 7 + 6 using mental arithmetic.
3. Students solve other problems: 8 + 7 + 12, 6 + 8 + 14, and 11 + 3 + 9.
4. Students read the *Addition Facts Strategies* Activity Pages in the *Student Guide* and do the problems in the Switching section.
5. Students discuss various solutions.

Part 3. Breaking Addends into Parts

1. Students partition addends to find groups of ten. They discuss and compare solutions.
2. Students solve two-digit addends in problems such as 11 + 5 + 3 and discuss their solutions.
3. Students complete the problems in the Breaking Addends into Parts section in the *Student Guide.*

Part 4. My Calculator Is Broken!

1. Students discuss how they might solve a problem on an imaginary calculator with a broken five key.
2. Students partition five so that a group of ten can be formed.
3. Students work additional problems that include addends such as 5, 15, or 25. Students list their keystrokes on the board or overhead.
4. Students practice predicting the calculator's answer before they key it into the calculator.
5. Students compare different keystroke sequences.

Homework

1. Assign the *Switch It!* Homework Page in the *Discovery Assignment Book.*
2. Assign the *Calculator Explorations* Homework Page.

Assessment

Students complete the *Calculator Challenges* Assessment Page.

Extension

Have students group three or four addends to make ten.

Answer Key is on pages 37–38.

Notes:

Calculator Challenges

Imagine the 7 key on your calculator is broken. What keys would you press to do the problems below? Look for tens. List your keystrokes and write the sum. You do not have to fill all the boxes.

1.   7 + 14 + 2 = _____

2.   15 + 7 + 4 = _____

3.   13 + 6 + 7 = _____

4.   7 + 18 + 1 = _____

5.   9 + 17 + 4 = _____

Copyright © Kendall/Hunt Publishing Company

Student Guide (p. 15)

Solution strategies may vary.

1. $16; 5 + 5 = 10; 10 + 6 = 16$
2. $27; 12 + 8 = 20; 20 + 7 = 27$
3. $25; 9 + 11 = 20; 20 + 5 = 25$
4. $27; 3 + 17 = 20; 20 + 7 = 27$
5. $31; 16 + 4 = 20; 20 + 10 + 1 = 31$
6. $36; 14 + 6 = 20; 20 + 16 = 36$
7. 24; break the 6 into $4 + 2$; $16 + 4 = 20$; $20 + 2 + 2 = 24$
8. 24; break the 5 into $2 + 3$; $3 + 7 = 10$; $10 + 12 + 2 = 24$
9. 23; break the 8 into $6 + 2$; $14 + 6 = 20$; $20 + 2 + 1 = 23$
10. 24; break the 2 into $1 + 1$; $9 + 1 = 10$; $10 + 1 + 13 = 24$
11. 30; break the 12 into $6 + 6$; $14 + 6 = 20$ and $6 + 4 = 10$; $10 + 20 = 30$
12. 43; break the 5 into $4 + 1$; $16 + 4 = 20$; $20 + 22 + 1 = 43$

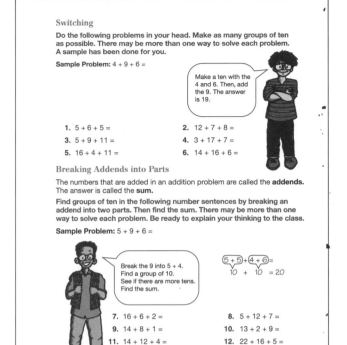

Student Guide - page 15

Discovery Assignment Book (p. 25)

Switch It!

Solution strategies will vary.

1. A. $26; 3 + 7 + 16 = 26$
   B. $27; 9 + 1 + 17 = 27$
   C. $21; 8 + 2 + 11 = 21$
   D. $26; 5 + 5 + 10 + 6 = 26$
   E. $27; 12 + 8 + 7 = 27$
2. Problems will vary.

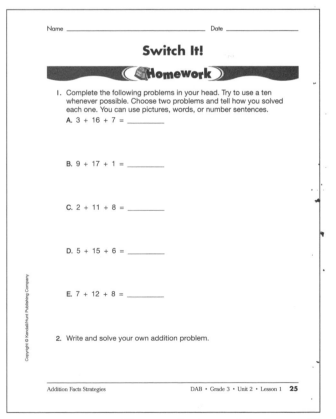

Discovery Assignment Book - page 25

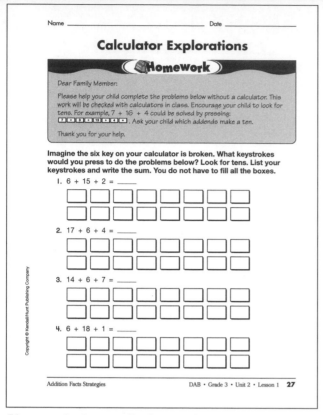

Discovery Assignment Book - page 27

Discovery Assignment Book (p. 27)

Calculator Explorations

Solution strategies/keystrokes will vary.

1. 23; $1 + 5 + 15 + 2 =$
2. 27; $17 + 3 + 3 + 4 =$
3. 27; $14 + 3 + 3 + 7 =$
4. 25; $4 + 2 + 18 + 1 =$

Calculator Challenges

Imagine the 7 key on your calculator is broken. What keys would you press to do the problems below? Look for tens. List your keystrokes and write the sum. You do not have to fill all the boxes.

1. $7 + 14 + 2 =$ _____

2. $15 + 7 + 4 =$ _____

3. $13 + 6 + 7 =$ _____

4. $7 + 18 + 1 =$ _____

5. $9 + 17 + 4 =$ _____

Copyright © Kendall/Hunt Publishing Company

36   URG • Grade 3 • Unit 2 • Lesson 1   Assessment Blackline Master

Unit Resource Guide - page 36

Unit Resource Guide (p. 36)

Calculator Challenges

Solution strategies/keystrokes will vary.

1. 23; $1 + 6 + 14 + 2 =$
2. 26; $15 + 5 + 2 + 4 =$
3. 26; $13 + 6 + 4 + 3 =$
4. 26; $5 + 2 + 18 + 1 =$
5. 30; $9 + 1 + 16 + 4 =$

Addition Facts Strategies

"There are many different ways to solve addition problems," said Miriam.

"I can think of at least two ways," said Eric. "You can count up using your fingers and toes, or you can use blocks or cubes."

"I like to find groups of ten, then add up what's left over," said Miriam.

Miriam and Eric used counters to help Tisha and Peter solve 6 + 10 + 4.

Copyright © Kendall/Hunt Publishing Company

Switching

Do the following problems in your head. Make as many groups of ten as possible. There may be more than one way to solve each problem. A sample has been done for you.

Sample Problem: 4 + 9 + 6 =

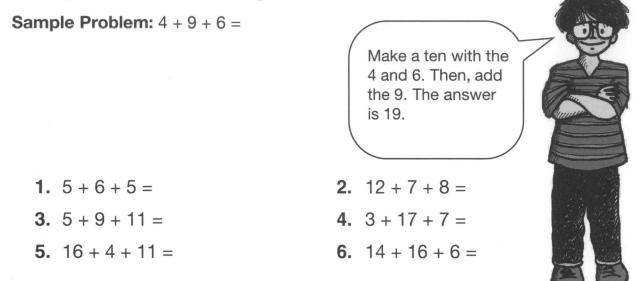

Make a ten with the 4 and 6. Then, add the 9. The answer is 19.

1. 5 + 6 + 5 =

2. 12 + 7 + 8 =

3. 5 + 9 + 11 =

4. 3 + 17 + 7 =

5. 16 + 4 + 11 =

6. 14 + 16 + 6 =

Breaking Addends into Parts

The numbers that are added in an addition problem are called the **addends.** The answer is called the **sum.**

Find groups of ten in the following number sentences by breaking an addend into two parts. Then find the sum. There may be more than one way to solve each problem. Be ready to explain your thinking to the class.

Sample Problem: 5 + 9 + 6 =

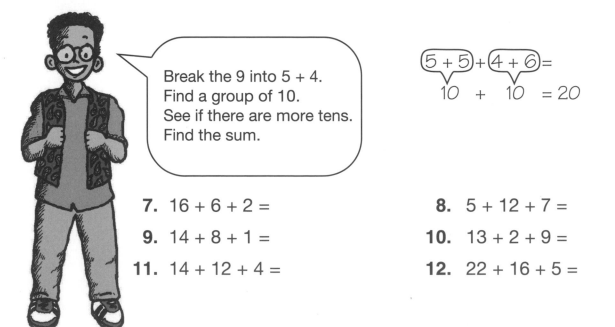

Break the 9 into 5 + 4. Find a group of 10. See if there are more tens. Find the sum.

$(5 + 5) + (4 + 6) =$
$10 \ + \ 10 \ = 20$

7. 16 + 6 + 2 =

8. 5 + 12 + 7 =

9. 14 + 8 + 1 =

10. 13 + 2 + 9 =

11. 14 + 12 + 4 =

12. 22 + 16 + 5 =

Copyright © Kendall/Hunt Publishing Company

Name _____   Date _____

Switch It!

I. Complete the following problems in your head. Try to use a ten whenever possible. Choose two problems and tell how you solved each one. You can use pictures, words, or number sentences.

   A. 3 + 16 + 7 = _____

   B. 9 + 17 + 1 = _____

   C. 2 + 11 + 8 = _____

   D. 5 + 15 + 6 = _____

   E. 7 + 12 + 8 = _____

2. Write and solve your own addition problem.

Copyright © Kendall/Hunt Publishing Company

Calculator Explorations

Homework

Dear Family Member:

Please help your child complete the problems below without a calculator. This work will be checked with calculators in class. Encourage your child to look for tens. For example, 7 + 16 + 4 could be solved by pressing: [7] [+] [3] [+] [13] [+] [4] [=] . Ask your child which addends make a ten.

Thank you for your help.

Imagine the six key on your calculator is broken. What keystrokes would you press to do the problems below? Look for tens. List your keystrokes and write the sum. You do not have to fill all the boxes.

1. 6 + 15 + 2 = _____

2. 17 + 6 + 4 = _____

3. 14 + 6 + 7 = _____

4. 6 + 18 + 1 = _____

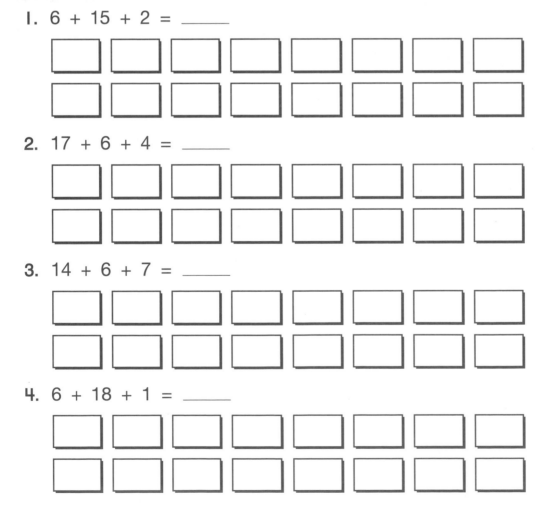

Copyright © Kendall/Hunt Publishing Company

Facts Distribution
Subtraction: Groups 1 & 2 • Weeks 3–5

Subtraction: Groups 1 & 2

Math Facts Groups	Weeks	Daily Practice and Problems	Home Practice	Flash Cards	Facts Quizzes and Tests
Subtraction: Groups 1 & 2	3–5	The lessons *Subtraction Facts Strategies* (Unit 2 Lesson 5) and *Assessing the Subtraction Facts* (Unit 2 Lesson 7) launch the practice and assessment of the subtraction facts in Grade 3. *Assessing the Subtraction Facts* introduces the flash cards and the *Subtraction Facts I Know* chart. Unit 2: items 2A, 2E, 2L, 2N, 2O, 2Q, 2R, 2T & 2U	Unit 2 Parts 1 & 2	Subtraction Flash Cards: Groups 1 & 2	The *Subtraction Facts I Know* chart is updated.

Students may solve the items individually, in groups, or as a class. The items may also be assigned for homework. The DPPs are also available on the Teacher Resource CD.

Student Questions	Teacher Notes

2A **Quick Addition**

Do these problems in your head. Write only the answers.

1. $4 + 9 =$

2. $40 + 90 =$

3. $20 + 90 =$

4. $20 + 30 =$

5. $30 + 50 =$

6. $40 + 60 =$

7. $10 + 90 =$

8. $60 + 80 =$

9. $80 + 70 =$

10. Explain your strategy for Question 9.

TIMS Bit

These problems provide an opportunity for students to review a few addition facts and relate them to adding multiples of ten.

1. 13
2. 130
3. 110
4. 50
5. 80
6. 100
7. 100
8. 140
9. 150
10. Possible strategy: Students may break apart 70 into 20 and 50. Then by joining 20 and 80 to make 100, the remaining 50 is added to equal 150.

Student Questions	Teacher Notes

2E Mental Arithmetic: Using Doubles

Solve these problems in your head. Write only the answers. Be ready to explain your answers.

1. $6 + 6 =$

2. $6 + 5 =$

3. $8 + 6 =$

4. $50 + 50 =$

5. $60 + 50 =$

6. $50 + 55 =$

7. $25 + 25 =$

8. $25 + 27 =$

9. $25 + 15 =$

10. Explain your strategy for Question 8.

TIMS Bit ⬛N ⬛ ⬛$\frac{5}{\times 7}$

These problems are grouped to encourage students to use doubles to find the answers. For example, $25 + 27$ can be solved by doubling 25 and adding two.

$(25 + 25 + 2 = 52)$

1. 12   2. 11

3. 14   4. 100

5. 110   6. 105

7. 50   8. 52

9. 40

10. Possible strategy: Students may think of adding two quarters to make 50 and then the remaining 2 to make 52.

2L Line Math Puzzle

Put the digits 4, 5, 6, 7, and 8 in the boxes so that the sum of each line is the same.

TIMS Task ⬛$\frac{5}{\times 7}$

One possible solution:

2N   Magic Square: 4, 5, 6

Complete the magic square using the digits 4, 4, 4, 5, 5, 5, 6, 6, and 6. Each row, column, and diagonal must have a sum of 15.

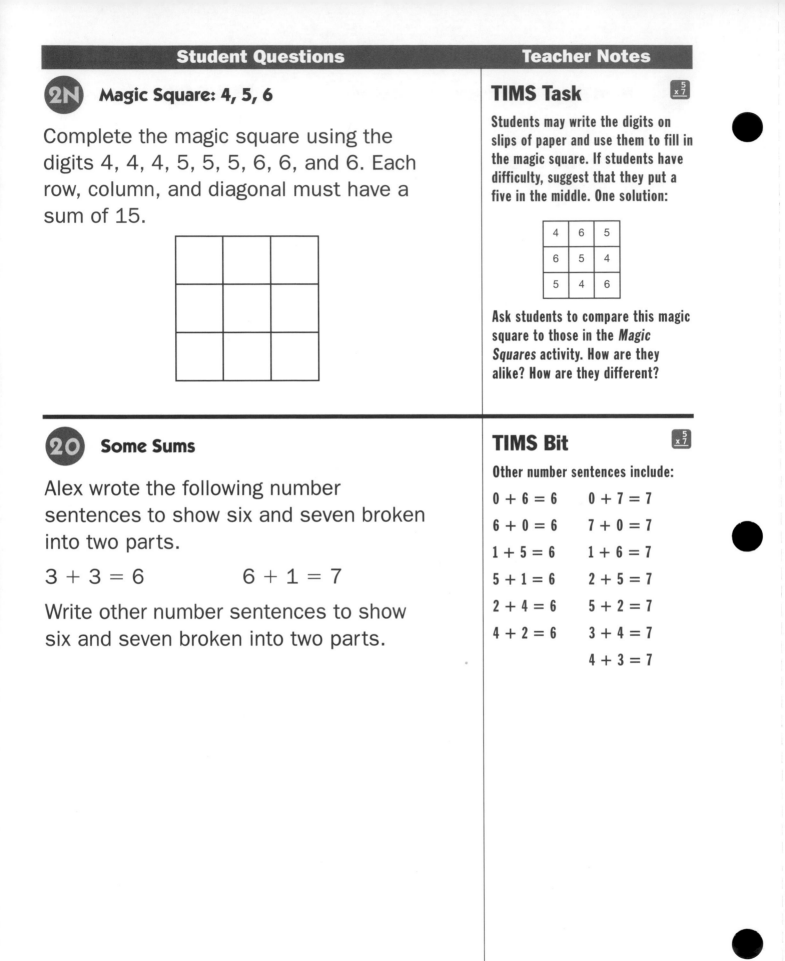

TIMS Task

Students may write the digits on slips of paper and use them to fill in the magic square. If students have difficulty, suggest that they put a five in the middle. One solution:

4	6	5
6	5	4
5	4	6

Ask students to compare this magic square to those in the *Magic Squares* activity. How are they alike? How are they different?

20   Some Sums

Alex wrote the following number sentences to show six and seven broken into two parts.

$3 + 3 = 6$ $6 + 1 = 7$

Write other number sentences to show six and seven broken into two parts.

TIMS Bit

Other number sentences include:

$0 + 6 = 6$	$0 + 7 = 7$
$6 + 0 = 6$	$7 + 0 = 7$
$1 + 5 = 6$	$1 + 6 = 7$
$5 + 1 = 6$	$2 + 5 = 7$
$2 + 4 = 6$	$5 + 2 = 7$
$4 + 2 = 6$	$3 + 4 = 7$
	$4 + 3 = 7$

2Q What's Your Strategy?

Bill has trouble remembering the answer to 15 − 8. What strategy might be helpful for Bill?

TIMS Bit $\boxed{\begin{smallmatrix}5\\\times 7\end{smallmatrix}}$

Bill might use ten:

from 8 to 10 is 2

from 10 to 15 is 5

So 15 − 8 = 7

or

15 − 5 = 10

10 − 3 = 7

2R Magic Square Mystery

Complete the magic square using the numbers 5, 6, 7, 10, and 11. Each row, column, and diagonal must have the same sum. What is the sum?

9	4	
	8	
	12	

TIMS Challenge $\boxed{\begin{smallmatrix}5\\\times 7\end{smallmatrix}}$

9	4	11
10	8	6
5	12	7

The sum is 24. Once students have found the solution, ask them to look at the magic square and look for patterns. Where are the odd and even numbers? (All of the odd numbers are on the corners.)

2T Magic Square: Sum = 15

Complete the magic square using 1, 2, 3, 4, 5, 6, 7, 8, and 9. Each row, column, and diagonal must have a sum of 15. This is the same magic square that Sun Feng had to do in the story *Yü the Great*.

TIMS Challenge

4	9	2
3	5	7
8	1	6

The solution above can also be found in the design on the turtle's back in the story *Yü the Great*. There are many solutions, but each solution has 5 in the center square. Challenge students to find more solutions. If students have difficulty, suggest that they put 5 in the middle.

2U Addition Sentences

Write two addition sentences for each of the following sums.

A. 13

B. 17

C. 10

D. 11

TIMS Bit

Students should compare solutions. Students may use different addends and a different number of addends. Some may need to check their work on a calculator.

Unit 2 Home Practice

Copyright © Kendall/Hunt Publishing Company

PART 1

1. A. $18 - 10 =$ _____
   B. $13 - 6 =$ _____
   C. $14 - 9 =$ _____

2. A. $4 + 4 + 8 =$ _____
   B. $7 + 9 + 8 =$ _____
   C. $15 + 7 + 4 =$ _____

3. Kyle received eight new books for his birthday. He now has fifty-two books. How many books did Kyle have before his birthday? Show how you found your answer.

   _____

   _____

   _____

   _____

PART 2

1. A. $15 + 5 +$ _____ $= 28$
   B. $20 + 5 +$ _____ $= 28$
   C. $17 +$ _____ $+ 3 = 28$
   D. $12 +$ _____ $+ 6 = 28$
   E. $5 + 9 +$ _____ $= 28$
   F. $13 + 8 +$ _____ $= 28$

2. For the food drive, Ron's class collected seventeen cans of vegetables, four cans of fruit, and nine cans of soup.
   A. How many cans did they collect?

   _____

   _____

   B. How many more cans of vegetables are there than soup?

   _____

   _____

Subtraction Facts Strategies

Lesson Overview

Estimated Class Sessions

2

This activity begins a review and practice of the subtraction facts. This focus will continue throughout the first half of the year. Students practice the facts as they encounter them in activities, labs, games, and the Daily Practice and Problems. Students' fluency is checked using quizzes in the DPP beginning in Unit 7.

The subtraction facts are organized by strategy into eight groups of nine facts. This lesson provides work with the first two groups of facts. These facts can be solved with the strategies using a ten, counting up, and thinking addition. Students will work with flash cards for these groups in Lesson 7. The additional six groups of facts will be introduced gradually through the Daily Practice and Problems. Appropriate strategies will be reviewed for each group.

Key Content

- Using strategies to learn subtraction facts.

Math Facts

DPP items N and O provide practice with math facts.

Homework

Students play *Nine, Ten* at home.

Assessment

1. Use DPP Task N to assess students' understanding of the Magic Square activity.
2. Use the *Observational Assessment Record* to note students' use of strategies to subtract.

Copyright © Kendall/Hunt Publishing Company

Materials List

Supplies and Copies

Student	Teacher
Supplies for Each Student Pair • 2 clear spinners (or pencils and paper clips)	**Supplies** • 2 clear spinners
Copies	**Copies/Transparencies** • 1 transparency of *Spinners 11–18 and 9–10* (*Discovery Assignment Book* Page 35)

All blackline masters including assessment, transparency, and DPP masters are also on the Teacher Resource CD.

Student Books
Subtraction Facts Strategies (*Student Guide* Pages 22–27)
Spinners 11–18 and 9–10 (*Discovery Assignment Book* Page 35)

Daily Practice and Problems and Home Practice
DPP items M–P (*Unit Resource Guide* Pages 23–24)

Note: Classrooms whose pacing differs significantly from the suggested pacing of the units should use the Math Facts Calendar in Section 4 of the *Facts Resource Guide* to ensure students receive the complete math facts program.

Assessment Tools
Observational Assessment Record (*Unit Resource Guide* Pages 15–16)

Copyright © Kendall/Hunt Publishing Company

Daily Practice and Problems

Suggestions for using the DPPs are on page 78.

M. Bit: 1 and 0 Are Broken (URG p. 23)

The "1" key and the "0" key are broken on the calculator. List the keys you would press to do these problems.

   A. 10 + 10

   B. 11 + 10

   C. 11 + 11

O. Bit: Some Sums (URG p. 24)

Alex wrote the following number sentences to show six and seven broken into two parts.

$$3 + 3 = 6 \qquad\qquad 6 + 1 = 7$$

Write other number sentences to show six and seven broken into two parts.

N. Task: Magic Square: 4, 5, 6
  (URG p. 24)

Complete the magic square using the digits 4, 4, 4, 5, 5, 5, 6, 6, and 6. Each row, column, and diagonal must have a sum of 15.

P. Task: Number Sentence Stories
  (URG p. 24)

Write a story for the following number sentence.

$$25 = 19 + \underline{\quad}$$

Copyright © Kendall/Hunt Publishing Company

Student Guide - page 22

Student Guide - page 23

Part 1 Subtraction Facts Strategies

Subtraction Facts Strategies in the *Student Guide* begins with a discussion between John, Suzanne, and their teacher about three subtraction facts, $15 - 10$, $13 - 10$, and $15 - 9$. Through their discussion, students review subtraction facts strategies. After students read the two pages of dialog, ask questions like the following:

- *What strategy do you use to solve the problem $15 - 10$?*

- *John thinks facts with tens are the easiest. He solves two of them. What are other examples of facts with tens?*

After listing a few facts with tens on the board, ask:

- *What are the answers to these subtraction facts?*

- *What patterns do you see?*

- *Explain to a friend why John might think these are easy.*

Refer to Suzanne's explanation to introduce "facts with nines." Ask the class to generate a list of problems similar to $15 - 9$, such as $13 - 9$ or $17 - 9$.

Ask:

- *What is $13 - 9$? How did you solve it?*

- *Use Suzanne's method of counting up to do $13 - 9$.*

- *Describe how Suzanne "used a ten" to help her do $15 - 9$.*

Class discussion of strategies helps students verbalize number relationships and encourages them to think about the problems in new ways. It is important to emphasize that a strategy that works well for one person may not be helpful to another. The strategies mentioned here are suggestions students may find useful. Encourage students to develop and share their own strategies as well. They will encounter helpful strategies that will make learning the subtraction facts easier. Students who already demonstrate fluency with the facts may find that using a strategy is more work. Emphasize that these strategies will be more helpful when they solve problems such as $25 - 9$ or $33 - 19$.

Ask student pairs to discuss the questions in the *Student Guide*. It is not necessary for students to remember the names of the strategies, but to remember how to use them. Students may use different strategies to do the same problem. Pairs can report their answers and methods in a class discussion.

Copyright © Kendall/Hunt Publishing Company

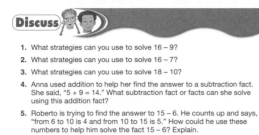

Discuss

1. What strategies can you use to solve 16 – 9?
2. What strategies can you use to solve 16 – 7?
3. What strategies can you use to solve 18 – 10?
4. Anna used addition to help her find the answer to a subtraction fact. She said, "5 + 9 = 14." What subtraction fact or facts can she solve using this addition fact?
5. Roberto is trying to find the answer to 15 – 6. He counts up and says, "from 6 to 10 is 4 and from 10 to 15 is 5." How could he use these numbers to help him solve the fact 15 – 6? Explain.
6. Sam said, "I know 5 – 2 = 3. I don't use any strategy for that fact. I just know it!" Name three subtraction facts you just know.

Nine, Ten

Players

This is a game for two players.

Materials

- *Spinners 11–18 and 9–10*
- 2 clear plastic spinners or 2 pencils with paper clips
- 2 game boards

24   SG • Grade 3 • Unit 2 • Lesson 5   Subtraction Facts Strategies

Student Guide - page 24 (Answers on p. 80)

Rules

The first person to fill in one of the columns on his or her game board is the winner.

1. Make two game boards, one for each player, like the one below.

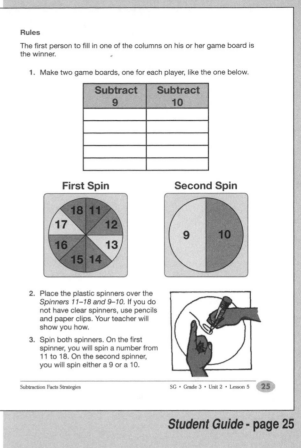

2. Place the plastic spinners over the *Spinners 11–18 and 9–10*. If you do not have clear spinners, use pencils and paper clips. Your teacher will show you how.

3. Spin both spinners. On the first spinner, you will spin a number from 11 to 18. On the second spinner, you will spin either a 9 or a 10.

Subtraction Facts Strategies   SG • Grade 3 • Unit 2 • Lesson 5   25

Student Guide - page 25

Journal Prompt

Describe a strategy you could use to help a friend find 17 – 9.

Part 2 Playing *Nine, Ten*

Students practice subtracting nine and ten while playing the game *Nine, Ten*. The game encourages the use of the strategies using a ten, counting up, and thinking addition.

Instruct students to read the directions for *Nine, Ten* in the *Student Guide*. As students play the game, circulate and listen to students as they solve the problems. If students are having trouble, encourage them to use strategies to help them write correct number sentences. Also, ask students to look for patterns on the game board as they fill in the columns. They may see that each difference in the "Subtract 10" column is the same as the ones digit of the first number in the sentence. They may also notice that each difference in the "Subtract 9" column is one more than the ones digit of the first number in the sentence.

---

4. Make a subtraction sentence with the two numbers you spin. Does your partner agree that your answer is correct? If so, write the number sentence in the game board column where it belongs. If it is not correct, do not write anything on the game board.

5. Take turns with your partner. The first player to fill in one of the columns on his or her game board is the winner.

Suzanne and John's Sample Game

Suzanne and John are playing *Nine, Ten*. Suzanne spins an 11 and a 9, so she says, "11 minus 9 equals 2." She answered correctly. She writes the number sentence in the column labeled "Subtract 9" on her game board.

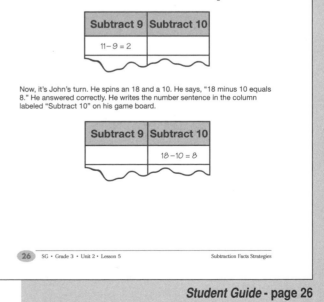

Now, it's John's turn. He spins an 18 and a 10. He says, "18 minus 10 equals 8." He answered correctly. He writes the number sentence in the column labeled "Subtract 10" on his game board.

26   SG • Grade 3 • Unit 2 • Lesson 5   Subtraction Facts Strategies

Student Guide - page 26

Copyright © Kendall/Hunt Publishing Company

After playing a while longer, the game boards looked like this:

Suzanne's Board

Subtract 9	Subtract 10
11 − 9 = 2	17 − 10 = 7
17 − 9 = 8	15 − 10 = 5
15 − 9 = 6	11 − 10 = 1
18 − 9 = 9	

John's Board

Subtract 9	Subtract 10
18 − 9 = 9	18 − 10 = 8
13 − 9 = 4	12 − 10 = 2
18 − 9 = 9	13 − 10 = 3
	16 − 10 = 6
	16 − 10 = 6

Notice that John recorded 16 − 10 = 6 twice. He spun the same numbers on two different turns. He answered the problem correctly both times. John completely filled in one column first. He won the game!

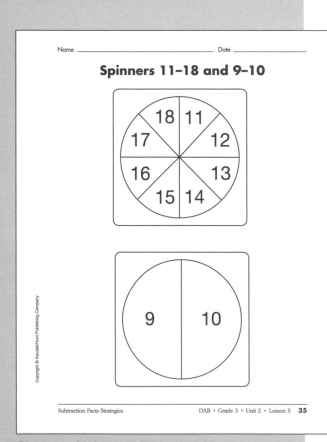

Play a game with a friend. Look for patterns in the number sentences on the game boards when you finish playing.

Subtraction Facts Strategies   SG • Grade 3 • Unit 2 • Lesson 5   27

Student Guide - page 27

Copyright © Kendall/Hunt Publishing Company

Name _____   Date _____

Spinners 11–18 and 9–10

Subtraction Facts Strategies   DAB • Grade 3 • Unit 2 • Lesson 5   **35**

Discovery Assignment Book - page 35

Math Facts

DPP item O provides practice with addition facts.

Homework and Practice

- Students can play *Nine, Ten* at home with their families.
- DPP items M and P build number sense and computation skills.

Assessment

- A plan for assessing fluency with subtraction facts is discussed in the Daily Practice and Problems Guide and in Lesson 7.
- Use the *Observational Assessment Record* to note students' use of strategies to subtract.
- DPP Task N can be used as an assessment of the Magic Square activities.

Extension

Write the following problems on the board, and read them aloud.

$$\begin{array}{r} 25 \\ -10 \end{array} \qquad \begin{array}{r} 25 \\ -9 \end{array} \qquad \begin{array}{r} 33 \\ -20 \end{array} \qquad \begin{array}{r} 33 \\ -19 \end{array} \qquad \begin{array}{r} 33 \\ -14 \end{array}$$

Ask students to solve these problems in their heads. Guide students to the notion that the strategies can be generalized to two-digit numbers. Then discuss possible strategies for solving these problems.

Copyright © Kendall/Hunt Publishing Company

At a Glance

Math Facts and Daily Practice and Problems

DPP items N and O provide practice with math facts. Items M and P build computation skills.

Part 1. Subtraction Facts Strategies

1. Students read *Subtraction Facts Strategies* in the *Student Guide*.
2. Discuss subtraction strategies. Students share their own methods.
3. Student pairs discuss **Questions 1–6** on the *Subtraction Facts Strategies* Activity Pages.

Part 2. Playing *Nine, Ten*

1. Students read the Nine, Ten section and the Suzanne and John's Game section in the *Student Guide*.
2. Student pairs play the game, discuss patterns, and share strategies.

Homework

Students play *Nine, Ten* at home.

Assessment

1. Use DPP Task N to assess students' understanding of the Magic Square activity.
2. Use the *Observational Assessment Record* to note students' use of strategies to subtract.

Extension

Write the following problems on the board and guide students to discover that strategies can be generalized to two-digit numbers.

$$
\begin{array}{ccccc}
25 & 25 & 33 & 33 & 33 \\
-10 & -\ 9 & -20 & -19 & -14 \\
\end{array}
$$

Answer Key is on page 80.

Notes:

Copyright © Kendall/Hunt Publishing Company

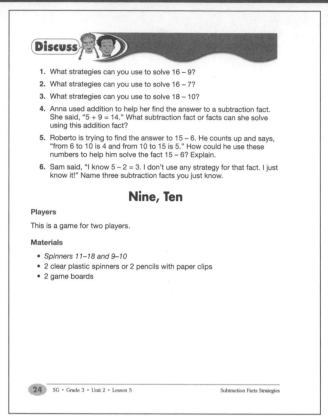

Student Guide - page 24

Student Guide (p. 24)

1. Answers will vary. Students may count up: From 9 to 10 is 1, from 10 to 16 is 6; $6 + 1 = 7$. Thinking addition: $9 + 7 = 16$ so $16 - 9 = 7$. Using a ten: $16 - 10 = 6$ so $16 - 9$ would be one more or 7. It is not necessary for students to remember the names of the strategies, but to remember how to use them.

2. Answers will vary. Counting up: From 7 to 10 is 3, from 10 to 16 is 6; $3 + 6 = 9$. Thinking addition: $7 + 9 = 16$ so $16 - 7 = 9$. Using a ten: $16 - 6 = 10$ so $16 - 7$ would be one less or 9.

3. Answers will vary. Thinking addition: $10 + 8 = 18$ so $18 - 10 = 8$. Counting up: $10 + 8 = 18$. The answer is the second digit in 18 (the number in the ones place).

4. $14 - 9 = 5$; $14 - 5 = 9$

5. Answers will vary. Roberto can add the 4 and 5 and get 9. $15 - 6 = 9$

6. Answers will vary.

Copyright © Kendall/Hunt Publishing Company

Subtraction Facts Strategies

Copyright © Kendall/Hunt Publishing Company

Copyright © Kendall/Hunt Publishing Company

Discuss

1. What strategies can you use to solve 16 – 9?

2. What strategies can you use to solve 16 – 7?

3. What strategies can you use to solve 18 – 10?

4. Anna used addition to help her find the answer to a subtraction fact. She said, "5 + 9 = 14." What subtraction fact or facts can she solve using this addition fact?

5. Roberto is trying to find the answer to 15 – 6. He counts up and says, "from 6 to 10 is 4 and from 10 to 15 is 5." How could he use these numbers to help him solve the fact 15 – 6? Explain.

6. Sam said, "I know 5 – 2 = 3. I don't use any strategy for that fact. I just know it!" Name three subtraction facts you just know.

Nine, Ten

Players

This is a game for two players.

Materials

- *Spinners 11–18 and 9–10*
- 2 clear plastic spinners or 2 pencils with paper clips
- 2 game boards

Copyright © Kendall/Hunt Publishing Company

Rules

The first person to fill in one of the columns on his or her game board is the winner.

1. Make two game boards, one for each player, like the one below.

Subtract 9	Subtract 10

First Spin

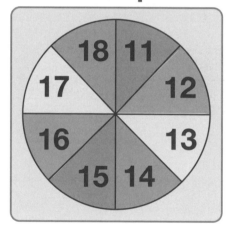

Second Spin

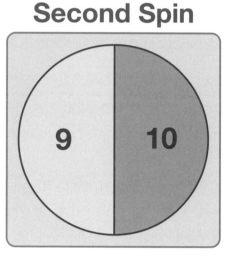

2. Place the plastic spinners over the *Spinners 11–18 and 9–10.* If you do not have clear spinners, use pencils and paper clips. Your teacher will show you how.

3. Spin both spinners. On the first spinner, you will spin a number from 11 to 18. On the second spinner, you will spin either a 9 or a 10.

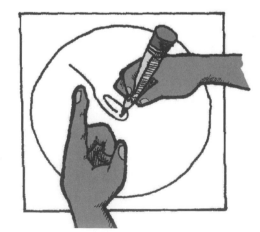

Copyright © Kendall/Hunt Publishing Company

4. Make a subtraction sentence with the two numbers you spin. Does your partner agree that your answer is correct? If so, write the number sentence in the game board column where it belongs. If it is not correct, do not write anything on the game board.

5. Take turns with your partner. The first player to fill in one of the columns on his or her game board is the winner.

Suzanne and John's Sample Game

Suzanne and John are playing *Nine, Ten.* Suzanne spins an 11 and a 9, so she says, "11 minus 9 equals 2." She answered correctly. She writes the number sentence in the column labeled "Subtract 9" on her game board.

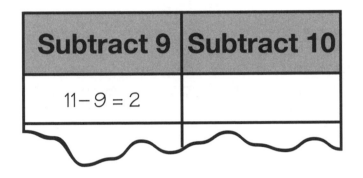

Subtract 9	Subtract 10
11 − 9 = 2	

Now, it's John's turn. He spins an 18 and a 10. He says, "18 minus 10 equals 8." He answered correctly. He writes the number sentence in the column labeled "Subtract 10" on his game board.

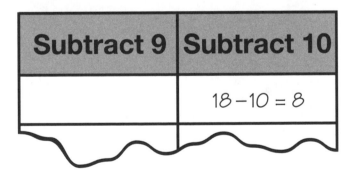

Subtract 9	Subtract 10
	18 − 10 = 8

Copyright © Kendall/Hunt Publishing Company

After playing a while longer, the game boards looked like this:

Suzanne's Board

Subtract 9	Subtract 10
11 − 9 = 2	17 − 10 = 7
17 − 9 = 8	15 − 10 = 5
15 − 9 = 6	11 − 10 = 1
18 − 9 = 9	

John's Board

Subtract 9	Subtract 10
18 − 9 = 9	18 − 10 = 8
13 − 9 = 4	12 − 10 = 2
18 − 9 = 9	13 − 10 = 3
	16 − 10 = 6
	16 − 10 = 6

Notice that John recorded 16 − 10 = 6 twice. He spun the same numbers on two different turns. He answered the problem correctly both times. John completely filled in one column first. He won the game!

Play a game with a friend. Look for patterns in the number sentences on the game boards when you finish playing.

Copyright © Kendall/Hunt Publishing Company

Spinners 11–18 and 9–10

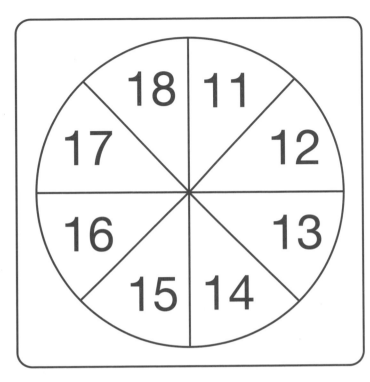

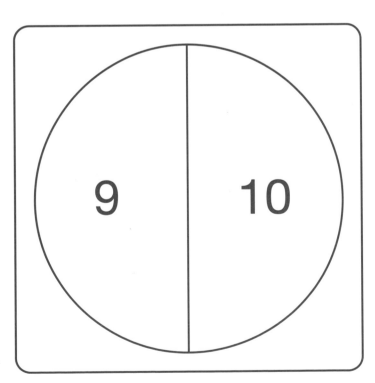

Copyright © Kendall/Hunt Publishing Company

Assessing the Subtraction Facts

Lesson Overview

Estimated Class Sessions

1

To facilitate learning, the subtraction facts are organized by strategy into eight groups of nine facts each. This activity involves the first two groups of facts that can be solved with the strategies using a ten, counting up, and thinking addition. The other six groups of facts will be reviewed gradually through the Daily Practice and Problems. Students are assessed on their knowledge of the subtraction facts in three ways:

1. through teacher observation;
2. through student self-assessment; and
3. through the use of written quizzes and tests.

The assessment of students' fluency with the subtraction facts is closely aligned with the philosophy and organization of its instruction as described in the Background and Daily Practice and Problems Guide of this unit.

Key Content

- Assessing knowledge of the subtraction facts.

Math Facts

DPP Bit U provides practice with addition facts.

Homework

Students take home the flash cards for Group 1 and Group 2 to practice the subtraction facts with a family member.

Copyright © Kendall/Hunt Publishing Company

Curriculum Sequence

Before This Unit

In Grade 2 Units 11–20 students practiced the subtraction facts using *Triangle Flash Cards.* After each time through the cards, they sorted them into three piles: those facts they knew quickly, those they knew using a strategy, and those they needed to study.

After This Unit

Students will continue to practice the subtraction facts in small groups in Units 3–10. They will take quizzes on these groups in Units 7–10. See Figure 10 for the distribution of the subtraction facts practice and assessment. See the Daily Practice and Problems Guide for this unit and the *Grade 3 Facts Resource Guide* for more information.

Copyright © Kendall/Hunt Publishing Company

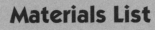

Materials List

Supplies and Copies

Student	Teacher
Supplies for Each Student • envelope for storing flash cards	**Supplies**
Copies • 1 copy of *Information for Parents: Grade 3 Math Facts Philosophy* per student (*Unit Resource Guide* Pages 13–14) • 1 back-to-back copy of *Subtraction Flash Cards: Group 1* per student, optional (*Unit Resource Guide* Pages 101–102) • 1 back-to-back copy of *Subtraction Flash Cards: Group 2* per student, optional (*Unit Resource Guide* Pages 103–104) **TIMS Tip** Copy each group of facts on different colored paper.	**Copies/Transparencies** • 1 transparency of *Subtraction Facts I Know,* optional (*Discovery Assignment Book* Page 43)

All blackline masters including assessment, transparency, and DPP masters are also on the Teacher Resource CD.

Student Books

Subtraction Flash Cards: Group 1 (*Discovery Assignment Book* Pages 37–38)
Subtraction Flash Cards: Group 2 (*Discovery Assignment Book* Pages 39–40)
Sorting Flash Cards (*Discovery Assignment Book* Page 41)
Subtraction Facts I Know (*Discovery Assignment Book* Page 43)

Daily Practice and Problems and Home Practice

DPP items U–V (*Unit Resource Guide* Page 26)

Note: Classrooms whose pacing differs significantly from the suggested pacing of the units should use the Math Facts Calendar in Section 4 of the *Facts Resource Guide* to ensure students receive the complete math facts program.

Copyright © Kendall/Hunt Publishing Company

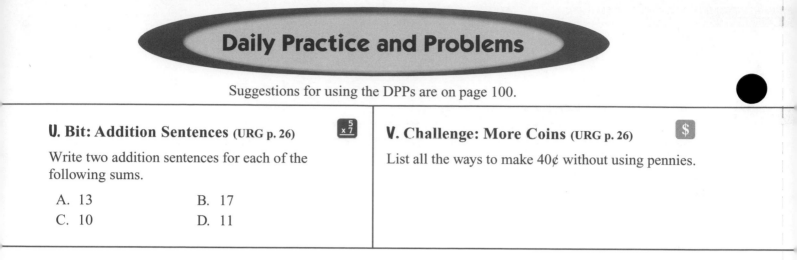

Daily Practice and Problems

Suggestions for using the DPPs are on page 100.

Suggestions for using the DPPs are on page 100.

U. Bit: Addition Sentences (URG p. 26)

Write two addition sentences for each of the following sums.

A. 13   B. 17
C. 10   D. 11

V. Challenge: More Coins (URG p. 26)

List all the ways to make 40¢ without using pennies.

Copyright © Kendall/Hunt Publishing Company

Before the Activity

Students cut out Groups 1 and 2 of *Subtraction Flash Cards* so each student has eighteen flash cards for this activity.

Teaching the Activity

Part 1 Strategies

Students discussed strategies for some of the subtraction facts from Groups 1 and 2 in Lesson 5. They can apply these strategies to the other facts in Groups 1 and 2. Write the following problems on the board or overhead: $13 - 4$, $15 - 6$, $14 - 5$, and $16 - 7$. Without referring to strategies, ask students for the answers to the facts. Then ask:

- *How did you solve $13 - 4$?*
- *Could you use a ten or count up to help you solve $13 - 4$? If so, describe how you would do so.* (Possible response: $13 - 3$ is 10, so $13 - 4$ is one less or 9.)
- *Could you use addition to help you solve the problem? If so, describe how you would do so.* (Since $4 + 9 = 13$, $13 - 9 = 4$.)

Part 2 Sorting Flash Cards

The eighteen facts in Groups 1 and 2 are grouped so students can use the subtraction strategies: using a ten, counting up, and thinking addition. Have student pairs put one deck of their flash cards away so they will not get mixed with those of their partners. Students will hold up one flash card at a time for their partner. Students use the *Sorting Flash Cards* Activity Page to sort the flash cards into three groups. If a student gives the correct answer quickly, then the flash card is laid on the first box labeled "Problems Answered Correctly and Quickly." If he or she answers correctly after thinking through a strategy, the flash card is laid on the second box labeled "Problems Answered Correctly after Thinking." If the student gives an incorrect answer, the flash card is laid on the third box labeled "Problems Answered Incorrectly."

After students finish sorting the flash cards, discuss the strategies they used to find the differences. Validate students' use of strategies unless they are inefficient. For example, if students are counting down from 15 to 9 by ones in order to solve $15 - 9$, encourage them to replace this strategy with a more efficient one, such as using a ten. Class discussion of strategies helps students verbalize the number relationships and encourages them to think about the problems in new ways.

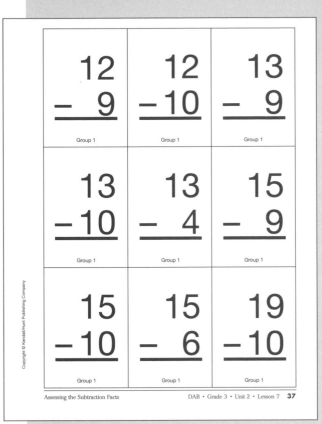

Discovery Assignment Book - page 37

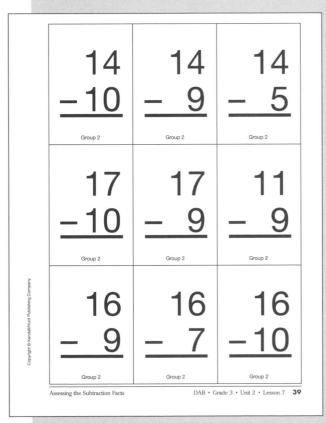

Discovery Assignment Book - page 39

Copyright © Kendall/Hunt Publishing Company

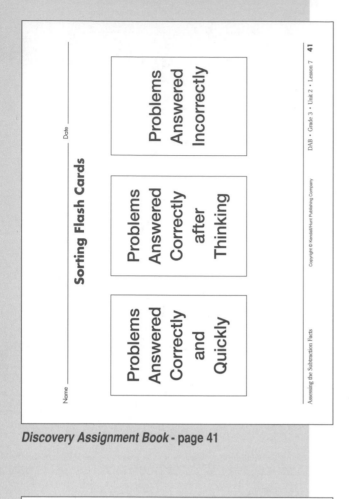

Discovery Assignment Book - page 41

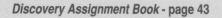

Discovery Assignment Book - page 43

Part 3 Subtraction Facts I Know

After sorting the flash cards, students record their current fluency with subtraction facts on their *Subtraction Facts I Know* charts found in the *Discovery Assignment Book*. Using their piles on *Sorting Flash Cards,* students should:

- circle the facts corresponding to the cards in the stack labeled "Problems Answered Correctly and Quickly";

- underline the facts corresponding to the cards in the stack labeled "Problems Answered Correctly after Thinking";

- do nothing to the facts corresponding to the cards in the stack labeled "Problems Answered Incorrectly."

TIMS Tip

To reduce the number of lost flash cards, students should write their initials on the back of each flash card and store them in an envelope. These flash cards will be used many times.

For more durable flash cards, copy the flash cards onto card stock or laminate the cards. You can also give each student two sets of cards, so they can take a set home and leave a set at school.

As students encounter all eight groups of facts in the Daily Practice and Problems, they should update their information on the chart by circling those problems they learn to answer quickly and underlining those facts they answer correctly after thinking.

To acquaint students with the *Subtraction Facts I Know* chart, ask students to look for patterns. Possible patterns include:

- the top numbers in each row get larger as you read from left to right;

- the top numbers in each column get larger as you read from top to bottom;

- all the subtraction facts that begin with eleven are in a diagonal that begins at the top right corner;

- the number to be subtracted is the same throughout each row, beginning with the 2 row, continuing with the 3 row, and so on;

- the differences increase by one as you read from left to right in each row.

Students can also refer to their *Subtraction Facts I Know* charts for facts they do not know as they encounter them in activities or labs. Students will see the number of facts that are circled or

Copyright © Kendall/Hunt Publishing Company

underlined grow as they learn more efficient strategies for finding the answers and as they use and practice the facts in activities, labs, and games.

Notes about Written Quizzes and Tests

There are four quizzes, each of which has eighteen subtraction facts. These quizzes are located in the DPP in Units 7–10 as shown in Figure 10.

In addition to these short quizzes, there is an inventory test of all seventy-two facts in Unit 10. This test is provided as part of the midyear assessments. More frequent testing may cause frustration or send the message that math is merely rote memorization of facts.

The Teacher Notes in the Daily Practice and Problems will remind you when to administer each quiz and the inventory test. Good performance on these assessments, however, is not a prerequisite for learning more complex mathematics. To solve more sophisticated problems, students can use strategies, manipulatives, calculators, or their *Subtraction Facts I Know* charts if they have difficulties.

Fluency with the subtraction facts will be maintained through the distributed practice outlined above and through the use of math facts in solving problems.

Copyright © Kendall/Hunt Publishing Company

Unit	Groups	Discussion Strategies	Distribution of Quizzes
2	1 and 2	Using a Ten, Thinking Addition	
3	3 and 4	Making a Ten	
4	5	Counting Strategies	
	6	Thinking Addition	
5	7 and 8	Using Doubles	
7	1 and 2	Using a Ten, Thinking Addition	A
8	3 and 4	Making a Ten	B
9	5	Counting Strategies	C
	6	Thinking Addition	
10	7 and 8	Using Doubles	D

Figure 10: *Subtraction Facts Practice and Assessment for Units 2–10*

Homework and Practice

- Students can take home the flash cards for Group 1 and Group 2 to practice.
- DPP Challenge V provides practice with money.

Estimated Class Sessions

1

At a Glance

Math Facts and Daily Practice and Problems

DPP Bit U provides practice with addition facts. Challenge V is a money problem.

Part 1. Strategies

Students discuss strategies for solving subtraction facts.

Part 2. Sorting Flash Cards

1. Students work in pairs to practice the subtraction facts in Group 1 and Group 2 using flash cards.
2. After going through all the cards, students sort the cards into three categories on the *Sorting Flash Cards* Activity Page.

Part 3. Subtraction Facts I Know

1. Students record their fluency with subtraction facts on the *Subtraction Facts I Know* chart.
2. Students update this chart throughout the year.

Homework

Students take home the flash cards for Group 1 and Group 2 to practice the subtraction facts with a family member.

Notes:

Copyright © Kendall/Hunt Publishing Company

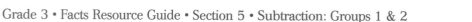

Copyright © Kendall/Hunt Publishing Company

Name _____

Date _____

Sorting Flash Cards

| Problems Answered Correctly and Quickly | Problems Answered Correctly after Thinking | Problems Answered Incorrectly |

Subtraction Facts I Know

Circle the subtraction facts you know and can answer quickly.
Underline those facts that you know when you use a strategy.
Do nothing to those facts that you still need to learn.

4 − 2 2	5 − 2 3	6 − 2 4	7 − 2 5	8 − 2 6	9 − 2 7	10 − 2 8	11 − 2 9
5 − 3 2	6 − 3 3	7 − 3 4	8 − 3 5	9 − 3 6	10 − 3 7	11 − 3 8	12 − 3 9
6 − 4 2	7 − 4 3	8 − 4 4	9 − 4 5	10 − 4 6	11 − 4 7	12 − 4 8	13 − 4 9
7 − 5 2	8 − 5 3	9 − 5 4	10 − 5 5	11 − 5 6	12 − 5 7	13 − 5 8	14 − 5 9
8 − 6 2	9 − 6 3	10 − 6 4	11 − 6 5	12 − 6 6	13 − 6 7	14 − 6 8	15 − 6 9
9 − 7 2	10 − 7 3	11 − 7 4	12 − 7 5	13 − 7 6	14 − 7 7	15 − 7 8	16 − 7 9
10 − 8 2	11 − 8 3	12 − 8 4	13 − 8 5	14 − 8 6	15 − 8 7	16 − 8 8	17 − 8 9
11 − 9 2	12 − 9 3	13 − 9 4	14 − 9 5	15 − 9 6	16 − 9 7	17 − 9 8	18 − 9 9
12 − 10 2	13 − 10 3	14 − 10 4	15 − 10 5	16 − 10 6	17 − 10 7	18 − 10 8	19 − 10 9

Copyright © Kendall/Hunt Publishing Company

Math Facts Groups	Weeks	Daily Practice and Problems	Home Practice	Flash Cards	Facts Quizzes and Tests
Subtraction: Groups 3 & 4 Multiplication: 5s & 10s	6–7	Unit 3: items 3A, 3C, 3E, 3F, 3G, 3I, 3K, 3M, 3N & 3O	Unit 3 Part 1	Subtraction Flash Cards: Groups 3 & 4	The *Subtraction Facts I Know* chart is updated.

Weeks 6–7

 **Daily Practice and Problems**

Students may solve the items individually, in groups, or as a class. The items may also be assigned for homework. The DPPs are also available on the Teacher Resource CD.

Student Questions	Teacher Notes
3A **Number of Toes** How many toes are in your classroom?	**TIMS Bit** Students can use counting strategies to find the answer.
3C **Subtraction: Making a Ten** Write the answers to these problems. 1. 10 − 8 = 2. 11 − 8 = 3. 9 − 5 = 4. 10 − 4 = 5. 11 − 4 = 6. 9 − 4 = 7. 10 − 6 = 8. 11 − 6 = 9. 11 − 5 =	**TIMS Bit** This bit reviews the facts in *Group 3* of the *Subtraction Flash Cards*. Ask students to describe strategies. Children are often comfortable with sums of 10 (e.g., 2 + 8, 6 + 4). They can use these facts to find differences from 10 (10 − 8 = 2, 10 − 4 = 6) or to find similar facts such as 11 − 4. 1. 2 2. 3 3. 4 4. 6 5. 7 6. 5 7. 4 8. 5 9. 6

3E Subtraction Flash Cards: Group 3

1. With a partner, sort the flash cards into three stacks: Facts I Know Quickly, Facts I Know Using a Strategy, and Facts I Need to Learn.

2. Update your *Subtraction Facts I Know* chart. Circle the facts that you answered quickly. Underline those you knew by using a strategy. Do nothing to those you still need to learn.

TIMS Bit

Pass out *Subtraction Flash Cards: Group 3.* After students sort, they should update the *Subtraction Facts I Know* chart. Students can take the cards for Group 3 home to practice with their families.

3F A Magic Square with Tens

Complete the magic square using the numbers 10, 20, 30, 40, 50, 60, 70, 80, and 90. Each row, column, and diagonal must have a sum of 150.

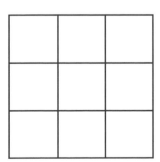

TIMS Challenge

This is the same magic square as the one in *Yü the Great* except the numbers are multiples of 10. One possible solution:

80	10	60
30	50	70
40	90	20

If students need a hint, remind them that the 5 was in the middle of the magic square in the story.

Student Questions	Teacher Notes

3G Subtraction: Making a Ten Again

Do these problems in your head. Write only the answers.

1. 10 − 7 =

2. 11 − 7 =

3. 9 − 7 =

4. 10 − 3 =

5. 11 − 3 =

6. 9 − 3 =

7. 100 − 20 =

8. 90 − 20 =

9. 9 − 6 =

TIMS Bit

This bit reviews the facts in *Group 4* of the *Subtraction Flash Cards*.

Ask students to describe the strategies they used to solve these problems. Possible strategies include making a ten, thinking addition, and using related facts. Knowing 10 − 3 = 7 helps solve 9 − 3 = 6. Knowing 10 − 2 = 8 helps solve 100 − 20 = 80. Class discussion can help students choose efficient strategies.

1. 3	2. 4
3. 2	4. 7
5. 8	6. 6
7. 80	8. 70
9. 3	

3I Subtraction Flash Cards: Group 4

1. With a partner, sort the flash cards into three stacks: Facts I Know Quickly, Facts I Know Using a Strategy, and Facts I Need to Learn.

2. Update your *Subtraction Facts I Know* chart. Circle the facts that you answered quickly. Underline those you knew by a strategy. Do nothing to those you still need to learn.

TIMS Bit

Pass out the *Subtraction Flash Cards: Group 4*. Students sort the cards with a partner and update their *Subtraction Facts I Know* charts. Students can take their flash cards for Group 4 home to practice with a family member.

Student Questions	Teacher Notes

3K **Pumpkins in Wagons**

This story problem was written by a third-grade student:

There are ten wagons and three pumpkins in each wagon. How many pumpkins are there? Solve the problem.

TIMS Bit $\boxed{x\frac{5}{7}}$

30 pumpkins

One good strategy for solving this problem is to draw a picture of the story.

3M **Making Groups**

You have thirty-seven beans. Make groups of five. Write a number sentence that shows your work. Don't forget about leftover beans.

TIMS Bit $\boxed{x\frac{5}{7}}$

Students might write:

$7 \times 5 + 2 = 37$

or

$5 \times 7 + 2 = 37$

3N **Subtraction Stories**

1. Write a story and draw a picture for $10 - 4$.

2. Write a story and draw a picture for $11 - 4$.

TIMS Task $\boxed{x\frac{5}{7}}$

Stories will vary.

3O **Frank's Hamburger Stand**

A hamburger and a soda cost $5.00 at Frank's Hamburger Stand. Derek, Sean, Karl, and Cindy each ordered a hamburger and a soda. What is the total cost? Write a number sentence to show your work.

TIMS Bit $\boxed{\$}$ $\boxed{x\frac{5}{7}}$

$5.00 + $5.00 + $5.00 + $5.00 = $20.00

or

$4 \times $5.00 = $20.00

Unit 3 Home Practice

PART 1

I. **A.** 9 – 5 = _____   2. **A.** 90 – 50 = _____

B. 11 – 7 = _____   **B.** 110 – 70 = _____

C. 10 – 2 = _____   **C.** 100 – 20 = _____

3. When the school bus arrived at school, Carla counted the number of people on it. There were twenty-four people. This was sixteen more than when she first got on. How many people were on the bus when Carla got on?

_____

_____

_____

_____

Copyright © Kendall/Hunt Publishing Company

Facts Distribution
Subtraction: Groups 5 & 6 and
Multiplication: 2s & 3s • Weeks 8–9

Subtraction:
Groups 5 & 6
and
Multiplication:
2s & 3s

Math Facts Groups	Weeks	Daily Practice and Problems	Home Practice	Flash Cards	Facts Quizzes and Tests
Subtraction: Groups 5 & 6 Multiplication: 2s & 3s	8–9	Unit 4: items 4B, 4C, 4D, 4E, 4F, 4G, 4H, 4K, 4M, 4S & 4T	Unit 4 Parts 1 & 2	Subtraction Flash Cards: Groups 5 & 6	The *Subtraction Facts I Know* chart is updated.

Weeks 8-9

Students may solve the items individually, in groups, or as a class. The items may also be assigned for homework. The DPPs are also available on the Teacher Resource CD.

Student Questions	Teacher Notes

4B Story Solving

Write a story and draw a picture about 3 × 8.

Write a number sentence about your picture.

TIMS Task

Answers will vary.

$3 \times 8 = 24$

$24 = 3 \times 8$

4C Calculator Counting with 2s and 3s

Work with a partner. One partner will count; the other will time how long the counting takes. Take turns.

A. Predict how long it will take to count by 2s to 30. Use a calculator to count by 2s to 60. Say the numbers quietly to yourself. How long did it take?

B. Predict how long it will take to count to 30 by 3s. Use a calculator to count by 3s to 30. Say the numbers quietly to yourself. How long did it take?

TIMS Bit

Pressing 2 + = = = on a calculator with a constant function will cause the calculator to count by 2s. (Note: Some calculators may use different keystrokes.)

Discuss patterns students notice as they count or discuss predictions they made. Did they predict the time for counting by 3s using information from another time they counted?

4D Guess My Number Puzzles

1. I am an even number. I am more than 5 and less than 10. I am not 6. Who am I?

2. I am an odd number. I am between 20 and 25. I am 3 times some number. Who am I?

TIMS Task

1. 8
2. 21

Student Questions	Teacher Notes

4E **Subtraction: Counting Strategies**

Do these problems in your head. Write only the answers.

1. $7 - 3 =$ 2. $11 - 2 =$

3. $8 - 6 =$ 4. $7 - 5 =$

5. $5 - 3 =$ 6. $8 - 2 =$

7. $40 - 20 =$ 8. $70 - 20 =$

9. $50 - 20 =$ 10. Explain your strategy for solving Question 6.

TIMS Bit

This Bit reviews the facts in Group 5. Ask students to describe strategies. Counting back and counting up are common strategies for solving these problems.

1. 4   2. 9   3. 2
4. 2   5. 2   6. 6
7. 20   8. 50   9. 30

10. Possible strategy: Thinking addition. $2 + 6 = 8$, so $8 - 2 = 6$. Note that these facts are related to $8 - 6 = 2$ in Question 3.

4F **Story Solving**

$7 \times 2 = ?$ Write a story and draw a picture about 7×2. Write a number sentence on your picture.

TIMS Task

Students may wish to share their stories with the class.

4G **Subtraction Flash Cards: Group 5**

1. With a partner, sort the flash cards into three stacks: Facts I Know Quickly, Facts I Know Using a Strategy, and Facts I Need to Learn.

2. Update your *Subtraction Facts I Know* chart. Circle the facts you answered quickly. Underline those you knew by using a strategy. Do nothing to those you still need to learn.

TIMS Bit

Students cut out *Subtraction Flash Cards: Group 5*. The flash cards are located in Section 7. After students sort, they should update the *Subtraction Facts I Know* chart. Students take the cards for Group 5 home to practice with their families.

4H Magic Square: Sum = 18

Complete the magic square using the numbers 2, 3, 4, 5, 6, 7, 8, 9, and 10. Each row, column, and diagonal must have a sum of 18.

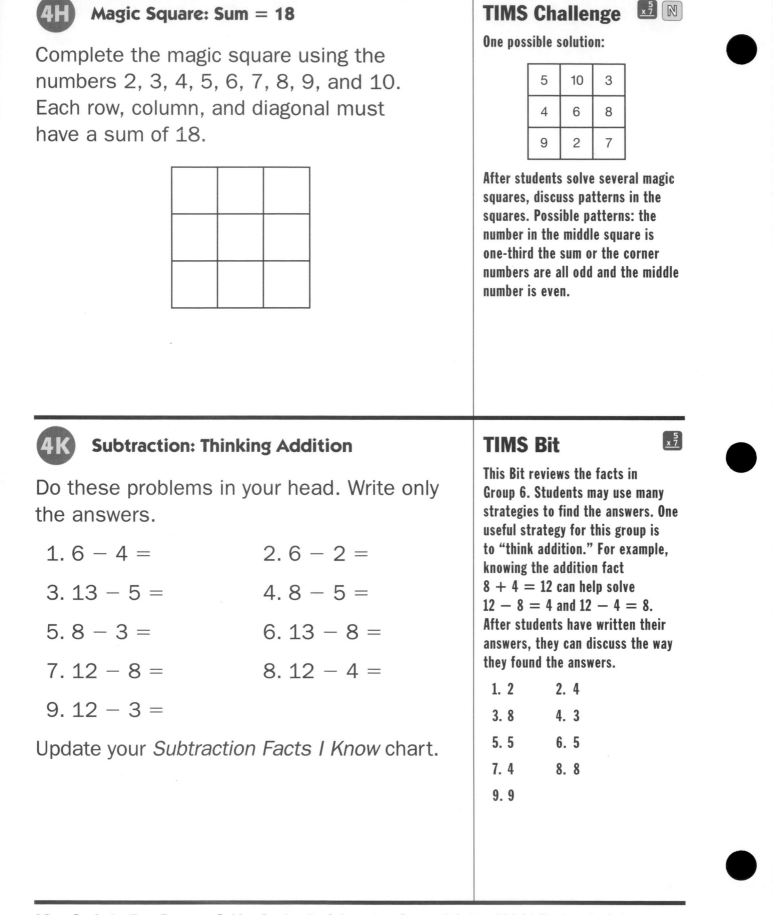

TIMS Challenge

One possible solution:

5	10	3
4	6	8
9	2	7

After students solve several magic squares, discuss patterns in the squares. Possible patterns: the number in the middle square is one-third the sum or the corner numbers are all odd and the middle number is even.

4K Subtraction: Thinking Addition

Do these problems in your head. Write only the answers.

1. 6 − 4 =   2. 6 − 2 =

3. 13 − 5 =   4. 8 − 5 =

5. 8 − 3 =   6. 13 − 8 =

7. 12 − 8 =   8. 12 − 4 =

9. 12 − 3 =

Update your *Subtraction Facts I Know* chart.

TIMS Bit

This Bit reviews the facts in Group 6. Students may use many strategies to find the answers. One useful strategy for this group is to "think addition." For example, knowing the addition fact 8 + 4 = 12 can help solve 12 − 8 = 4 and 12 − 4 = 8. After students have written their answers, they can discuss the way they found the answers.

1. 2   2. 4

3. 8   4. 3

5. 5   6. 5

7. 4   8. 8

9. 9

Student Questions	**Teacher Notes**

4M **Subtraction Flash Cards: Group 6**

1. With a partner, sort the flash cards into three stacks: Facts I Know Quickly, Facts I Know Using a Strategy, and Facts I Need to Learn.

2. Update your *Subtraction Facts I Know* chart. Circle the facts you answered quickly. Underline those you knew by using a strategy. Do nothing to those you still need to learn.

TIMS Bit

Students cut out *Subtraction Flash Cards: Group 6*. The flash cards are located in Section 7. After students sort, they should update the *Subtraction Facts I Know* chart. Have students take the cards for Groups 5 and 6 home to practice with their families.

4S **More Subtraction**

Do these problems in your head. Write only the answers.

1. 60 − 40 =	2. 60 − 20 =
3. 500 − 200 =	4. 80 − 60 =
5. 80 − 50 =	6. 80 − 30 =
7. 12 − 3 =	8. 120 − 30 =
9. 110 − 20 =	

TIMS Bit

These problems use the facts from Groups 5 and 6. Students can skip count by tens to solve these problems.

1. 20	2. 40	3. 300
4. 20	5. 30	6. 50
7. 9	8. 90	9. 90

4T **Story Solving**

3 × 6 = ? Write a story and draw a picture about 3 × 6. Write a number sentence on your picture.

TIMS Task

Students may wish to share their stories with the class.

Unit 4 **Home Practice**

PART 1

1. **A.** 12 – 4 = _____   2. **A.** 3 + 8 = _____

   B. 52 – 4 = _____   **B.** 43 + 8 = _____

   C. 72 – 4 = _____   **C.** 123 + 8 = _____

3. Alicia's class has 34 students in it. Draw a picture to show how many teams of four can be formed. Write a number sentence to describe this problem.

4. **A.** Skip count by tens from 100 to 300.

   _____

   B. Skip count by hundreds from 100 to 1000.

   _____

PART 2

1. **A.** 80 – 20 = _____   2. **A.** 110 – 20 = _____

   B. 30 + 40 = _____   **B.** 30 + 90 = _____

   C. 50 – 30 = _____   **C.** 130 – 50 = _____

3. Break the following numbers into two, three, or four parts.

   A. 79 = _____ + _____

   B. 507 = _____ + _____

      507 = _____ + _____ + _____

   C. 1551 = _____ + _____ + _____

      1551 = _____ + _____ + _____ + _____

Copyright © Kendall/Hunt Publishing Company

Facts Distribution

Section 5

Subtraction: Groups 7 & 8 and Multiplication: Square Numbers • Weeks 10–11

Weeks 10–11

Math Facts Groups	Weeks	Daily Practice and Problems	Home Practice	Flash Cards	Facts Quizzes and Tests
Subtraction: Groups 7 & 8 Multiplication: Square Numbers	10–11	Unit 5: items 5A, 5C, 5H, 5I, 5J, 5K, 5O & 5P	Unit 5 Part 1	Subtraction Flash Cards: Groups 7 & 8	The *Subtraction Facts I Know* chart is updated.

 **Daily Practice and Problems**

Students may solve the items individually, in groups, or as a class. The items may also be assigned for homework. The DPPs are also available on the Teacher Resource CD.

Student Questions	Teacher Notes

5A **Subtraction: Using Doubles**

Do these problems in your head. Write only the answers.

1. 14 − 7 =

2. 14 − 6 =

3. 14 − 8 =

4. 12 − 6 =

5. 12 − 7 =

6. 12 − 5 =

7. 100 − 50 =

8. 13 − 7 =

9. 13 − 6 =

10. Explain your strategy for solving Question 6.

TIMS Bit $\frac{5}{\times 7}$

This bit corresponds to *Subtraction Flash Cards: Group 7*. Students are usually quite comfortable with addition "doubles." They can solve the facts in this group by "thinking addition" with doubles. (14 − 7 = 7 because 7 + 7 = 14) Students can also use doubles to figure out "near doubles" such as 14 − 6 = 8.

1. 7
2. 8
3. 6
4. 6
5. 5
6. 7
7. 50
8. 6
9. 7
10. Possible strategy: Students can use the subtraction fact 12 − 6 = 6 to reason that 12 − 5 will be one more or 7 (12 − 5 = 7).

5C   **Subtraction Flash Cards: Group 7**

1. With a partner, sort the flash cards into three stacks: Facts I Know Quickly, Facts I Know Using a Strategy, and Facts I Need to Learn.

2. Update your *Subtraction Facts I Know* chart. Circle the facts you answered quickly. Underline those you knew by using a strategy. Do nothing to those you still need to learn.

TIMS Bit

Students cut out the *Subtraction Flash Cards: Group 7*. The flash cards are in Section 7. After students sort the flash cards, they should update the *Subtraction Facts I Know* chart. Students take the cards for Group 7 home to practice with their families.

5H   **Kim's Savings**

1. Kim earns $7 each week mowing lawns. She wants to buy jeans that cost $45. The tax will be $3. How long will she have to save to buy the jeans?

   Will she have to save longer than a month?

2. Leila earns $10 each week babysitting. How much money will she earn in 10 weeks?

TIMS Task

1. Kim will have to save for 7 weeks, which is longer than a month.

One possible strategy for solving this problem is to skip count by sevens:

Weeks:

1	2	3	4	5	6	7
$7	$14	$21	$28	$35	$42	$49

2. $100

Student Questions	Teacher Notes

5I Subtraction: Using Doubles

Do these problems in your head. Write only the answers.

1. $16 - 8 =$

2. $17 - 8 =$

3. $15 - 8 =$

4. $18 - 9 =$

5. $18 - 10 =$

6. $15 - 7 =$

7. $8 - 4 =$

8. $7 - 4 =$

9. $60 - 30 =$

10. Explain your strategy for solving Question 4.

TIMS Bit

This bit reviews the facts in Group 8 of the *Subtraction Flash Cards*. Students can solve them by "thinking addition" using doubles, although other strategies would be as useful. Let students tell the class how they found the answers. Discuss which strategies are most efficient.

1. 8	2. 9
3. 7	4. 9
5. 8	6. 8
7. 4	8. 3
9. 30	

10. Possible strategy: Students may use the addition double $9 + 9$.

5J Story Solving

$8 \times 8 = ?$ Write a story and draw a picture about 8×8.

Write a number sentence on your picture.

TIMS Task

Students may wish to share their stories with the class.

Student Questions	**Teacher Notes**

5K Subtraction Flash Cards: Group 8

TIMS Bit

1. With a partner, sort the flash cards into three stacks: Facts I Know Quickly, Facts I Know Using a Strategy, and Facts I Need to Learn.

2. Update your *Subtraction Facts I Know* chart. Circle the facts you answered quickly. Underline those you knew by using a strategy. Do nothing to those you still need to learn.

Students cut out *Subtraction Flash Cards: Group 8*. After sorting the flash cards, they should update the *Subtraction Facts I Know* chart. Have students take the cards for Groups 7 and 8 home to practice with their families.

50 Subtraction: Strategies

TIMS Bit

Do these problems in your head. Write only the answers.

1. $15 - 7 =$

2. $11 - 6 =$

3. $14 - 6 =$

4. $13 - 4 =$

5. $11 - 3 =$

6. $17 - 8 =$

7. $16 - 7 =$

8. $13 - 8 =$

9. $17 - 9 =$

Update your *Subtraction Facts I Know* chart.

This set of subtraction facts problems is taken from all the groups of subtraction facts. Students can use a variety of strategies to learn them. In a class discussion, compare strategies; is one more efficient than another?

1. 8
2. 5
3. 8
4. 9
5. 8
6. 9
7. 9
8. 5
9. 8

Student Questions	Teacher Notes

5P **More Story Solving**

$9 \times 9 = ?$ Write a story and draw a picture about 9×9.

Write a number sentence on your picture.

TIMS Task

Students may wish to share their stories with the class.

Unit 5 Home Practice

PART 1

I. **A.** Half of 120 is _____ **B.** Half of 130 is _____

C. Twice 80 is _____ **D.** Twice 95 is _____

2. For each of the problems below, write another number sentence that has the same difference.

Example: $8 - 4$ is the same as $10 - 6$. We write $8 - 4 = 10 - 6$.

A. $14 - 7 =$ _____

B. $17 - 8 =$ _____

C. $12 - 5 =$ _____

Copyright © Kendall/Hunt Publishing Company

Facts Distribution
Multiplication: 9s • Weeks 12–14

Math Facts Groups	Weeks	Daily Practice and Problems	Home Practice	Flash Cards	Facts Quizzes and Tests
Multiplication: 9s	12–14	Unit 6: items 6B, 6C, 6D, 6F, 6H, 6V & 6DD	Unit 6 Part 1		

Unit 6 Daily Practice and Problems

Students may solve the items individually, in groups, or as a class. The items may also be assigned for homework. The DPPs are also available on the Teacher Resource CD.

Student Questions	Teacher Notes

6B Guess My Number Puzzles

TIMS Task

1. I am more than 3 × 9 and less than 4 × 9. I am odd. The sum of my digits is 4. Who am I?

2. The sum of my digits is nine. If you skip count by 5s, you hit me. Who am I?

3. I am odd. I am more than half of 22 and less than half of 30. Who am I?

1. 31
2. 45
3. 13

6C Subtraction: Using Doubles

Do the following problems in your head. Write only the answers.

1. 50 − 25 =

2. 51 − 25 =

3. 100 − 50 =

4. 100 − 48 =

5. 180 − 90 =

6. 160 − 80 =

7. Explain your strategy for Question 4.

TIMS Bit

These problems can be solved by thinking addition with doubles. (Since 25 + 25 = 50, then 50 − 25 = 25.) However, students will probably solve them in many ways. Ask them to describe their strategies, helping them verbalize their thinking.

1. 25
2. 26
3. 50
4. 52
5. 90
6. 80
7. Possible strategy: Students may count up from 48 to 50 and then use the double 50 + 50 to find the missing part.

6D School Clothes

Jerry likes to wear T-shirts and shorts to school. He has three T-shirts: a red one, a blue one, and a white one. He has two pairs of shorts: a blue pair and a black pair. How many different outfits does Jerry have for school?

TIMS Challenge

6 outfits:

Shirts	Shorts
red	blue
red	black
blue	blue
blue	black
white	blue
white	black

6F Multiplication Strategies

Dima says that he finds 6×9 this way, "I think 6 tens are 60, so 6 nines will be 6 less." $6 \times 10 = 60$ and $60 - 6 = 54$.

1. Use Dima's strategy to find 2×9.

2. Use his strategy to find 7×9.

3. Find 9×9.

TIMS Task

1. $2 \times 10 = 20$ and $20 - 2 = 18$

2. $7 \times 10 = 70$ and $70 - 7 = 63$

3. 81

(6H) Cold Cafe

The Cold Cafe is an ice cream parlor. The cafe has three kinds of cones: plain, sugar, and waffle. There are four flavors of ice cream: chocolate, vanilla, strawberry, and mint. How many different one-scoop cones can you get?

TIMS Challenge

Solution: 12 cones

Students can draw pictures or make diagrams to solve the problems.

Plain: Ch, Van, Str, Mt

Waffle: Ch, Van, Str, Mt

Sugar: Ch, Van, Str, Mt

(6V) Story Solving

Write a story and draw a picture about 8 × 9. Write a number sentence on your picture.

TIMS Task

Stories will vary.

(6DD) Jonah's Class Project

Jonah's class is recycling aluminum cans to raise money for a field trip. If he finds 9 cans a day for an entire week, how many cans will he have for his class?

The class needs $3 more to pay for the bus. If Jonah receives 5 cents for each can he collected during the week, will they have enough?

TIMS Challenge

Jonah will have 63 cans by the end of the week. The 63 cans will earn his class $3.15. Therefore, they will have the money they need to rent the bus.

To find the number of cans, students might skip count by nines.

cans: 9 18 27 36 45 54 63

days: 1   2   3   4   5   6   7

To find out how much money he earned students might use a calculator or repeated addition.
63 + 63 + 63 + 63 + 63 = 315

Unit 6 Home Practice

PART 1

1. **A.** 15 – 9 = _____ **B.** 17 – 10 = _____

   C. 9 – 4 = _____ **D.** 11 – 7 = _____

   E. 7 – 2 = _____ **F.** 12 – 3 = _____

   G. 14 – 8 = _____ **H.** 18 – 9 = _____

2. Leah has a hard time finding the answer to 1G. How did you find the answer to this subtraction fact? Share your method.

Copyright © Kendall/Hunt Publishing Company

Facts Distribution

Subtraction: Groups 1 & 2 and Multiplication: Last Six Facts • Weeks 15–16

Weeks 15–16

Math Facts Groups	Weeks	Daily Practice and Problems	Home Practice	Flash Cards	Facts Quizzes and Tests
Subtraction: Groups 1 & 2 Multiplication: Last Six Facts	15–16	Unit 7: items 7A, 7B, 7C, 7F, 7G, 7I, 7P, 7Q & 7U	Unit 7 Parts 1 & 2	Subtraction Flash Cards: Groups 1 & 2	DPP item 7U is a quiz on the subtraction facts in Groups 1 & 2. The *Subtraction Facts I Know* chart is updated.

Students may solve the items individually, in groups, or as a class. The items may also be assigned for homework. The DPPs are also available on the Teacher Resource CD.

Student Questions	Teacher Notes

7A Subtraction Facts: Group 1

Do the following problems in your head. Write only the answers.

1. $12 - 10 =$

2. $13 - 10 =$

3. $15 - 10 =$

4. $12 - 9 =$

5. $13 - 9 =$

6. $15 - 9 =$

7. $19 - 10 =$

8. $13 - 4 =$

9. $15 - 6 =$

TIMS Bit $\boxed{\frac{5}{\times 7}}$

1. 2	2. 3
3. 5	4. 3
5. 4	6. 6
7. 9	8. 9
9. 9	

Students begin a review of each of the Subtraction Facts Groups. (See the Unit 2 Lesson 7 Lesson Guide for an outline of the study of the facts throughout the year.) To focus practice on this group, students should work with the flash cards for Group 1 only. These facts focus on using a ten and thinking addition. Discuss these and other strategies that help students with these facts and ask them to practice using the strategies at home.

7B Story Solving

1. Write a story and draw a picture about 8×7. Write a number sentence on your picture.

2. Write a story and draw a picture about 8×4. Write a number sentence on your picture.

TIMS Task

Students can share their stories with the class. If a computer with a drawing program is available, students may choose to draw their pictures on the computer.

7C Subtraction Flash Cards: Group 1

1. With a partner, sort the *Subtraction Flash Cards: Group 1* into three stacks: Facts I Know Quickly, Facts I Know Using a Strategy, and Facts I Need to Learn.

2. Update your *Subtraction Facts I Know* chart. Circle the facts you answered quickly. Underline those you know by using a strategy. Do nothing to those you still need to learn.

TIMS Bit

Have students sort *Subtraction Flash Cards: Group 1*. After students sort, they should update the *Subtraction Facts I Know* chart. Students can take the cards for Group 1 home to practice with their families. The flash cards for Group 1 were distributed in the *Discovery Assignment Book* in Unit 2. These flash cards are available in Section 7.

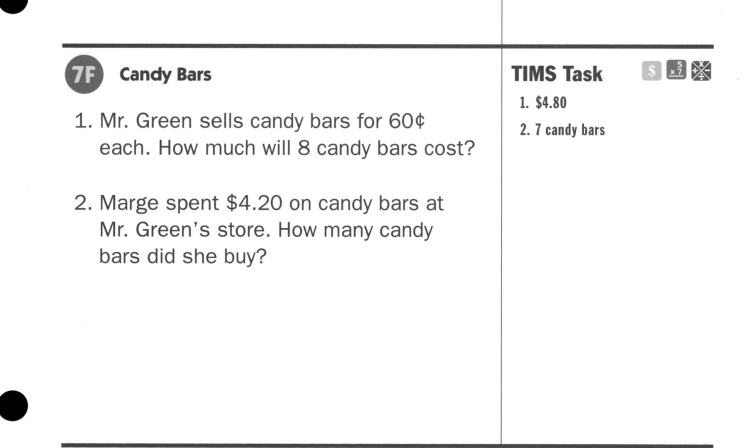

7F Candy Bars

1. Mr. Green sells candy bars for 60¢ each. How much will 8 candy bars cost?

2. Marge spent $4.20 on candy bars at Mr. Green's store. How many candy bars did she buy?

TIMS Task

1. $4.80

2. 7 candy bars

Student Questions	Teacher Notes

7G Subtraction Facts: Group 2

Do the following problems in your head.
Write only the answers.

1. $14 - 10 =$

2. $16 - 10 =$

3. $17 - 10 =$

4. $14 - 9 =$

5. $16 - 9 =$

6. $17 - 9 =$

7. $14 - 5 =$

8. $16 - 7 =$

9. $11 - 9 =$

TIMS Bit

1. 4
2. 6
3. 7
4. 5
5. 7
6. 8
7. 9
8. 9
9. 2

Ask students to use *Subtraction Flash Cards: Group 2* to study these facts, applying appropriate strategies for learning the facts. Possible strategies include using a ten and thinking addition.

7I Subtraction Flash Cards: Group 2

1. With a partner, sort the *Subtraction Flash Cards: Group 2* into three stacks: Facts I Know Quickly, Facts I Know Using a Strategy, and Facts I Need to Learn.

2. Update your *Subtraction Facts I Know* chart. Circle the facts you answered quickly. Underline those you know by using a strategy. Do nothing to those you still need to learn.

TIMS Bit

Have students sort *Subtraction Flash Cards: Group 2* and update their *Subtraction Facts I Know* charts. Have students take the cards for Group 2 home to practice with their families. The flash cards for Group 2 were distributed in the *Discovery Assignment Book* in Unit 2. The cards are also available in Section 7.

Tell students when you will give *Subtraction Facts Quiz A,* which is made up of facts from Groups 1 and 2. After the quiz, students should update their *Subtraction Facts I Know* charts. Quiz A is in DPP Bit 7U.

7P **Sharing Muffins**

1. You want to share 24 muffins equally among 6 friends. How many muffins does each person get?

2. Two friends move away. You want to share 24 muffins equally among 4 friends. How many muffins does each person get?

3. The dog ate 3 muffins. You want to share 21 muffins equally among 6 friends. How many muffins does each friend get?

TIMS Task $\boxed{\frac{5}{\times 7}}$

Students can use counters or paper circles to help solve the problems.

1. $24 \div 6 = 4$ muffins

2. $24 \div 4 = 6$ muffins

3. $21 \div 6 = 3$ R3 or $3\frac{1}{2}$ muffins

7Q **Marathon Mark**

Mark is training for the Chicago Marathon in October. He can run 7 miles in one hour. How far will he run in 4 hours?

The marathon is 26.2 miles long. Will he be able to finish in 4 hours?

TIMS Bit $\boxed{\frac{5}{\times 7}}$

In 4 hours Mark can run 28 miles.

Students can skip count by sevens or use repeated addition.

Yes, Mark will be able to run the marathon in under four hours.

7U **Subtraction Facts Quiz A**

Students take *Subtraction Facts Quiz A*, which corresponds to *Subtraction Flash Cards: Groups 1* and *2.* Then students update their *Subtraction Facts I Know* charts.

TIMS Bit

Subtraction Facts Quiz A is at the end of this set of DPP items. Ask students to have two pens or pencils of different colors ready. During the first minute of the quiz, they should write their answers using one color pen or pencil. After a minute passes, tell students to write their answers with the other color pen or pencil. Give students a reasonable time to complete the rest of the problems, then they should check their work.

3	6	9	6	2	9
5	4	9	2	9	3
9	7	8	4	7	5

Subtraction Facts Quiz A

You will need two pens or pencils of different colors. Use the first color when you begin the test. When your teacher tells you to switch pens or pencils, finish the test using the second color.

13 − 10	15 − 9	13 − 4	16 − 10	11 − 9	19 − 10
15 − 10	13 − 9	15 − 6	12 − 10	14 − 5	12 − 9
16 − 7	17 − 10	17 − 9	14 − 10	16 − 9	14 − 9

Teacher: These facts correspond with *Subtraction Flash Cards: Groups 1* and *2*.

Copyright © Kendall/Hunt Publishing Company

Unit 7 Home Practice

PART 1

1. **A.** 12 + 8 + 5 = ____   2. **A.** 100 – 90 = ____

   B. 17 + 3 + 5 = ____   **B.** 110 – 90 = ____

   C. 5 + 16 + 4 = ____   **C.** 150 – 90 = ____

3. Sara said that she used the addition facts strategy "making a ten" to solve Questions 1A–1C. Explain how you could "make a ten" to solve each problem.

   _____

   _____

   _____

PART 2

1. **A.** 160 – 90 = ____   2. **A.** 160 + 40 = ____

   B. 160 – 100 = ____   **B.** 160 + 60 = ____

   C. 160 – 70 = ____   **C.** 160 + 80 = ____

3. Enrique and Derek bought ice cream. Together, they had $1.50. Derek bought a chocolate cone for $0.60 and Enrique bought a double-decker strawberry cone for $0.80.

   A. How much money will they have left after buying the ice cream

   cones? _____

   B. If they split the change evenly, how much money should each

   person get? _____

4. Erik wants to buy pencils at the school store. Each pencil costs 7 cents.

   How many pencils could he buy with 50 cents? _____
   Show how you solved the problem.

Copyright © Kendall/Hunt Publishing Company

 **Section 5**

Facts Distribution
Subtraction: Groups 3 & 4 and
Multiplication: 2s, 5s & 10s • Weeks 17–18

Math Facts Groups	Weeks	Daily Practice and Problems	Home Practice	Flash Cards	Facts Quizzes and Tests
Subtraction: Groups 3 & 4 Multiplication: 2s, 5s & 10s	17–18	Unit 8: items 8A, 8B, 8C, 8D, 8G, 8H, 8I, 8L & 8M		Subtraction Flash Cards: Groups 3 & 4	DPP item 8M is a quiz on the subtraction facts in Groups 3 & 4. The *Subtraction Facts I Know* chart is updated.

Weeks 17–18

 **Daily Practice and Problems**

Students may solve the items individually, in groups, or as a class. The items may also be assigned for homework. The DPPs are also available on the Teacher Resource CD.

Student Questions	Teacher Notes

8A Subtraction Facts: Group 3

Do the following problems in your head. Write answers only.

1. $10 - 4 =$ 2. $10 - 6 =$

3. $10 - 8 =$ 4. $9 - 4 =$

5. $11 - 6 =$ 6. $11 - 8 =$

7. $11 - 4 =$ 8. $11 - 5 =$

9. $9 - 5 =$

TIMS Bit

To focus practice on these facts, students can work with *Subtraction Flash Cards: Group 3*. These flash cards are located in Section 7 and in the *Discovery Assignment Book* for Unit 3. Students can use the strategies making a ten and reasoning from known facts. Discuss students' strategies.

1. 6   2. 4   3. 2

4. 5   5. 5   6. 3

7. 7   8. 6   9. 4

8B Story Solving

Write a story and draw a picture about 10×4. Write a number sentence on your picture.

TIMS Task

Students may wish to share their stories with the class.

8C Subtraction Flash Cards: Group 3

1. With a partner, sort the flash cards into three stacks: Facts I Know Quickly, Facts I Know Using a Strategy, and Facts I Need to Learn.

2. Update your *Subtraction Facts I Know* chart. Circle the facts you answered quickly. Underline those you know by using a strategy. Do nothing to those you still need to learn.

TIMS Bit

Have students sort *Subtraction Flash Cards: Group 3*. After students sort, they should update the *Subtraction Facts I Know* chart. Students can take the cards for Group 3 home to practice with their families. The flash cards for Group 3 were distributed in the *Discovery Assignment Book* in Unit 3. These flash cards are available in Section 7 and in the *Unit Resource Guide*.

8D **Mathhoppers**

1. A +8 mathhopper started at 0 and made 5 hops. On what number did it land?

2. A +8 mathhopper started on 6 and made 2 hops. On what number did it land?

3. A +8 mathhopper landed on 100 after making 10 hops. On what number did it start?

TIMS Task

Encourage students to sketch a number line or use a measuring tape or meterstick to solve the problems. Ask for a number sentence for each problem.

1. 40
2. 22
3. 20

8G **Subtraction Facts: Group 4**

Do these problems in your head. Write answers only.

1. 11 − 7 =   2. 10 − 3 =

3. 10 − 7 =   4. 10 − 2 =

5. 9 − 2 =   6. 9 − 7 =

7. 9 − 3 =   8. 11 − 3 =

9. 9 − 6 =

TIMS Bit

Students can study this group of facts with the *Subtraction Flash Cards: Group 4*. The flash cards are located in Section 7 and in the *Discovery Assignment Book* in Unit 3.

Tell students when you will give *Subtraction Facts Quiz B*, which is made up of facts from *Groups 3* and *4*.

1. 4   2. 7
3. 3   4. 8
5. 7   6. 2
7. 6   8. 8
9. 3

8H Money Jar

TIMS Task

The Franklins saved $4.00 in dimes. They have 6 people in the family.

1. If they share the dimes equally, how much money will each family member receive?

2. Can the Franklins trade in the leftover dimes for other coins so they can share the leftover money? How much money will each family member receive? Explain.

Have play money available for students to use. *Money Masters* are in Unit 7 Lesson 5.

1. $4.00 in dimes is the same as 40 dimes. Each member receives 6 dimes or 60¢; 4 dimes or 40¢ are left over.

2. The four dimes can be traded in for 8 nickels. Each person could receive one nickel. Two nickels remain. If traded for pennies, each person could receive one penny. Four pennies would be left over. Each family member receives 6¢ more.

8I Subtraction Flash Cards: Group 4

TIMS Bit

1. With a partner, sort the flash cards into three stacks: Facts I Know Quickly, Facts I Know Using a Strategy, and Facts I Need to Learn.

2. Update your *Subtraction Facts I Know* chart. Circle the facts you answered quickly. Underline those you know by using a strategy. Do nothing to those you still need to learn.

Have students sort *Subtraction Flash Cards: Group 4.* After students sort, they should update the *Subtraction Facts I Know* chart. Have students take the cards for Group 4 home to practice with their families. Remind students when the quiz on Groups 3 and 4 will be given. The flash cards for Group 4 are in Section 7 and in the *Discovery Assignment Book* in Unit 3. These flash cards are also available in the *Unit Resource Guide.*

Student Questions	Teacher Notes

8L Facts Problems

1. $5 \times 3 =$ 2. $10 \times 3 =$ 3. $15 + 15 =$

4. $5 \times 5 =$ 5. $10 \times 5 =$ 6. $25 + 25 =$

7. $5 \times 7 =$ 8. $10 \times 7 =$ 9. $35 + 35 =$

10. $5 \times 9 =$ 11. $10 \times 9 =$ 12. $45 + 45 =$

TIMS Task

Students can skip count to find the products. Encourage students to identify and describe patterns.

1. 15	2. 30	3. 30
4. 25	5. 50	6. 50
7. 35	8. 70	9. 70
10. 45	11. 90	12. 90

8M Subtraction Facts Quiz B

Students take *Subtraction Facts Quiz B*, which corresponds to *Subtraction Flash Cards: Groups 3* and *4.*

TIMS Bit

Quiz B is at the end of this set of DPP items. Ask students to have two pens or pencils of different colors ready. During the first minute of the quiz, they should write their answers using one color pen or pencil. After you tell the students that a minute has passed, they should begin writing their answers with the other color pen or pencil. After students have been given a reasonable time to complete the rest of the problems, they should check their work.

Subtraction Facts Quiz B

You will need two pens or pencils of different colors. Use the first color when you begin the test. When your teacher tells you to switch pens or pencils, finish the test using the second color.

10 − 4	10 − 2	9 − 4	11 − 5	11 − 4	9 − 6
10 − 6	9 − 5	11 − 8	10 − 7	11 − 6	9 − 2
9 − 3	10 − 3	11 − 7	10 − 8	9 − 7	11 − 3

Teacher: These facts correspond with *Subtraction Flash Cards Groups 3* and *4.*

Copyright © Kendall/Hunt Publishing Company

Facts Distribution
Subtraction: Groups 5 & 6 and Multiplication: 3s, 9s & Square Numbers • Weeks 19–20

Subtraction:
Groups 5 & 6
and
Multiplication:
3s, 9s & Square
Numbers

Math Facts Groups	Weeks	Daily Practice and Problems	Home Practice	Flash Cards	Facts Quizzes and Tests
Subtraction: Groups 5 & 6 Multiplication: 3s, 9s & Square Numbers	19–20	Unit 9: items 9A, 9B, 9C, 9E, 9G, 9I, 9J, 9K, 9L & 9M	Unit 9 Part 2	Subtraction Flash Cards: Groups 5 & 6	DPP item 9M is a quiz on the subtraction facts in Groups 5 & 6. The *Subtraction Facts I Know* chart is updated.

Students may solve the items individually, in groups, or as a class. The items may also be assigned for homework. The DPPs are also available on the Teacher Resource CD.

Student Questions	Teacher Notes

9A Subtraction Facts: Group 5

Do these problems in your head. Write only the answers.

1. 11 − 2 =
2. 70 − 20 =
3. 70 − 50 =
4. 8 − 2 =
5. 7 − 3 =
6. 5 − 3 =
7. 8 − 6 =
8. 5 − 2 =
9. 400 − 200 =

TIMS Bit [×5/7] [N]

1. 9
2. 50
3. 20
4. 6
5. 4
6. 2
7. 2
8. 3
9. 200

This set of subtraction problems corresponds to *Subtraction Flash Cards: Group 5*. The answers to these problems can often be found by using counting strategies, although other strategies may work as well. Students use the flash cards to study for *Subtraction Facts: Quiz C.*

9B Boxes

What do you notice about these boxes?

```
3 ┌─────┐ 3    5 ┌─────┐ 5    4 ┌─────┐ 4
  │  12  │        │  20  │        │  16  │
3 └─────┘ 3    5 └─────┘ 5    4 └─────┘ 4
```

1. Make up a box like these with a 10 on a corner.

2. Make up a box like these with 36 on the inside.

3. Make up other boxes like these.

TIMS Task [×5/7] [N]

1. A box with a 10 on each corner will have 40 inside. All the numbers on the inside are multiples of four. Students may express this as, *"They are all four times something."*

2. A box with 36 in the middle will have nines on each corner.

3. Answers will vary, but the numbers on the corners must all be the same.

Student Questions	Teacher Notes

9C Subtraction Flash Cards: Group 5

TIMS Bit

1. With a partner, sort the flash cards for Group 5 into three stacks: Facts I Know Quickly, Facts I Know Using a Strategy, and Facts I Need to Learn.

2. Update your *Subtraction Facts I Know* chart. Circle the facts you answered quickly. Underline those you know by using a strategy. Do nothing to those you still need to learn.

Have students sort *Subtraction Flash Cards: Group 5*. After students sort, they update the *Subtraction Facts I Know* chart. Have students take the cards for Group 5 home to practice with their families. *Subtraction Flash Cards: Group 5* were distributed in Unit 4 in the *Discovery Assignment Book*. They are also available in Section 7.

9E Subtraction Facts: Group 6

TIMS Bit

Do these problems in your head. Write only the answers.

1. $12 - 8 =$ 2. $13 - 8 =$

3. $6 - 4 =$ 4. $12 - 4 =$

5. $8 - 5 =$ 6. $12 - 3 =$

7. $6 - 2 =$ 8. $13 - 5 =$

9. $8 - 3 =$

1. 4   2. 5
3. 2   4. 8
5. 3   6. 9
7. 4   8. 8
9. 5

Students study this group of facts with the flash cards for Group 6, discussing the strategies they use to remember them.

9G Subtraction Flash Cards: Group 6

1. With a partner, sort the flash cards for Group 6 into three stacks: Facts I Know Quickly, Facts I Know Using a Strategy, and Facts I Need to Learn.

2. Update your *Subtraction Facts I Know* chart. Circle the facts you answered quickly. Underline those you know by using a strategy. Do nothing to those you still need to learn.

TIMS Bit

Have students sort *Subtraction Flash Cards: Group 6*. After students sort, they update the *Subtraction Facts I Know* chart. Have students take the cards for Group 6 home to practice with their families. Tell students when you will give *Subtraction Facts: Quiz C*. This quiz is at the end of this set of DPP items. The quiz is assigned in Bit 9M. The flash cards for Group 6 were distributed in the *Discovery Assignment Book* in Unit 4. The flash cards are also in Section 7.

9I The House of Sevens

A. Jerry's house has 7 windows in it. Each window has 9 panes of glass. How many panes of glass are in Jerry's house?

B. Jerry's house has 7 shelves. Each shelf has 7 books. How many books are in Jerry's house?

C. Jerry's house has 7 lamps. Each lamp has 3 lightbulbs. How many lightbulbs are in Jerry's house?

TIMS Bit

A. 63 panes of glass

B. 49 books

C. 21 lightbulbs

Student Questions	Teacher Notes

9J **Granola**

1. Trish made 72 grams of granola. It takes 9 grams of granola to make one cookie. How many cookies can she make?

2. Bill has 60 grams of granola. It takes 9 grams for one cookie. How many cookies can he make?

3. Mary has 210 grams of granola. She wants to make 7 big cookies. How much granola can she put in each cookie?

TIMS Task

1. 8 cookies

2. 6 cookies with 6 grams of granola left over

3. 30 grams

9K **Toy Car**

A toy car balances nine 6-gram masses and three 5-gram masses. What is the mass of the car?

TIMS Bit

$9 \times 6 g + 3 \times 5 g = 69 g$

Discuss various student solution strategies.

9L **Mouse Chow**

Professor Peabody has 450 grams of mouse chow for his pet mouse Milo.

1. If he wants the mouse chow to last for 9 days, how much should he feed to Milo every day?

2. If 100 grams of mouse chow cost $1, how much did 450 grams of mouse chow cost?

TIMS Challenge

1. 50 g

2. $4.50

9M Subtraction Facts: Quiz C

Students take *Subtraction Facts: Quiz C*, which corresponds to *Subtraction Flash Cards: Groups 5* and *6.*

TIMS Bit

Subtraction Facts: Quiz C is at the end of this set of DPP items. Ask students to have two pens or pencils of different colors ready. During the first minute of the quiz, they write their answers using one color pen or pencil. When a minute has passed, they write their answers with the other color. After a reasonable time to complete the problems, students check their work. Students then update their *Subtraction Facts I Know* chart.

Name _____   Date _____

Subtraction Facts: Quiz C

You will need two pens or pencils of different colors. Use the first color when you begin the test. When your teacher tells you to switch pens or pencils, finish the test using the second color.

4 − 2	8 − 6	13 − 8	7 − 3	11 − 2	7 − 5
5 − 2	13 − 5	6 − 4	12 − 4	8 − 3	12 − 8
6 − 2	8 − 5	7 − 2	12 − 3	8 − 2	5 − 3

Teacher: These facts correspond with *Subtraction Flash Cards Groups 5* and *6*.

Copyright © Kendall/Hunt Publishing Company

Unit 9 Home Practice

PART 2

1. A ball balances nine 10-gram masses and three 5-gram masses.

   What is the mass of the ball? _____

2. A marker balances three 10-gram masses, nine 5-gram masses, and three 1-gram masses. What is the mass of the marker?

   _____

3. A box that has 3 crayons in it has a total mass of 60 grams. What is

   the mass of one crayon? _____

Copyright © Kendall/Hunt Publishing Company

Facts Distribution

Subtraction: Groups 7 & 8 and
Multiplication: Last Six Facts• Weeks 21–22

Math Facts Groups	Weeks	Daily Practice and Problems	Home Practice	Flash Cards	Facts Quizzes and Tests
Subtraction: Groups 7 & 8 Multiplication: Last Six Facts	21–22	Unit 10: items 10A, 10C, 10E, 10F, 10G, 10I, 10J, 10K & 10L	Unit 10 Part 1	Subtraction Flash Cards: Groups 7 & 8	DPP item 10I is a quiz on the subtraction facts in Groups 7 & 8. Item 10K is an inventory test on all the subtraction facts. The *Subtraction Facts I Know* chart is updated.

Students may solve the items individually, in groups, or as a class. The items may also be assigned for homework. The DPPs are also available on the Teacher Resource CD.

Student Questions	Teacher Notes

10A Subtraction Facts: Group 7

Do these problems in your head. Write only the answers.

1. $14 - 7 =$

2. $14 - 8 =$

3. $14 - 6 =$

4. $12 - 6 =$

5. $12 - 7 =$

6. $12 - 5 =$

7. $13 - 6 =$

8. $13 - 7 =$

9. $10 - 5 =$

TIMS Bit

To focus practice on these facts, students can work with *Subtraction Flash Cards: Group 7*. Students can use the flash cards to study for *Subtraction Facts Quiz D* in Bit 10I, which has facts from Groups 7 and 8. Ask students to describe strategies they use. They can use doubles and reason from known facts (doubles) to solve these facts. TIMS Bits 10E and 10G review Group 8. Students will take an inventory test on Groups 1–8 in Bit 10K.

1. 7	2. 6	3. 8
4. 6	5. 5	6. 7
7. 7	8. 6	9. 5

10C **Subtraction Flash Cards: Group 7**

1. With a partner, sort the Flash Cards for Group 7 into three stacks: Facts I Know Quickly, Facts I Know Using a Strategy, and Facts I Need to Learn.

2. Update your *Subtraction Facts I Know* chart. Circle the facts you answered quickly. Underline those you know by using a strategy. Do nothing to those you still need to learn.

TIMS Bit

Have students sort *Subtraction Flash Cards* for *Group 7*. After students sort, they should update the *Subtraction Facts I Know* charts. Students can take the cards for Group 7 home to practice with their families. The flash cards for Group 7 were distributed in the *Discovery Assignment Book* in Unit 5. They are also available in Section 7.

Tell students when you will give *Subtraction Facts Quiz D*, which is made up of facts from Groups 7 and 8. Quiz D is at the end of this set of DPP items. The quiz is assigned in Bit 10I.

10E **Subtraction Facts: Group 8**

Do these problems in your head. Write only the answers.

1. $16 - 8 =$ 2. $17 - 8 =$

3. $15 - 8 =$ 4. $18 - 9 =$

5. $18 - 10 =$ 6. $15 - 7 =$

7. $8 - 4 =$ 8. $7 - 4 =$

9. $6 - 3 =$

TIMS Bit

Students can study this group of facts with the flash cards for Group 8, discussing the strategies they use to remember them. Tell students when you will give *Subtraction Facts Quiz D*, which is made up of facts from Groups 7 and 8. Quiz D is at the end of this set of DPP items. The quiz is assigned in Bit 10I.

1. 8   2. 9
3. 7   4. 9
5. 8   6. 8
7. 4   8. 3
9. 3

Student Questions	Teacher Notes

10F **Masses**

Suppose we use these standard masses to measure mass using a two-pan balance: 8-gram masses, 4-gram masses, and 1-gram masses. How many of each would you need to use to balance an apple with a mass of 62 grams? Find as many solutions as you can.

TIMS Task

There are many solutions to the problem and many ways to find and express answers. Here are two possibilities:

$7 \times 8\,g + 6 \times 1\,g = 62\,g$

$5 \times 8\,g + 5 \times 4\,g + 2 \times 1\,g = 62\,g$

10G **Subtraction Flash Cards: Group 8**

1. With a partner, sort the Flash Cards for Group 8 into three stacks: Facts I Know Quickly, Facts I Know Using a Strategy, and Facts I Need to Learn.

2. Update your *Subtraction Facts I Know* chart. Circle the facts you answered quickly. Underline those you know by using a strategy. Do nothing to those you still need to learn.

TIMS Bit

Have students sort *Subtraction Flash Cards: Group 8*. After students sort, they should update the *Subtraction Facts I Know* charts. Students can take the cards for Group 8 home to practice with their families. The flash cards for Group 8 were distributed in the *Discovery Assignment Book* in Unit 5. They are also available in Section 7.

Students can study this group of facts with the flash cards for Group 7, discussing the strategies they use to remember them. Tell students when you will give *Subtraction Facts Quiz D,* which is made up of facts from Groups 7 and 8. Quiz D is at the end of this set of DPP items. The quiz is assigned in Bit 10I.

10I Subtraction Facts Quiz D

Students take *Subtraction Facts Quiz D,* which corresponds to *Subtraction Flash Cards: Groups 7* and *8.*

Quiz D is at the end of this set of DPP items. Ask students to have two pens or pencils of different colors ready. During the first minute of the quiz, they should write their answers using one color pen or pencil. After you tell students that a minute has passed, they should begin writing their answers with the other color pen or pencil. After students have been given a reasonable amount of time to complete the rest of the problems, they should check their work. Students should update their *Subtraction Facts I Know* charts using the results of the quiz.

DPP Bit 10K is an inventory test on all the subtraction facts. Encourage students to study for the test using their flash cards. Students should concentrate on those facts that are not yet marked on their *Subtraction Facts I Know* charts.

10J Moe and Joe Smart

1. Moe Smart is helping his brother Joe with his homework. Joe says, "Seven times eight is 54." How can Moe show Joe he is wrong?

2. Joe Smart says, "Six times eight is 46." How can Moe show Joe he is wrong?

TIMS Task

Students can use manipulatives or drawings to show that $8 \times 7 = 56$ and $6 \times 8 = 48$.

Student Questions	Teacher Notes

10K **Subtraction Facts Inventory**

Students take an inventory test of the 72 subtraction facts that were studied in Groups 1–8 throughout Units 2–10.

TIMS Bit $\boxed{\frac{5}{x\,7}}$

The *Subtraction Facts Inventory* is at the end of this set of DPP items. Ask students to have two pens or pencils of different colors ready. During the first four minutes of the test, students should write their answers using one color pen or pencil. After four minutes, students should begin writing their answers with the other color pen or pencil. Give students a reasonable amount of time to finish the test.

10L **Double Doubles**

1. $2 \times 6 =$ 2. $2 \times 2 \times 6 =$

3. $4 \times 6 =$ 4. $2 \times 7 =$

5. $2 \times 2 \times 7 =$ 6. $4 \times 7 =$

7. $2 \times 8 =$ 8. $2 \times 2 \times 8 =$

9. $4 \times 8 =$ 10. $3 \times 7 =$

11. $2 \times 3 \times 7 =$ 12. $6 \times 7 =$

13. $3 \times 8 =$ 14. $2 \times 3 \times 8 =$

15. $6 \times 8 =$

TIMS Task $\boxed{\frac{5}{x\,7}}$

Ask students to describe patterns that will help them learn these facts.

1. 12	2. 24
3. 24	4. 14
5. 28	6. 28
7. 16	8. 32
9. 32	10. 21
11. 42	12. 42
13. 24	14. 48
15. 48	

Name _____ Date _____

Subtraction Facts Quiz D

You will need two pens or pencils of different colors. Use the first color when you begin the test. When your teacher tells you to switch pens or pencils, finish the test using the second color.

14 − 7	16 − 8	12 − 7	6 − 3	14 − 8	13 − 6
12 − 6	14 − 6	13 − 7	10 − 5	18 − 10	7 − 4
8 − 4	12 − 5	15 − 7	17 − 8	15 − 8	18 − 9

Teacher: These facts correspond with *Subtraction Flash Cards*: *Groups 7* and *8.*

Copyright © Kendall/Hunt Publishing Company

Subtraction Facts Inventory

You will need two pens or pencils of different colors. Use the first color when you begin the test. When your teacher tells you to switch pens or pencils, finish the test using the second color.

9 − 2	11 − 9	7 − 3	16 − 7	11 − 4	11 − 2	7 − 4	14 − 10
10 − 2	14 − 7	16 − 9	12 − 4	13 − 7	11 − 5	8 − 2	4 − 2
10 − 8	11 − 7	13 − 10	8 − 6	5 − 3	13 − 8	12 − 10	16 − 8
9 − 3	7 − 5	6 − 2	11 − 6	17 − 9	10 − 3	13 − 5	16 − 10
14 − 5	15 − 7	10 − 6	9 − 5	11 − 3	13 − 6	8 − 5	12 − 7
5 − 2	12 − 8	9 − 4	12 − 9	10 − 7	12 − 3	9 − 6	10 − 5
13 − 4	8 − 3	15 − 6	17 − 10	18 − 9	14 − 9	17 − 8	6 − 3
19 − 10	15 − 8	15 − 10	6 − 4	11 − 8	13 − 9	9 − 7	15 − 9
14 − 6	12 − 6	14 − 8	18 − 10	10 − 4	8 − 4	12 − 5	7 − 2

Copyright © Kendall/Hunt Publishing Company

Unit 10 Home Practice

PART 1

Do these problems in your head. Write only the answers.

1. 16 – 8 = _____   2. 17 – 8 = _____   3. 170 – 80 = _____

4. 18 – 9 = _____   5. 18 – 10 = _____   6. 150 – 70 = _____

7. 14 – 7 = _____   8. 14 – 8 = _____   9. 120 – 70 = _____

10. 14 – 6 = _____   11. 12 – 5 = _____   12. 120 – 50 = _____

13. 100
    – 50

14.   80
    – 40

15. 150
    – 80

Copyright © Kendall/Hunt Publishing Company

Facts Distribution
Multiplication: 5s & 10s • Weeks 23–24

Math Facts Groups	Weeks	Daily Practice and Problems	Home Practice	Flash Cards	Facts Quizzes and Tests
Multiplication: 5s & 10s	23–24	Part 2 of the lesson *Completing the Table* (Unit 11 Lesson 4) launches the assessment of the multiplication facts in Grade 3. This lesson also introduces the *Multiplication Facts I Know* chart. Unit 11: items 11B, 11C, 11D, 11E, 11F, 11J, 11L, 11N, 11O, 11P, 11Q, 11R, 11S & 11T	Unit 11 Parts 1 & 2	*Triangle Flash Cards: 5s & 10s*	DPP item 11S is a quiz on the multiplication facts for the 5s and 10s. The *Multiplication Facts I Know* chart is updated.

Daily Practice and Problems

Students may solve the items individually, in groups, or as a class. The items may also be assigned for homework. The DPPs are also available on the Teacher Resource CD.

Student Questions	Teacher Notes
11B Multiplication Story	**TIMS Task**
1. Write a story and draw a picture about 3 × 5. Write a number sentence on your picture.	1. 3 × 5 = 15 2. 9 × 5 = 45 Students may wish to share their stories with the class.
2. Write a story and draw a picture about 9 × 5. Write a number sentence for your picture.	Discuss students' pictures. Ask students if they can use their pictures to solve 3 × 15.

11C Fives and Tens

A. 5 × 2 =   B. 10 × 2 =

C. 5 × 4 =   D. 10 × 4 =

E. 5 × 6 =   F. 10 × 6 =

G. 5 × 8 =   H. 10 × 8 =

I. 5 × 10 =   J. 10 × 10 =

What patterns do you see?

TIMS Bit

A.	10	B.	20
C.	20	D.	40
E.	30	F.	60
G.	40	H.	80
I.	50	J.	100

Students may see that 10 times a number is twice 5 times that number (because 10 is twice 5). They may also see that solutions in the first column skip count by tens and solutions in the second column skip count by twenty.

Student Questions	**Teacher Notes**

11D Guess My Number

1. I am less than 3×4. I am greater than 2×3. I am an even number. I am not 10.

2. I am less than 4×5. I am greater than 2×7. I am 3 times some number. I am not 15.

TIMS Task

1. 8
2. 18

11E Multiplication Facts: 0s and 1s

A. $5 \times 0 =$ B. $5 \times 1 =$

C. $10 \times 0 =$ D. $1 \times 10 =$

E. $0 \times 47 =$ F. $47 \times 1 =$

G. $0 \times 736 =$ H. $1 \times 736 =$

I. Use your calculator to check your answers.

J. What can you say about multiplying numbers by 0?

K. What can you say about multiplying numbers by 1?

TIMS Bit

After students complete these questions discuss them with the class.

A. 0   B. 5

C. 0   D. 10

E. 0   F. 47

G. 0   H. 736

J. Numbers multiplied by 0 equal 0.

K. Numbers multiplied by 1 equal themselves.

11F More Fives and Tens

A. $5 \times 3 =$ B. $10 \times 3 =$

C. $5 \times 5 =$ D. $10 \times 5 =$

E. $5 \times 7 =$ F. $10 \times 7 =$

G. $5 \times 9 =$ H. $10 \times 9 =$

What patterns do you see?

TIMS Task

A. 15   B. 30

C. 25   D. 50

E. 35   F. 70

G. 45   H. 90

Refer to the Teacher Notes for Bit 11C.

Student Questions	Teacher Notes

11J   Nickels and Dimes

You may use real or pretend money to help you solve the following problems.

1. What is the total value of 6 nickels and 4 dimes?

2. A. The total value of 55¢ is made up of 2 dimes and how many nickels?

   B. Name three other ways you can make 55¢ using only nickels and dimes.

TIMS Task

1. 70¢

2. A. 7 nickels

   B. Students should list at least 3 of the following five other ways:

   5 dimes and 1 nickel

   4 dimes and 3 nickels

   3 dimes and 5 nickels

   1 dime and 9 nickels

   0 dimes and 11 nickels

11L   More Nickels and Dimes

True or false? Explain how you know.

1. 4 dimes $<$ 6 nickels

2. 7 dimes and 4 nickels $=$ 9 dimes

3. 15 nickels $>$ 6 dimes

TIMS Task

Have real or pretend money available to help students solve the problems.

1. False; 4 dimes is 40 cents, 6 nickels is 30 cents.

2. True; the 4 nickels can be exchanged for 2 dimes.

3. True; $.75 is greater than $.60.

(11N) Multiplication and Rectangles

A rectangle is made from 3 rows with 8 tiles in each row.

1. Draw this rectangle on *Centimeter Grid Paper.*

2. How many tiles make up the rectangle? Write a number sentence to show your answer.

3. Make a different rectangle with the same number of tiles. How many rows? How many tiles in each row?

TIMS Task

1.

2. 3 × 8 = 24 tiles

3. Answers will vary.

Possible responses:
1 row of 24 tiles;

2 rows of 12 tiles;

4 rows of 6 tiles;

6 rows of 4 tiles;

8 rows of 3 tiles;

12 rows of 2 tiles;

24 rows of 1 tile

(11O) Lizardland

Use the picture of Lizardland in the *Student Guide* to help you solve the following problems.

Find the Lizardland wall at the entrance to the park.

1. How many bricks are behind the Lizardland sign? Tell how you know.

2. How many bricks are covered by the sign listing the admission prices? Tell how you know.

TIMS Bit

1. 5 × 6 = 30 bricks
2. 6 × 4 = 24 bricks

11P **How Much and How Many?**

A. Moe spent 9 nickels and 7 dimes to buy ice cream. How much money did he spend? Show how you found your answer.

B. Joe has 5 shirts. Each shirt has 3 pockets. How many pockets are on Joe's shirts? Write a number sentence.

C. Flo has 7 braids in her hair. Each braid has 5 beads. How many beads are in Flo's hair? Write a number sentence.

TIMS Task $\boxed{\$}$ $\boxed{\frac{5}{\times 7}}$

A. $1.15;

   9×5 cents $= 45$ cents

   7×10 cents $= 70$ cents

   45 cents $+ 70$ cents
   $= 115$ cents

B. $3 \times 5 = 15$ pockets

C. $7 \times 5 = 35$ beads

11Q **Mathhoppers**

1. A $+3$ mathhopper starts at 0 and hops six times. Where does it land?

2. A $+5$ mathhopper starts at 0 and hops eight times. Where does it land?

3. A $+5$ mathhopper starts at 0 and wants to eat a sunflower seed on 163. Will it be able to land on the sunflower seed? Why or why not? Think about the patterns you found in your multiplication table.

TIMS Bit $\boxed{\frac{5}{\times 7}}$ $\boxed{N}$

1. 18

2. 40

3. No, a $+5$ mathhopper lands only on numbers ending in 0 or 5. It will land on 160 and then 165. It will jump right over the sunflower seed.

Student Questions	Teacher Notes

11R **A Product of 36**

Write 36 as a product of two numbers in as many ways as you can.

TIMS Task

Have tiles and graph paper available so students can work with arrays to find the answers.

  1×36 2×18 3×12

  4×9 6×6

11S **Quiz on 5s and 10s**

A. $5 \times 2 =$ B. $3 \times 10 =$

C. $5 \times 0 =$ D. $8 \times 10 =$

E. $6 \times 10 =$ F. $5 \times 3 =$

G. $10 \times 9 =$ H. $7 \times 5 =$

I. $10 \times 2 =$ J. $10 \times 7 =$

K. $6 \times 5 =$ L. $5 \times 10 =$

M. $8 \times 5 =$ N. $9 \times 5 =$

O. $4 \times 10 =$ P. $4 \times 5 =$

Q. $10 \times 10 =$ R. $5 \times 5 =$

TIMS Bit

This quiz is on the first group of multiplication facts, the 5s and 10s.

We recommend 2 minutes for this test. Allow students to change pens after the time is up and complete the remaining problems in a different color.

After students take the test, have them update their *Multiplication Facts I Know* charts.

11T Mathhopper

You may use a calculator to solve the problems. A +8 mathhopper starts at 0.

1. There is a frog at 97. Will the mathhopper land on the frog and be eaten? Tell how you know. If it does not land on the frog, how close does it get?

2. How many hops does the mathhopper need to take to get to a daisy at 224? Tell how you know.

TIMS Task

1. Discuss the patterns of the multiples of 8. Since they are even, it will not land on 97. It lands on 96; one away from the frog. If your calculator has the constant feature press: 8 + 8 = = = = etc. Each time you press =, the constant number (8) and operation (addition) are repeated.

2. 28 hops.

   With the constant feature press: 8 + 8 = = = = etc. Count the number of times you press the equal sign.

   Help students recognize that division can be used. Using the calculator, press: 224 ÷ 8 =.

   Alternatively, 10 hops gets the mathhopper to 80, 20 hops to 160, 30 hops to 240. That's too far. Two hops back is 224, so the answer is 28 hops.

   Other strategies that may be used are repeated subtraction and trial and error.

 Unit 11 Home Practice

PART 1

1. 160 − 70 = _____   2. 120 − 50 = _____   3. 140 − 60 = _____

4. 82 + _____ = 100   5. 53 + _____ = 100   6. 44 + _____ = 100

7. When Tony cleaned his mom's car he found some coins under the seats. His mom let him keep the coins and gave him $.25 more for cleaning the car. Now he has $2.00.

   A. How much money did Tony find in the car? _____

   B. What coins and how many of each could he have found? Give two possible answers.

PART 2

1. 600 + 700 = _____   2. 400 + 800 = _____   3. 500 + 900 = _____

4. 1000 − _____ = 450   5. 1000 − _____ = 343

6. Tina's high school graduating class has 321 students. Rita's junior high graduating class has 132 students. Sara, who is graduating from kindergarten, is in a class of 42 students.

   A. How many more students are in Tina's class than in Rita's?

   B. If all three classes attend the same ceremony, how many students would be graduating?

Copyright © Kendall/Hunt Publishing Company

Lesson 4

Completing the Table

Lesson Overview

Estimated Class Sessions
2

In Part 1, students complete their multiplication tables by finding the remaining multiplication facts through skip counting or using a calculator. Symmetry in the table is discussed as well as patterns for multiples of 9. In Part 2, students learn how to use the *Triangle Flash Cards: 5s* and *10s* to practice the facts. They begin their *Multiplication Facts I Know* charts.

Key Content

- Identifying patterns for multiples of nine.
- Investigating symmetry in the multiplication table.

Key Vocabulary

- symmetry

Math Facts

DPP items J and L provide practice with multiplication facts.

Homework

1. Assign the Homework section of the *Completing the Table* Activity Pages.
2. Students take home their lists of facts they need to study and the *Triangle Flash Cards* to practice the facts with a family member.
3. Assign Parts 1 and 2 of the Home Practice.

Curriculum Sequence

Before This Unit

In Units 2–10, students reviewed and were assessed on the subtraction facts primarily through the Daily Practice and Problems. They also developed strategies for the multiplication facts.

After This Unit

In Units 12–20, students will continue to practice and assess the multiplication facts. In each unit, they will study a small group of facts in the Daily Practice and Problems. In Grade 4 students will review the multiplication facts and develop fluency with the division facts.

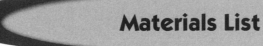

Materials List

Supplies and Copies

Student	Teacher
Supplies for Each Student • calculator, optional • envelope for storing flash cards	**Supplies**
Copies • 2 *Small Multiplication Tables* (1 for class and 1 for home) per student, optional (*Unit Resource Guide* Page 67) • 1 copy of *My Multiplication Table,* completed in Lessons 2 and 3 per student (*Discovery Assignment Book* Page 159)	**Copies/Transparencies** • 1 transparency of *My Multiplication Table,* completed in Lessons 2 and 3 (*Discovery Assignment Book* Page 159) • 1 transparency of *Multiplication Table* (*Unit Resource Guide* Page 66)

All blackline masters including assessment, transparency, and DPP masters are also on the Teacher Resource CD.

Student Books

Completing the Table (*Student Guide* Pages 149–151)
Triangle Flash Cards: 5s (*Discovery Assignment Book* Page 165)
Triangle Flash Cards: 10s (*Discovery Assignment Book* Page 167)
Multiplication Facts I Know (*Discovery Assignment Book* Page 169)

Daily Practice and Problems and Home Practice

DPP items I–L (*Unit Resource Guide* Pages 20–21)
Home Practice Parts 1–2 (*Discovery Assignment Book* Page 156)

Note: Classrooms whose pacing differs significantly from the suggested pacing of the units should use the Math Facts Calendar in Section 4 of the *Facts Resource Guide* to ensure students receive the complete math facts program.

I. Bit: Lizardland Picnic (URG p. 20)

At Lizardland, eight people can sit at a table in Picnic Park. If your class had a picnic there (including your teacher), how many tables would you need? Draw a picture to show your answer.

K. Bit: Cookies (URG p. 21)

At Max and Cora's cookie stand, one cookie costs 35¢. How many different ways can you pay exact change for one cookie using only nickels, dimes, and quarters?

J. Task: Nickels and Dimes
(URG p. 20)

You may use real or pretend money to help you solve the following problems.

1. What is the total value of 6 nickels and 4 dimes?
2. A. The total value of 55¢ is made up of 2 dimes and how many nickels?
   B. Name three other ways you can make 55¢ using only nickels and dimes.

L. Task: More Nickels and Dimes
(URG p. 21)

True or false? Explain how you know.

1. 4 dimes < 6 nickels
2. 7 dimes and 4 nickels = 9 dimes
3. 15 nickels > 6 dimes

Teaching the Activity

Part 1 Patterns for Nine

The *Completing the Table* Activity Pages in the *Student Guide* begin by pointing out that students only need to find a few more facts to complete their multiplication tables. Remind them that when they find a fact, such as 4 × 6, they can also record its turn-around fact, 6 × 4. When students begin the lesson, they should have 20 blank squares left (from the original 121) in their multiplication tables. Because of the turn-around rule of multiplication, they actually have only 10 facts remaining.

Have students figure out the remaining facts in any manner they wish. Some good strategies include using skip counting, a calculator, a number line, or counters. Another good strategy is to use known facts to derive the new ones. For example, a student might add to the known fact 5 × 4 = 20 to derive the new fact 6 × 4 = 24:

"I know that 5 × 4 = 20. So, 6 × 4 is 4 more—24." A student might subtract from the known fact 5 × 8 = 40 to derive the new fact 4 × 8 = 32: "I know that 5 × 8 is 40. So, 4 × 8 is 8 less—32."

After completing their multiplication tables, students look for patterns in their tables. They have already looked for patterns in earlier activities, but will probably see new ones in the completed table.

Question 1 asks students to look for patterns with nines. In discovering patterns in *Question 2,* students might observe the following:

1. When the products are listed in a column, as below, it is easy to see that the digits in the ten's place count up by ones (0, 1, 2, 3 . . .) and that the digits in the one's place count down by ones (9, 8, 7 . . .).

   9
   18
   27
   36
   45
   54
   63
   72
   81

Completing the Table

You should have only 20 blank squares left in your multiplication table. Use any strategy you like—skip counting, a calculator, a number line, or counters—to find the remaining facts.

When you find a fact, such as 4 × 6, you can also record its turn-around fact—in this case, 6 × 4.

Patterns for Nine

1. Copy and complete the list of facts for 9. Then write the products in a column, one on each line.

   0 × 9 = ?

   1 × 9 = ?

   2 × 9 = ?

   3 × 9 = ?

   4 × 9 = ?

   5 × 9 = ?

   6 × 9 = ?

   7 × 9 = ?

   8 × 9 = ?

   9 × 9 = ?

2. What patterns do you see in your list?

Completing the Table   SG • Grade 3 • Unit 11 • Lesson 4   149

Student Guide - page 149 (Answers on p. 68)

TIMS Tip

To remember 9s facts it often helps to see how simple it is to derive them from the familiar 10s facts. For example, "10 × 4 is 40. So, 9 × 4 is 4 less: 40 − 4 = 36" and "10 × 5 is 50. So, 9 × 5 is 5 less: 50 − 5 = 45."

Student Guide - page 150 (Answers on p. 68)

Student Guide - page 150 content:

3. Use your calculator to find the products below. Then add the digits in each product. Repeat adding the digits until you get a one digit number.

Example: $9 \times 634 = 5706$ $5 + 7 + 0 + 6 = 18$ $1 + 8 = 9$

A. 9×47	B. 9×83
C. 9×89	D. 9×92
E. 9×123	F. 9×633
G. 9×697	H. 9×333

4. Describe what happens when you add the digits of a multiple of 9.

Multiplication Facts and Triangle Flash Cards

Practice multiplication facts with a partner. Use your *Triangle Flash Cards: 5s* and *Triangle Flash Cards: 10s*, and follow the directions below.

- One partner covers the shaded number, the largest number on the card. This number will be the answer to the multiplication problem. It is called the **product**.

$5 \times 4 = ?$
$4 \times 5 = ?$

- The second person multiplies the two uncovered numbers (one in a circle, one in a square). These are the two **factors.** It doesn't matter which of the factors is said first. 4×5 and 5×4 both equal 20.

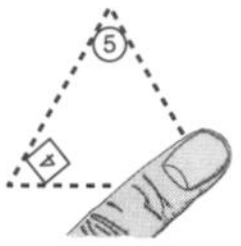

- Divide the cards into three piles: those facts you know and can answer quickly, those you can figure out with a strategy, and those you need to learn.

150   SG • Grade 3 • Unit 11 • Lesson 4   Completing the Table

---

Discovery Assignment Book - page 169 content:

Name _____   Date _____

Multiplication Facts I Know

- Circle the facts you know well.
- Keep this table and use it to help you multiply.
- As you learn more facts, you may circle them too.

×	0	1	2	3	4	5	6	7	8	9	10
0	0	0	0	0	0	0	0	0	0	0	0
1	0	1	2	3	4	5	6	7	8	9	10
2	0	2	4	6	8	10	12	14	16	18	20
3	0	3	6	9	12	15	18	21	24	27	30
4	0	4	8	12	16	20	24	28	32	36	40
5	0	5	10	15	20	25	30	35	40	45	50
6	0	6	12	18	24	30	36	42	48	54	60
7	0	7	14	21	28	35	42	49	56	63	70
8	0	8	16	24	32	40	48	56	64	72	80
9	0	9	18	27	36	45	54	63	72	81	90
10	0	10	20	30	40	50	60	70	80	90	100

Completing the Table   DAB • Grade 3 • Unit 11 • Lesson 4 **169**

Discovery Assignment Book - page 169

---

2. The sums of the two digits in each of the products listed is nine. For example, $3 + 6 = 9$ and $7 + 2 = 9$. In fact, the sum of the digits of any multiple of 9 is also a multiple of 9. Furthermore, the process of adding digits can be repeated until nine itself results. As illustrated in **Question 3,** $9 \times 634 = 5706$. Adding the product's digits provides a multiple of nine: $5 + 7 + 0 + 6 = 18$. Adding the new answer's digits results in nine: $1 + 8 = 9$. In **Question 3,** students work with other multiples of nine to discover that this pattern is consistent.

Students may notice other patterns in their multiplication tables. They may notice that the diagonal line from the top left corner to the bottom right corner is a line of symmetry formed by the square numbers. To see this, students can circle a number above the line and connect it to its matching number on the bottom half, as in Figure 6.

×	0	1	2	3	4	5	6	7	8	9	10
0	0	0	0	0	0	0	0	0	0	0	0
1	0	1	2	3	4	5	6	7	8	9	10
2	0	2	4	6	8	10	12	14	16	18	20
3	0	3	6	9	12	15	18	21	(24)	27	30
4	0	4	8	12	16	20	(24)	28	32	36	40
5	0	5	10	15	20	25	30	35	40	45	50
6	0	6	12	18	(24)	30	36	42	48	54	60
7	0	7	14	21	28	35	42	49	56	63	70
8	0	8	16	(24)	32	40	48	56	64	72	80
9	0	9	18	27	36	45	54	63	72	81	90
10	0	10	20	30	40	50	60	70	80	90	100

Figure 6: *Symmetry in the multiplication table*

TIMS Tip

Adding the digits of the product of a 9s fact to see whether they add up to nine can be a strategy for remembering 9s facts. For example, a student might think, "Let me see, does 9×6 equal 54 or 56? It must be 54 since $5 + 4$ is 9, but $5 + 6$ is not 9."

Journal Prompt

Describe the patterns in your multiplication table.

Part 2 Multiplication Facts and Triangle Flash Cards

The *Triangle Flash Cards: 5s* and *Triangle Flash Cards: 10s* are located in the *Discovery Assignment Book.* The *Student Guide* outlines how students use the *Triangle Flash Cards* for practicing the multiplication facts. Partners cover the number that is shaded (the largest number on the card). This is the **product,** the answer to the multiplication problem that the other two numbers—the **factors**—present. The student being quizzed multiplies the two numbers showing, gives the answer, and the answer is checked.

As their partners quiz them on the facts, students sort the cards into three piles—those facts they can answer quickly, those they know using a strategy, and those they need to learn. Then each student begins a *Multiplication Facts I Know* chart found in the *Discovery Assignment Book.* Students circle the facts they know and can answer quickly on the chart. Remind students that if they know a fact, they also know its turn-around fact. So if they circle $5 \times 3 = 15$, they can also circle $3 \times 5 = 15$.

Review with students what they learned in Lesson 2 about multiplication by zero and one. Students can also circle these facts.

Students list the facts they did not circle on their charts. They take this list home along with their flash cards to practice the facts they need to study with a family member. Students will take a quiz on the multiplication facts for the fives and tens in DPP Bit S at the end of this unit. After the quiz, they update their charts.

As students encounter multiplication problems with the facts in the activities and labs, encourage them to share their strategies. The fives and tens are easily solved using skip counting. For descriptions of other multiplication facts strategies, see the TIMS Tutor: *Math Facts* in the *Teacher Implementation Guide.*

Instruct students to keep their *Multiplication Facts I Know* charts in a safe place. They will use the charts to track their progress learning the multiplication facts as they continue to study them in Units 12–20.

TIMS Tip

Use the *Small Multiplication Tables* Page to make a small multiplication table for each student. (There are four tables on each page.) Students can tape them to their desks or notebooks for easy reference so they have ready access to all the facts while they are working on activities or playing games.

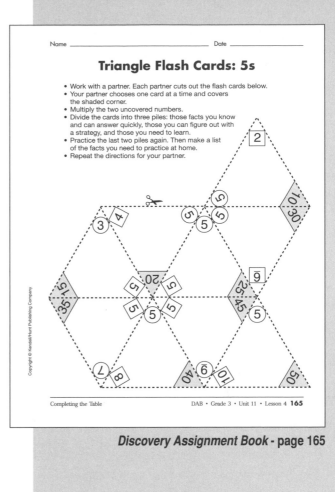

Discovery Assignment Book - page 165

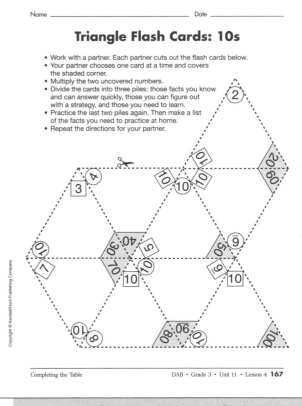

Discovery Assignment Book - page 167

Student Guide page content (left column, top):

- Discuss how you can figure out facts that you do not recall right away. Share your strategies with your partner.

- Practice the last two piles again. Then make a list of the facts you need to practice at home for homework.

- Circle the facts you know quickly on your *Multiplication Facts I Know* chart. Remember that if you know one fact, you also know its turn-around fact. Circle both on your chart.

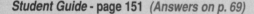

Multiplication Facts I Know

×	0	1	2	3	4	5	6	7	8	9	10
0	0	0	0	0	0	0	0	0	0	0	0
1	0	1	2	3	4	5	6	7	8	9	10
2	0	2	4	6	8	10	12	14	16	18	20
3	0	3	6	9	12	15	18	21	24	27	30
4	0	4	8	12	16	20	24	28	32	36	40
5	0	5	10	15	20	25	30	35	40	45	50
6	0	6	12	18	24	30	36	42	48	54	60
7	0	7	14	21	28	35	42	49	56	63	70
8	0	8	16	24	32	40	48	56	64	72	80
9	0	9	18	27	36	45	54	63	72	81	90
10	0	10	20	30	40	50	60	70	80	90	100

Homework

Find these products.

1. $3 \times 4 = ?$
2. $6 \times 7 = ?$
3. $6 \times 5 = ?$
4. $5 \times 4 = ?$
5. $7 \times 9 = ?$
6. $4 \times 2 = ?$
7. $8 \times 5 = ?$
8. $8 \times 8 = ?$
9. $7 \times 4 = ?$
10. $0 \times 6 = ?$
11. $7 \times 3 = ?$
12. $9 \times 6 = ?$
13. $6 \times 8 = ?$
14. $7 \times 8 = ?$
15. $9 \times 9 = ?$

16. $\begin{array}{r} 7 \\ \times 5 \\ \hline \end{array}$
17. $\begin{array}{r} 6 \\ \times 9 \\ \hline \end{array}$
18. $\begin{array}{r} 3 \\ \times 8 \\ \hline \end{array}$

19. $\begin{array}{r} 4 \\ \times 6 \\ \hline \end{array}$
20. $\begin{array}{r} 8 \\ \times 3 \\ \hline \end{array}$
21. $\begin{array}{r} 9 \\ \times 1 \\ \hline \end{array}$

22. $\begin{array}{r} 8 \\ \times 4 \\ \hline \end{array}$
23. $\begin{array}{r} 6 \\ \times 6 \\ \hline \end{array}$
24. $\begin{array}{r} 7 \\ \times 7 \\ \hline \end{array}$

25. Choose one of the facts in Questions 1–24. Write a multiplication story about it. Draw a picture to go with your story.

Completing the Table — SG • Grade 3 • Unit 11 • Lesson 4 — **151**

Student Guide - page 151 (Answers on p. 69)

Math Facts

DPP items J and L provide practice with the multiplication facts for the fives and tens using problems with nickels and dimes.

Homework and Practice

- Assign the Homework section in the *Student Guide.* Allow students to take home their completed multiplication tables.

- DPP Bit I builds number sense through a division word problem. Bit K is a problem involving money.

- Remind students to practice the multiplication facts for the fives and tens throughout the rest of this unit using their *Triangle Flash Cards.*

- Parts 1 and 2 of the Home Practice can be assigned for homework. They provide addition and subtraction practice.

Answers for Parts 1 and 2 of the Home Practice are in the Answer Key at the end of this lesson and at the end of this unit.

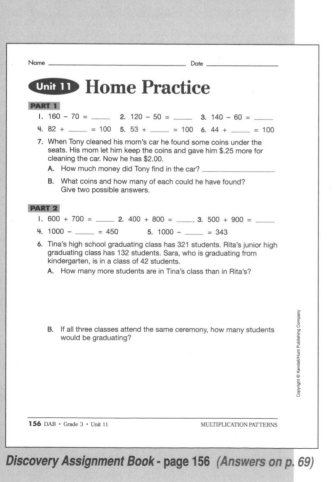

Name _____ Date _____

Unit 11 Home Practice

PART 1

1. $160 - 70 =$ _____
2. $120 - 50 =$ _____
3. $140 - 60 =$ _____
4. $82 +$ _____ $= 100$
5. $53 +$ _____ $= 100$
6. $44 +$ _____ $= 100$

7. When Tony cleaned his mom's car he found some coins under the seats. His mom let him keep the coins and gave him $.25 more for cleaning the car. Now he has $2.00.
   A. How much money did Tony find in the car? _____
   B. What coins and how many of each could he have found? Give two possible answers.

PART 2

1. $600 + 700 =$ _____
2. $400 + 800 =$ _____
3. $500 + 900 =$ _____
4. $1000 -$ _____ $= 450$
5. $1000 -$ _____ $= 343$

6. Tina's high school graduating class has 321 students. Rita's junior high graduating class has 132 students. Sara, who is graduating from kindergarten, is in a class of 42 students.
   A. How many more students are in Tina's class than in Rita's?

   B. If all three classes attend the same ceremony, how many students would be graduating?

156 DAB • Grade 3 • Unit 11 — MULTIPLICATION PATTERNS

Copyright © Kendall/Hunt Publishing Company

Discovery Assignment Book - page 156 (Answers on p. 69)

Math Facts and Daily Practice and Problems

Bits I and K are word problems. DPP items J and L provide practice with multiplication facts.

Part 1. Patterns for Nines

1. Using any method they choose, students fill in ten of the blank spaces on *My Multiplication Table* for Lessons 2 and 3.
2. Students use turn-around facts to fill in the remaining blank spaces.
3. Students look for patterns with multiples of nine and discuss using the patterns to learn the facts.
4. Students look for symmetry in their multiplication tables. Use the *Multiplication Table* Transparency Master to model the table's symmetry.
5. Students complete *Questions 1–4* of the *Completing the Table* Activity Pages in the *Student Guide*.

Part 2. Multiplication Facts and Triangle Flash Cards

1. Following the directions in the *Student Guide,* students practice the facts for the fives and tens using *Triangle Flash Cards.*
2. Students sort their cards into three piles according to how well they know each fact. They begin their *Multiplication Facts I Know* charts by circling the facts they know well and can answer quickly.
3. Students list the fives and tens they still need to learn.
4. Students review multiplication by zero and one and circle these facts on their charts.

Homework

1. Assign the Homework section of the *Completing the Table* Activity Pages.
2. Students take home their lists of facts they need to study and the *Triangle Flash Cards* to practice the facts with a family member.
3. Assign Parts 1 and 2 of the Home Practice.

Answer Key is on pages 68–69.

Notes:

Multiplication Table

×	0	1	2	3	4	5	6	7	8	9	10
0	0	0	0	0	0	0	0	0	0	0	0
1	0	1	2	3	4	5	6	7	8	9	10
2	0	2	4	6	8	10	12	14	16	18	20
3	0	3	6	9	12	15	18	21	24	27	30
4	0	4	8	12	16	20	24	28	32	36	40
5	0	5	10	15	20	25	30	35	40	45	50
6	0	6	12	18	24	30	36	42	48	54	60
7	0	7	14	21	28	35	42	49	56	63	70
8	0	8	16	24	32	40	48	56	64	72	80
9	0	9	18	27	36	45	54	63	72	81	90
10	0	10	20	30	40	50	60	70	80	90	100

Copyright © Kendall/Hunt Publishing Company

Name _____   Date _____

Small Multiplication Tables

×	0	1	2	3	4	5	6	7	8	9	10
0	0	0	0	0	0	0	0	0	0	0	0
1	0	1	2	3	4	5	6	7	8	9	10
2	0	2	4	6	8	10	12	14	16	18	20
3	0	3	6	9	12	15	18	21	24	27	30
4	0	4	8	12	16	20	24	28	32	36	40
5	0	5	10	15	20	25	30	35	40	45	50
6	0	6	12	18	24	30	36	42	48	54	60
7	0	7	14	21	28	35	42	49	56	63	70
8	0	8	16	24	32	40	48	56	64	72	80
9	0	9	18	27	36	45	54	63	72	81	90
10	0	10	20	30	40	50	60	70	80	90	100

×	0	1	2	3	4	5	6	7	8	9	10
0	0	0	0	0	0	0	0	0	0	0	0
1	0	1	2	3	4	5	6	7	8	9	10
2	0	2	4	6	8	10	12	14	16	18	20
3	0	3	6	9	12	15	18	21	24	27	30
4	0	4	8	12	16	20	24	28	32	36	40
5	0	5	10	15	20	25	30	35	40	45	50
6	0	6	12	18	24	30	36	42	48	54	60
7	0	7	14	21	28	35	42	49	56	63	70
8	0	8	16	24	32	40	48	56	64	72	80
9	0	9	18	27	36	45	54	63	72	81	90
10	0	10	20	30	40	50	60	70	80	90	100

×	0	1	2	3	4	5	6	7	8	9	10
0	0	0	0	0	0	0	0	0	0	0	0
1	0	1	2	3	4	5	6	7	8	9	10
2	0	2	4	6	8	10	12	14	16	18	20
3	0	3	6	9	12	15	18	21	24	27	30
4	0	4	8	12	16	20	24	28	32	36	40
5	0	5	10	15	20	25	30	35	40	45	50
6	0	6	12	18	24	30	36	42	48	54	60
7	0	7	14	21	28	35	42	49	56	63	70
8	0	8	16	24	32	40	48	56	64	72	80
9	0	9	18	27	36	45	54	63	72	81	90
10	0	10	20	30	40	50	60	70	80	90	100

×	0	1	2	3	4	5	6	7	8	9	10
0	0	0	0	0	0	0	0	0	0	0	0
1	0	1	2	3	4	5	6	7	8	9	10
2	0	2	4	6	8	10	12	14	16	18	20
3	0	3	6	9	12	15	18	21	24	27	30
4	0	4	8	12	16	20	24	28	32	36	40
5	0	5	10	15	20	25	30	35	40	45	50
6	0	6	12	18	24	30	36	42	48	54	60
7	0	7	14	21	28	35	42	49	56	63	70
8	0	8	16	24	32	40	48	56	64	72	80
9	0	9	18	27	36	45	54	63	72	81	90
10	0	10	20	30	40	50	60	70	80	90	100

Copyright © Kendall/Hunt Publishing Company

Completing the Table

You should have only 20 blank squares left in your multiplication table. Use any strategy you like—skip counting, a calculator, a number line, or counters—to find the remaining facts.

When you find a fact, such as 4 × 6, you can also record its turn-around fact—in this case, 6 × 4.

Patterns for Nine

1. Copy and complete the list of facts for 9. Then write the products in a column, one on each line.

   0 × 9 = ?

   1 × 9 = ?

   2 × 9 = ?

   3 × 9 = ?

   4 × 9 = ?

   5 × 9 = ?

   6 × 9 = ?

   7 × 9 = ?

   8 × 9 = ?

   9 × 9 = ?

2. What patterns do you see in your list?

Completing the Table — SG • Grade 3 • Unit 11 • Lesson 4 — 149

Student Guide - page 149

3. Use your calculator to find the products below. Then add the digits in each product. Repeat adding the digits until you get a one digit number.

   Example: 9 × 634 = 5706   5 + 7 + 0 + 6 = 18   1 + 8 = 9

   A. 9 × 47   **B.** 9 × 83

   C. 9 × 89   **D.** 9 × 92

   E. 9 × 123   **F.** 9 × 633

   G. 9 × 697   **H.** 9 × 333

4. Describe what happens when you add the digits of a multiple of 9.

Multiplication Facts and Triangle Flash Cards

Practice multiplication facts with a partner. Use your *Triangle Flash Cards: 5s* and *Triangle Flash Cards: 10s,* and follow the directions below.

- One partner covers the shaded number, the largest number on the card. This number will be the answer to the multiplication problem. It is called the **product.**

  5 × 4 = ?

  4 × 5 = ?

- The second person multiplies the two uncovered numbers (one in a circle, one in a square). These are the two **factors.** It doesn't matter which of the factors is said first. 4 × 5 and 5 × 4 both equal 20.

- Divide the cards into three piles: those facts you know and can answer quickly, those you can figure out with a strategy, and those you need to learn.

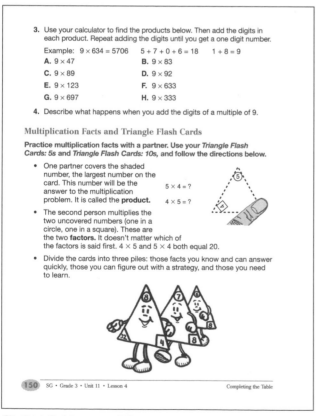

150   SG • Grade 3 • Unit 11 • Lesson 4   Completing the Table

Student Guide - page 150

Student Guide (p. 149)

1. 0, 9, 18, 27, 36, 45, 54, 63, 72, 81
2. Answers will vary.*

Student Guide (p. 150)

3. **A.** 423; 4 + 2 + 3 = 9*

   B. 747; 7 + 4 + 7 = 18*

   C. 801; 8 + 0 + 1 = 9

   D. 828; 8 + 2 + 8 = 18

   E. 1107; 1 + 1 + 0 + 7 = 9

   F. 5697; 5 + 6 + 9 + 7 = 27

   G. 6273; 6 + 2 + 7 + 3 = 18

   H. 2997; 2 + 9 + 9 + 7 = 27

4. The sum is a multiple of 9.

*Answers and/or discussion are included in the Lesson Guide.

Student Guide (p. 151)

Homework

1. 12	2. 42
3. 30	4. 20
5. 63	6. 8
7. 40	8. 64
9. 28	10. 0
11. 21	12. 54
13. 48	14. 56
15. 81	16. 35
17. 54	18. 24
19. 24	20. 24
21. 9	22. 32
23. 36	24. 49

25. Answers will vary.

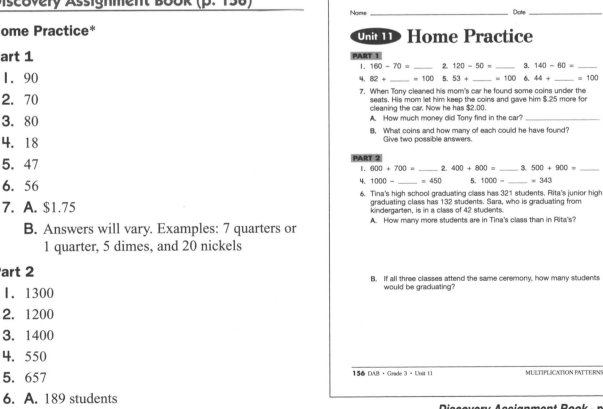

Student Guide - page 151

Discovery Assignment Book (p. 156)

Home Practice*

Part 1

1. 90
2. 70
3. 80
4. 18
5. 47
6. 56
7. A. $1.75
   B. Answers will vary. Examples: 7 quarters or 1 quarter, 5 dimes, and 20 nickels

Part 2

1. 1300
2. 1200
3. 1400
4. 550
5. 657
6. A. 189 students
   B. 495 students

Discovery Assignment Book - page 156

*Answers for all the Home Practice in the *Discovery Assignment Book* are at the end of the unit.

Completing the Table

You should have only 20 blank squares left in your multiplication table. Use any strategy you like—skip counting, a calculator, a number line, or counters—to find the remaining facts.

When you find a fact, such as 4×6, you can also record its turn-around fact—in this case, 6×4.

Patterns for Nine

1. Copy and complete the list of facts for 9. Then write the products in a column, one on each line.

   $0 \times 9 = ?$

   $1 \times 9 = ?$

   $2 \times 9 = ?$

   $3 \times 9 = ?$

   $4 \times 9 = ?$

   $5 \times 9 = ?$

   $6 \times 9 = ?$

   $7 \times 9 = ?$

   $8 \times 9 = ?$

   $9 \times 9 = ?$

2. What patterns do you see in your list?

Copyright © Kendall/Hunt Publishing Company

3. Use your calculator to find the products below. Then add the digits in each product. Repeat adding the digits until you get a one digit number.

Example: $9 \times 634 = 5706$ $5 + 7 + 0 + 6 = 18$ $1 + 8 = 9$

A. 9×47 **B.** 9×83

C. 9×89 **D.** 9×92

E. 9×123 **F.** 9×633

G. 9×697 **H.** 9×333

4. Describe what happens when you add the digits of a multiple of 9.

Multiplication Facts and Triangle Flash Cards

Practice multiplication facts with a partner. Use your *Triangle Flash Cards: 5s* and *Triangle Flash Cards: 10s,* and follow the directions below.

- One partner covers the shaded number, the largest number on the card. This number will be the answer to the multiplication problem. It is called the **product.**

$5 \times 4 = ?$

$4 \times 5 = ?$

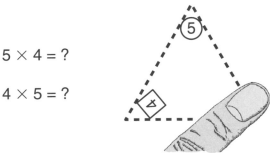

- The second person multiplies the two uncovered numbers (one in a circle, one in a square). These are the two **factors.** It doesn't matter which of the factors is said first. 4×5 and 5×4 both equal 20.

- Divide the cards into three piles: those facts you know and can answer quickly, those you can figure out with a strategy, and those you need to learn.

Copyright © Kendall/Hunt Publishing Company

- Discuss how you can figure out facts that you do not recall right away. Share your strategies with your partner.

- Practice the last two piles again. Then make a list of the facts you need to practice at home for homework.

- Circle the facts you know quickly on your *Multiplication Facts I Know* chart. Remember that if you know one fact, you also know its turn-around fact. Circle both on your chart.

Multiplication Facts I Know

×	0	1	2	3	4	5	6	7	8	9	10
0	0	0	0	0	0	0	0	0	0	0	0
1	0	1	2	3	4	5	6	7	8	9	10
2	0	2	4	6	8	10	12	14	16	18	20
3	0	3	6	9	12	15	18	21	24	27	30
4	0	4	8	12	16	20	24	28	32	36	40
5	0	5	10	15	20	25	30	35	40	45	50
6	0	6	12	18	24	30	36	42	48	54	60
7	0	7	14	21	28	35	42	49	56	63	70
8	0	8	16	24	32	40	48	56	64	72	80
9	0	9	18	27	36	45	54	63	72	81	90
10	0	10	20	30	40	50	60	70	80	90	100

Homework

Find these products.

1. $3 \times 4 = ?$

2. $6 \times 7 = ?$

3. $6 \times 5 = ?$

4. $5 \times 4 = ?$

5. $7 \times 9 = ?$

6. $4 \times 2 = ?$

7. $8 \times 5 = ?$

8. $8 \times 8 = ?$

9. $7 \times 4 = ?$

10. $0 \times 6 = ?$

11. $7 \times 3 = ?$

12. $9 \times 6 = ?$

13. $6 \times 8 = ?$

14. $7 \times 8 = ?$

15. $9 \times 9 = ?$

16.
$$\begin{array}{r} 7 \\ \times 5 \\ \hline \end{array}$$

17.
$$\begin{array}{r} 6 \\ \times 9 \\ \hline \end{array}$$

18.
$$\begin{array}{r} 3 \\ \times 8 \\ \hline \end{array}$$

19.
$$\begin{array}{r} 4 \\ \times 6 \\ \hline \end{array}$$

20.
$$\begin{array}{r} 8 \\ \times 3 \\ \hline \end{array}$$

21.
$$\begin{array}{r} 9 \\ \times 1 \\ \hline \end{array}$$

22.
$$\begin{array}{r} 8 \\ \times 4 \\ \hline \end{array}$$

23.
$$\begin{array}{r} 6 \\ \times 6 \\ \hline \end{array}$$

24.
$$\begin{array}{r} 7 \\ \times 7 \\ \hline \end{array}$$

25. Choose one of the facts in Questions 1–24. Write a multiplication story about it. Draw a picture to go with your story.

Copyright © Kendall/Hunt Publishing Company

Name _____   Date _____

Multiplication Facts I Know

- Circle the facts you know well.
- Keep this table and use it to help you multiply.
- As you learn more facts, you may circle them too.

×	0	1	2	3	4	5	6	7	8	9	10
0	0	0	0	0	0	0	0	0	0	0	0
1	0	1	2	3	4	5	6	7	8	9	10
2	0	2	4	6	8	10	12	14	16	18	20
3	0	3	6	9	12	15	18	21	24	27	30
4	0	4	8	12	16	20	24	28	32	36	40
5	0	5	10	15	20	25	30	35	40	45	50
6	0	6	12	18	24	30	36	42	48	54	60
7	0	7	14	21	28	35	42	49	56	63	70
8	0	8	16	24	32	40	48	56	64	72	80
9	0	9	18	27	36	45	54	63	72	81	90
10	0	10	20	30	40	50	60	70	80	90	100

Copyright © Kendall/Hunt Publishing Company

Facts Distribution
Multiplication: 2s & 3s •
Weeks 25–26

Math Facts Groups	Weeks	Daily Practice and Problems	Home Practice	Flash Cards	Facts Quizzes and Tests
Multiplication: 2s & 3s	25–26	Unit 12: items 12A, 12C, 12J, 12K & 12M		*Triangle Flash Cards: 2s & 3s*	DPP item 12M is a quiz on the multiplication facts for the 2s and 3s. The *Multiplication Facts I Know* chart is updated.

Daily Practice and Problems

Students may solve the items individually, in groups, or as a class. The items may also be assigned for homework. The DPPs are also available on the Teacher Resource CD.

Student Questions	Teacher Notes

 Triangle Flash Cards: 2s and 3s

With a partner, use your *Triangle Flash Cards* to quiz each other on the multiplication facts for the twos and threes. One partner covers the corner containing the highest number. This number will be the product. The second person multiplies the two uncovered numbers.

Separate the used cards into three piles: those facts you know and can answer quickly, those you can figure out with a strategy, and those you need to learn. Practice the last two piles again and then make a list of the facts you need to practice at home for homework.

Circle the facts you know and can answer quickly on your *Multiplication Facts I Know* chart.

TIMS Bit

The *Triangle Flash Cards* follow the Home Practice for this unit in the *Discovery Assignment Book.* Remind students to take home the list of the facts they need to practice and their *Triangle Flash Cards* to study with a family member.

Have students record the facts they know well on their *Multiplication Facts I Know* charts. Students should circle the facts they know and can answer quickly. Since these charts can also be used as multiplication tables, students should have them available to use as needed.

Inform students when you will give the quiz on the 2s and 3s. This quiz appears in Bit 12M.

12C Using Twos

Do these problems in your head. Write only the answers.

A. $2 \times 9 =$ B. $3 \times 20 =$

C. $2 \times 100 =$ D. $8 \times 2 =$

E. $5 \times 20 =$ F. $20 \times 2 =$

G. $4 \times 2 =$ H. $6 \times 2 =$

I. $2 \times 7 =$ J. $2 \times 0 =$

TIMS Bit $\boxed{\times \frac{5}{7}}$

Ask students what strategies they use for solving these problems.

A. 18	B. 60
C. 200	D. 16
E. 100	F. 40
G. 8	H. 12
I. 14	J. 0

12J Story Solving

1. $3 \times 9 = ?$ Write a story and draw a picture about 3×9. Write a number sentence on your picture.

2. $3 \times \frac{1}{2} = ?$ Write a story, and draw a picture about $3 \times \frac{1}{2}$. Write a number sentence on your picture.

TIMS Task $\boxed{\times}$ $\boxed{N}$ $\boxed{\times \frac{5}{7}}$

1. 27; Stories will vary.

2. $1\frac{1}{2}$; Students may wish to share their stories with the class. If there is a computer with a drawing program available, students may choose to draw their picture and tell their story on the computer.

12K **Using Threes**

Do these problems in your head. Write only the answers.

A. $3 \times 5 =$

B. $7 \times 3 =$

C. $9 \times 3 =$

D. $3 \times 2 =$

E. $10 \times 3 =$

F. $3 \times 6 =$

G. $4 \times 3 =$

H. $3 \times 3 =$

I. $3 \times 1 =$

J. $8 \times 3 =$

Describe a strategy for 8×3.

TIMS Bit

Ask students what strategies they use for solving these problems.

A. 15   B. 21

C. 27   D. 6

E. 30   F. 18

G. 12   H. 9

I. 3   J. 24

Two possible strategies: skip count by 3s; $4 \times 3 = 12$, so 8×3 is double 12, or 24.

12M **Quiz on 2s and 3s**

A. $4 \times 2 =$

B. $3 \times 2 =$

C. $5 \times 3 =$

D. $2 \times 10 =$

E. $6 \times 3 =$

F. $2 \times 5 =$

G. $10 \times 3 =$

H. $7 \times 2 =$

I. $8 \times 3 =$

J. $3 \times 3 =$

K. $8 \times 2 =$

L. $2 \times 2 =$

M. $9 \times 2 =$

N. $6 \times 2 =$

O. $3 \times 7 =$

P. $4 \times 3 =$

Q. $3 \times 9 =$

R. $3 \times 1 =$

TIMS Bit

This quiz is on the second group of multiplication facts, the 2s and 3s. We recommend 5 minutes for this quiz. You might want to allow students to change pens or pencils after the time is up and complete the remaining problems in a different color.

After students take the quiz, have them update their *Multiplication Facts I Know* charts.

Facts Distribution

Multiplication:
Square Numbers • Week 27

Math Facts Groups	Week	Daily Practice and Problems	Home Practice	Flash Cards	Facts Quizzes and Tests
Multiplication: Square Numbers	27	Unit 13: items 13A, 13D, 13E, 13F & 13K		*Triangle Flash Cards: Square Numbers*	DPP item 13K is a quiz on the multiplication facts for the square numbers. The *Multiplication Facts I Know* chart is updated.

 **Daily Practice and Problems**

Students may solve the items individually, in groups, or as a class. The items may also be assigned for homework. The DPPs are also available on the Teacher Resource CD.

Student Questions	Teacher Notes

 Triangle Flash Cards: Square Numbers

With a partner, use your *Triangle Flash Cards* to quiz each other on the multiplication facts for the square numbers. One partner covers the corner containing the highest number with his or her thumb. The second person multiplies the two uncovered numbers.

Separate the used cards into three piles: those facts you know and can answer quickly, those you can figure out with a strategy, and those you need to learn. Practice the last two piles again and then make a list of the facts you need to practice at home for homework.

Circle the facts you know and can answer quickly on your *Multiplication Facts I Know* chart.

TIMS Bit

The *Triangle Flash Cards* follow the Home Practice for this unit in the *Discovery Assignment Book*. Students should take them home for practice.

Have students record the facts they know well on their *Multiplication Facts I Know* chart. Since these charts can also be used as multiplication tables, students should have them available to use as needed.

Inform students when you will give the quiz on the square numbers. This quiz appears in Bit 13K.

13D Square Care

Help Professor Peabody fill in the missing information on his "Exploring Square Numbers" chart from Unit 11 Lesson 3.

Number on a side	Number in Square	Multiplication Fact
2	4	2 × 2 = 4
3	◯	3 × 3 = 9
◯	16	4 × 4 = 16
5	25	◯
6	◯	6 × 6 = ◯
7	◯	7 × ◯ = 49
◯	64	8 × 8 = ◯
9	◯	9 × 9 = ◯

TIMS Task $\boxed{\times \tfrac{5}{7}}$

Ask students what strategies they use for finding the missing information.

Number on a side	Number in Square	Multiplication Fact
2	4	2 × 2 = 4
3	9	3 × 3 = 9
4	16	4 × 4 = 16
5	25	5 × 5 = 25
6	36	6 × 6 = 36
7	49	7 × 7 = 49
8	64	8 × 8 = 64
9	81	9 × 9 = 81

13E Multiplying with Ending Zeros

A. 5 × 5 =

B. 5 × 50 =

C. 8 × 8 =

D. 8 × 80 =

E. 2 × 2 =

F. 2 × 20 =

G. 4 × 4 =

H. 4 × 40 =

I. 40 × 40 =

J. 40 × 400 =

What patterns do you see?

TIMS Bit $\boxed{\times \tfrac{5}{7}}$ $\boxed{N}$ $\boxed{\times}$

A. 25	B. 250
C. 64	D. 640
E. 4	F. 40
G. 16	H. 160
I. 1600	J. 16,000

The answer is the product of the two non-zero numbers plus the number of zeros in the two factors.

Student Questions	Teacher Notes

13F How Many Times More

A. Shana lives 6 blocks from her grandmother. Manuel lives six times as far from his grandmother. How far does Manuel live from his grandmother?

B. Ivor's family bought 3 books at the book fair. Gwen's family bought 3 times as many books at the book fair. How many books did Gwen's family buy at the book fair?

C. Karen is 7 years old. Her father is seven times as old. How old is Karen's father?

D. Write a story about 9×9.

TIMS Task $\boxed{\begin{smallmatrix}5\\ \times 7\end{smallmatrix}}$

A. 36 blocks

B. 9 books

C. 49 years old

D. Stories will vary.

13K Quiz on the Square Numbers

A. $4 \times 4 =$

B. $7 \times 7 =$

C. $1 \times 1 =$

D. $10 \times 10 =$

E. $3 \times 3 =$

F. $5 \times 5 =$

G. $6 \times 6 =$

H. $8 \times 8 =$

I. $9 \times 9 =$

J. $2 \times 2 =$

TIMS Bit $\boxed{\begin{smallmatrix}5\\ \times 7\end{smallmatrix}}$

This quiz is on the third group of multiplication facts, the square numbers. We recommend 1 minute for this test. Allow students to change pens or pencils after the time is up and complete the remaining problems in a different color.

After students take the test, have them update their *Multiplication Facts I Know* charts.

Facts Distribution
Multiplication: 9s •
Week 28

Math Facts Groups	Week	Daily Practice and Problems	Home Practice	Flash Cards	Facts Quizzes and Tests
Multiplication: 9s	28	Unit 14: items 14A, 14C, 14D, 14E, 14G & 14J		*Triangle Flash Cards: 9s*	DPP item 14G is a quiz on the multiplication facts for the 9s. The *Multiplication Facts I Know* chart is updated.

Students may solve the items individually, in groups, or as a class. The items may also be assigned for homework. The DPPs are also available on the Teacher Resource CD.

Student Questions	Teacher Notes

 Triangle Flash Cards: 9s

With a partner, use your *Triangle Flash Cards* to quiz each other on the multiplication facts for the nines. One partner covers the corner containing the highest number. The second person multiplies the two uncovered numbers.

Separate the used cards into three piles: those facts you know and can answer quickly, those you can figure out with a strategy, and those you need to learn. Practice the last two piles again and then, for homework, make a list of the facts you need to practice at home.

Circle the facts you know quickly on your *Multiplication Facts I Know* chart.

TIMS Bit

The *Triangle Flash Cards* follow the Home Practice in the *Discovery Assignment Book*. They should be sent home for practice.

Have students record the facts they know well on their *Multiplication Facts I Know* charts. Students should circle the facts they know and can answer quickly. Since these charts can also be used as multiplication tables, students should have them available to use as needed.

Inform students when you will give the quiz on the nines. This quiz appears in DPP Bit 14G.

14C Triples

1. A. $3 \times 2 =$
   B. $3 \times 3 \times 2 =$
   C. $9 \times 2 =$

2. A. $3 \times 3 =$
   B. $3 \times 3 \times 3 =$
   C. $9 \times 3 =$

3. A. $3 \times 4 =$
   B. $3 \times 3 \times 4 =$
   C. $9 \times 4 =$

4. A. $3 \times 5 =$
   B. $3 \times 3 \times 5 =$
   C. $9 \times 5 =$

TIMS Bit

1. A. 6
   B. 18
   C. 18

2. A. 9
   B. 27
   C. 27

3. A. 12
   B. 36
   C. 36

4. A. 15
   B. 45
   C. 45

Encourage students to describe any patterns they see.

14D Multiples of 10 and 100

Use the patterns you found in your multiplication table for multiplying by 10 and 100 to do the following problems.

1. $2 \times 9 =$

2. $2 \times 90 =$

3. $2 \times 900 =$

4. $9 \times 7 =$

5. $9 \times 70 =$

6. $9 \times 700 =$

7. $4 \times 9 =$

8. $4 \times 90 =$

9. $4 \times 900 =$

TIMS Task

1. 18   2. 180
3. 1800   4. 63
5. 630   6. 6300
7. 36   8. 360
9. 3600

14E Fine Nines

Do these problems in your head. Write only the answers.

A. $9 \times 1 =$ B. $9 \times 7 =$

C. $8 \times 9 =$ D. $9 \times 2 =$

E. $6 \times 9 =$ F. $9 \times 4 =$

G. $10 \times 9 =$ H. $9 \times 9 =$

I. $9 \times 3 =$ J. $5 \times 9 =$

K. $9 \times 0 =$

TIMS Bit

Ask students what strategies they use to solve these problems. One possible strategy for finding nine times a number is to multiply the number by ten, then subtract the number from the total. (Example: $9 \times 6 = 10 \times 6 - 6$)

A. 9   B. 63

C. 72   D. 18

E. 54   F. 36

G. 90   H. 81

I. 27   J. 45

K. 0

14G Multiplication Quiz: 9s

A. $3 \times 9 =$ B. $9 \times 7 =$

C. $10 \times 9 =$ D. $0 \times 9 =$

E. $5 \times 9 =$ F. $9 \times 8 =$

G. $6 \times 9 =$ H. $4 \times 9 =$

I. $9 \times 9 =$ J. $9 \times 2 =$

K. $9 \times 1 =$

TIMS Bit

This quiz is on the fourth group of multiplication facts, the nines. We recommend 2 minutes for this quiz. Allow students to change pens after the time is up and complete the remaining problems in a different color.

After students take the test, have them update their *Multiplication Facts I Know* charts.

A. 27   B. 63

C. 90   D. 0

E. 45   F. 72

G. 54   H. 36

I. 81   J. 18

K. 9

14J **Square Numbers**

1. What square number is shown by all the small squares below?

2. What other square numbers do you see?

3. Bob thinks 8 is a square number. Show him why it is not.

TIMS Task

1. 16

2. 1, 4, and 9

3. 4 is 2 × 2 and 9 is 3 × 3. So, there are no square numbers between 4 and 9.

Facts Distribution

Multiplication: Last Six Facts •
Weeks 29–30

Math Facts Groups	Weeks	Daily Practice and Problems	Home Practice	Flash Cards	Facts Quizzes and Tests
Multiplication: Last Six Facts	29–30	Unit 15: items 15A, 15B, 15I, 15J, 15K & 15M		*Triangle Flash Cards: Last Six Facts*	DPP item 15M is a quiz on the multiplication facts for the last six facts. The *Multiplication Facts I Know* chart is updated.

 **Daily Practice and Problems**

Students may solve the items individually, in groups, or as a class. The items may also be assigned for homework. The DPPs are also available on the Teacher Resource CD.

Student Questions	Teacher Notes

 Triangle Flash Cards: The Last Six Facts

With a partner, use your *Triangle Flash Cards* to quiz each other on the multiplication facts for the last six facts. One partner covers the corner containing the highest number with his or her thumb. The second person multiplies the two uncovered numbers.

Separate the used cards into three piles: those facts you know and can answer quickly, those you can figure out with a strategy, and those you will need to learn. Practice the last two piles again and then make a list of the facts you need to practice at home for homework.

Circle the facts you know quickly on your *Multiplication Facts I Know* chart.

TIMS Bit

The *Triangle Flash Cards* follow the Home Practice for this unit in the *Discovery Assignment Book*. Send the *Triangle Flash Cards* home for practice with family members.

Have students record the facts they know well on their *Multiplication Facts I Know* charts. Since these charts can also be used as multiplication tables, students should have them available to use as needed.

Inform students when you will give the quiz on the last six facts. This quiz appears in DPP Bit 15M.

Student Questions	Teacher Notes

15B **Break Apart Facts**

Kevin said, "To multiply 6×7, I break apart 7 into $5 + 2$. Then I multiply $6 \times 5 = 30$ and $6 \times 2 = 12$ and add $30 + 12 = 42$."

Use Kevin's method to multiply:

1. 6×8

2. 8×7

3. 4×8

TIMS Task $\boxed{^5_{\times\,7}}$

Possible strategies:

1. $6 \times 8 = 6 \times (5 + 3)$
   $\qquad = 6 \times 5 + 6 \times 3$
   $\qquad = 30 + 18$
   $\qquad = 48$

2. $8 \times 7 = 8 \times (5 + 2)$
   $\qquad = (8 \times 5) + (8 \times 2)$
   $\qquad = 40 + 16$
   $\qquad = 56$

3. $4 \times 8 = 4 \times (5 + 3)$
   $\qquad = (4 \times 5) + (4 \times 3)$
   $\qquad = 20 + 12$
   $\qquad = 32$

15I **Multiplication: The Last Six Facts**

Do these problems in your head. Write only the answers.

A. $8 \times 4 =$ B. $6 \times 7 =$

C. $8 \times 7 =$ D. $4 \times 7 =$

E. $6 \times 4 =$ F. $8 \times 6 =$

Explain your strategy for Question D.

TIMS Bit $\boxed{^5_{\times\,7}}$

Ask students what strategies they use for solving these problems.

A. 32

B. 42

C. 56

D. 28

E. 24

F. 48

Possible strategy:
$2 \times 7 = 14$,
so $4 \times 7 = 2 \times 2 \times 7$
or
$2 \times 14 = 28$.

Student Questions	Teacher Notes

15J **Triangles and Rectangles**

1. How many corners do ten separate triangles have?

2. How many corners do eight separate rectangles have?

3. How many corners do nine separate triangles have?

4. How many corners do six separate rectangles have?

5. How many corners do eight separate hexagons have?

TIMS Task $\boxed{\times \frac{5}{7}}$ ⬚

1. 30
2. 32
3. 27
4. 24
5. 48

15K **Story Solving**

Write a story and draw a picture about 8 × 7. Write a number sentence for your picture.

TIMS Bit $\boxed{\times \frac{5}{7}}$

56; Ask students to share their stories with the class.

15M **Multiplication Quiz: The Last Six Facts**

A. 8 × 4 =

B. 6 × 7 =

C. 4 × 7 =

D. 7 × 8 =

E. 6 × 8 =

F. 4 × 6 =

TIMS Bit $\boxed{\times \frac{5}{7}}$

This quiz is on the fifth and final group of multiplication facts, the last six facts. We recommend 1 minute for this quiz. You might want to allow students to change pens or pencils after the time is up and complete the remaining problems in a different color.

After students take the test, have them update their *Multiplication Facts I Know* charts.

A. 32	B. 42
C. 28	D. 56
E. 48	F. 24

Math Facts Groups	Week	Daily Practice and Problems	Home Practice	Flash Cards	Facts Quizzes and Tests
Multiplication: 2s, 5s & 10s	31	Unit 16: items 16C, 16E, 16G, 16J & 16K		*Triangle Flash Cards: 2s, 5s & 10s*	DPP item 16K is a quiz on the multiplication facts for the 2s, 5s and 10s. The *Multiplication Facts I Know* chart is updated.

Week 31

Students may solve the items individually, in groups, or as a class. The items may also be assigned for homework. The DPPs are also available on the Teacher Resource CD.

Student Questions	Teacher Notes

16C Doubles

A. $2 \times 6 =$

B. $12 + 12 =$

C. $4 \times 6 =$

D. $2 \times 5 =$

E. $10 + 10 =$

F. $4 \times 5 =$

G. $2 \times 10 =$

H. $20 + 20 =$

I. $4 \times 10 =$

What patterns do you see? Describe a strategy for multiplying a number by 4.

TIMS Bit

One strategy for multiplying a number by 4 is to multiply first by 2. Then double the answer. These problems are designed to help students see this pattern. Ask students if they have other patterns for finding the answers to these fact problems.

Remind students to take home their *Triangle Flash Cards: 2s, 5s, and 10s* to practice the multiplication facts for these groups. Tell them when you will give the Multiplication Quiz: 2s, 5s, and 10s.

16E Multiplication Patterns

A. $1 \times 5 =$ $2 \times 5 =$ $3 \times 5 =$

$4 \times 5 =$ $5 \times 5 =$ $6 \times 5 =$

$7 \times 5 =$ $8 \times 5 =$ $9 \times 5 =$

$10 \times 5 =$

B. $1 \times 10 =$ $2 \times 10 =$ $3 \times 10 =$

$4 \times 10 =$ $5 \times 10 =$ $6 \times 10 =$

$7 \times 10 =$ $8 \times 10 =$ $9 \times 10 =$

$10 \times 10 =$

What patterns do you see in both sets of problems?

TIMS Bit

A. The multiples of five are the same numbers found skip counting by fives. An even number multiplied by 5 ends in zero. An odd number multiplied by 5 ends in five.

B. The multiples of ten are the numbers found skip counting by tens. All multiples of ten end in zero. When a number is multiplied by ten, the answer is that number with a zero added to the end.

Student Questions	Teacher Notes

16G **More Doubles**

A. $3 \times 7 =$

B. $21 + 21 =$

C. $6 \times 7 =$

D. $3 \times 8 =$

E. $24 + 24 =$

F. $6 \times 8 =$

G. $3 \times 10 =$

H. $30 + 30 =$

I. $6 \times 10 =$

What patterns do you see? Describe a strategy for multiplying a number by 6.

TIMS Bit

One strategy for multiplying a number by 6 is to multiply first by 3. Then, double the answer. These problems are designed to help students see this pattern. Ask students if they have other patterns for finding the answers to these fact problems.

16J **Mother's Helpers**

1. After school, Jan helps her neighbor with her new baby and earns 2 dollars each day. How much does Jan earn if she helps 4 days? 9 days? 7 days? 3 days?

2. Tony helps by going to the store for the neighbor and earns 50 cents each time. How much will Tony earn if he goes to the store 4 times? 5 times? 8 times? 9 times? Write the number sentences.

TIMS Task

1. 8 dollars

   18 dollars

   14 dollars

   6 dollars

2. 2 dollars;
   4×50 cents $= 200$¢ or $2

   $2.50; 5×50¢ $= $2.50

   $4.00; 8×50 cents $= 400$¢ or $4

   $4.50; 9×50 cents $= 450$¢ or $4.50

16K Multiplication Quiz: 2s, 5s, and 10s

A. $2 \times 5 =$ B. $5 \times 7 =$

C. $3 \times 10 =$ D. $10 \times 8 =$

E. $8 \times 5 =$ F. $2 \times 7 =$

G. $5 \times 3 =$ H. $4 \times 5 =$

I. $2 \times 8 =$ J. $10 \times 4 =$

K. $9 \times 2 =$ L. $5 \times 5 =$

M. $5 \times 9 =$ N. $10 \times 5 =$

O. $2 \times 6 =$ P. $6 \times 10 =$

Q. $5 \times 6 =$ R. $4 \times 2 =$

S. $10 \times 7 =$ T. $10 \times 2 =$

U. $5 \times 1 =$ V. $4 \times 2 =$

W. $0 \times 2 =$ X. $10 \times 10 =$

Y. $3 \times 2 =$ Z. $10 \times 9 =$

TIMS Bit

We recommend 2 minutes for this quiz. Have students continue with a different colored pen or pencil when the two minutes are up. After a reasonable time, have students check their work and update their *Multiplication Facts I Know* charts.

Section 5

Facts Distribution
Multiplication: 3s & 9s • Week 32

Math Facts Groups	Week	Daily Practice and Problems	Home Practice	Flash Cards	Facts Quizzes and Tests
Multiplication: 3s & 9s	32	Unit 17: items 17A, 17I, 17J & 17K		*Triangle Flash Cards: 3s & 9s*	DPP item 17K is a quiz on the multiplication facts for the 3s and 9s. The *Multiplication Facts I Know* chart is updated.

Students may solve the items individually, in groups, or as a class. The items may also be assigned for homework. The DPPs are also available on the Teacher Resource CD.

Student Questions	Teacher Notes

17A   **Facts: 3s and 9s**

A. $5 \times 3 =$ B. $3 \times 7 =$

C. $5 \times 9 =$ D. $3 \times 0 =$

E. $7 \times 9 =$ F. $8 \times 3 =$

G. $3 \times 3 =$ H. $10 \times 9 =$

I. $9 \times 9 =$ J. $9 \times 2 =$

K. $1 \times 9 =$ L. $2 \times 3 =$

Explain your strategies for Questions E and F.

TIMS Bit $\frac{5}{\times 7}$

A. 15	B. 21
C. 45	D. 0
E. 63	F. 24
G. 9	H. 90
I. 81	J. 18
K. 9	L. 6

Discuss strategies students use to solve the facts, emphasizing those that are more efficient than others. For example, skip counting for 3×3 (3, 6, 9) may be efficient; however, skip counting for 7×9 is not. Alternatively, to solve 7×9, students might use $7 \times 10 = 70$ and then subtract 7 to get 63. Knowing one fact may help in solving another. For example, by doubling the answer to 4×3, one can quickly get the answer to 8×3. Students also may say, "I just know it." Recall is obviously an efficient strategy.

Tell students to take home the *Triangle Flash Cards: 3s* and *9s* to study for the quiz in DPP Bit 17K. The flash cards for these groups were distributed in Units 12 and 14 in the *Discovery Assignment Book* following the Home Practice. Flash cards are also available in Section 7.

17I **Facts: 3s and 9s Again**

A. $3 \times 1 =$ B. $3 \times 9 =$

C. $9 \times 4 =$ D. $8 \times 3 =$

E. $8 \times 9 =$ F. $3 \times 7 =$

G. $3 \times 5 =$ H. $4 \times 3 =$

I. $9 \times 6 =$ J. $10 \times 3 =$

K. $0 \times 9 =$ L. $3 \times 6 =$

Explain your strategies for Questions E and F.

TIMS Bit $\boxed{\times\frac{5}{7}}$

A. 3   B. 27

C. 36   D. 24

E. 72   F. 21

G. 15   H. 12

I. 54   J. 30

K. 0   L. 18

Discuss strategies students use to solve the facts, emphasizing those that are more efficient than others. By subtracting 8 from the answer to 8×10 or 80, a student can quickly get the answer to 8×9. Knowing one fact may help in solving another. If a student knows $3 \times 6 = 18$, he or she can add 3 more to get the answer to 3×7.

Remind students to use the flash cards to study at home and tell them when you will give the quiz on these facts. The quiz is in DPP Bit 17K.

17J **Multiples of 10 and 100**

1. Solve the following problems.

A. $3 \times 4 =$ B. $3 \times 40 =$

C. $3 \times 400 =$ D. $400 \times 9 =$

E. $300 \times 6 =$ F. $5 \times 60 =$

G. $5 \times 59 =$ H. $4 \times 40 =$

I. $4 \times 39 =$

2. Choose one of the problems. Draw a picture and write a story about it.

TIMS Task $\boxed{N}$ $\boxed{\times}$ $\boxed{\times\frac{5}{7}}$

The answer to Question F is 300. To do Question G, think: $5 \times 60 - 5 \times 1$. Discuss other strategies used to solve Questions 1G and 1I.

1. A. 12   B. 120

   C. 1200   D. 3600

   E. 1800   F. 300

   G. 295   H. 160

   I. 156

2. Stories will vary.

17K Multiplication Quiz: 3s and 9s

Do these problems in your head. Write only the answers.

A. $3 \times 0 =$ B. $9 \times 4 =$

C. $9 \times 3 =$ D. $3 \times 7 =$

E. $0 \times 9 =$ F. $9 \times 8 =$

G. $4 \times 3 =$ H. $9 \times 2 =$

I. $9 \times 6 =$ J. $3 \times 8 =$

K. $3 \times 3 =$ L. $9 \times 5 =$

M. $9 \times 7 =$ N. $3 \times 2 =$

O. $6 \times 3 =$ P. $9 \times 9 =$

Q. $10 \times 3 =$ R. $5 \times 3 =$

S. $9 \times 10 =$ T. $9 \times 1 =$

TIMS Bit

We recommend 2 minutes for this quiz. Allow students to change pens or pencils after the time is up and complete the remaining problems in a different color. After students take the quiz, have them update their *Multiplication Facts I Know* charts.

A	0	B.	36
C.	27	D.	21
E.	0	F.	72
G.	12	H.	18
I.	54	J.	24
K.	9	L.	45
M.	63	N.	6
O.	18	P.	81
Q.	30	R.	15
S.	90	T.	9

Facts Distribution
Multiplication: Square Numbers • Week 33

Week 33

Math Facts Groups	Week	Daily Practice and Problems	Home Practice	Flash Cards	Facts Quizzes and Tests
Multiplication: Square Numbers	33	Unit 18: items 18A, 18B, 18E, 18G, 18I & 18K		*Triangle Flash Cards: Square Numbers*	DPP item 18K is a quiz on the multiplication facts for the square numbers. The *Multiplication Facts I Know* chart is updated.

Daily Practice and Problems

Students may solve the items individually, in groups, or as a class. The items may also be assigned for homework. The DPPs are also available on the Teacher Resource CD.

Student Questions	Teacher Notes

18A Multiplication: Squares

Do these problems in your head. Write only the answers.

A. $6 \times 6 =$

B. $5 \times 5 =$

C. $2 \times 2 =$

D. $9 \times 9 =$

E. $7 \times 7 =$

F. $3 \times 3 =$

G. $4 \times 4 =$

H. $8 \times 8 =$

I. $10 \times 10 =$

J. $1 \times 1 =$

TIMS Bit

Discuss strategies with students. Tell students to practice the multiplication facts for the square numbers at home using the *Triangle Flash Cards*. The flash cards for this group were distributed in Unit 13 in the *Discovery Assignment Book* following the Home Practice. The cards are also in Section 7. Advise students when you will give the quiz on the square numbers. Bit 18K is a quiz on these facts.

18B **Squares**

Find the area of the squares.

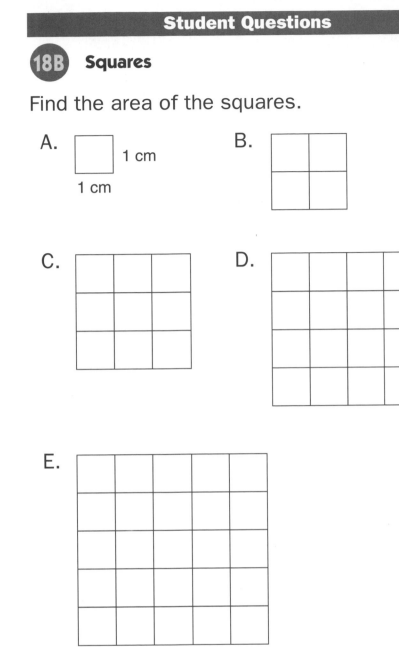

A. [ ] 1 cm
   1 cm

B.

C.

D.

E.

F. What is the area of a 6 cm × 6 cm square?

G. What is the area of a 7 cm × 7 cm square?

H. Why do we call the square numbers *square numbers?* Give an example.

TIMS Task

A. 1 sq cm

B. 4 sq cm

C. 9 sq cm

D. 16 sq cm

E. 25 sq cm

F. 36 sq cm

G. 49 sq cm

H. Possible response: 25 is a square number because 5 × 5 = 25. You can multiply 5 times itself and get 25. The area of a square that has sides equal to 5 cm is 25 sq cm.

(18E) Story Solving

Write a story and draw a picture about 8×8. Write a number sentence for your picture.

TIMS Bit $\boxed{\begin{smallmatrix}5\\ \times 7\end{smallmatrix}}$

Discuss students' stories with the class.

(18G) Quick Addition

Do these problems in your head. Write only the answers.

1. $5 + 6 =$

2. $50 + 60 =$

3. $60 + 40 =$

4. $60 + 30 =$

5. $40 + 70 =$

6. $20 + 80 =$

TIMS Bit $\boxed{\times}$ $\boxed{N}$ $\boxed{\begin{smallmatrix}5\\ \times 7\end{smallmatrix}}$

1. 11
2. 110
3. 100
4. 90
5. 110
6. 100

These problems provide an opportunity for students to review a few addition facts and to relate them to adding multiples of 10.

18I More Squares

For each problem the numbers in the squares must be the same.

A. 64 = ☐ × ☐

B. 36 = ☐ × ☐

C. 9 = ☐ × ☐

D. 25 = ☐ × ☐

E. 49 = ☐ × ☐

F. 81 = ☐ × ☐

G. 100 = ☐ × ☐

H. 16 = ☐ × ☐

I. 4 = ☐ × ☐

J. 1 = ☐ × ☐

TIMS Bit   ⬚⁵⁷ Ⓝ

A. 8
B. 6
C. 3
D. 5
E. 7
F. 9
G. 10
H. 4
I. 2
J. 1

18K Multiplication Quiz: Squares

Do these problems in your head. Write only the answers.

A. $5 \times 5 =$

B. $4 \times 4 =$

C. $9 \times 9 =$

D. $7 \times 7 =$

E. $10 \times 10 =$

F. $8 \times 8 =$

G. $3 \times 3 =$

H. $1 \times 1 =$

I. $6 \times 6 =$

J. $2 \times 2 =$

TIMS Bit   ⬚⁵⁷

This quiz is on the squares. We recommend 1 minute for this quiz. Allow students to change pens or pencils after this time is up and complete the remaining problems in a different color. After students take the quiz, have them update their *Multiplication Facts I Know* charts.

Math Facts Groups	Week	Daily Practice and Problems	Home Practice	Flash Cards	Facts Quizzes and Tests
Multiplication: Last Six Facts	34	Unit 19: items 19A, 19E, 19H, 19K, 19P & 19Q		*Triangle Flash Cards: Last Six Facts*	DPP item 19Q is a quiz on the multiplication facts for the last six facts. The *Multiplication Facts I Know* chart is updated.

 **Daily Practice and Problems**

Students may solve the items individually, in groups, or as a class. The items may also be assigned for homework. The DPPs are also available on the Teacher Resource CD.

Student Questions	Teacher Notes

19A Facts: The Last Six Facts

A. $4 \times 8 =$

B. $4 \times 7 =$

C. $7 \times 6 =$

D. $4 \times 6 =$

E. $8 \times 6 =$

F. $8 \times 7 =$

Explain your strategy for Question C.

TIMS Bit $\boxed{\frac{5}{\times 7}}$

Discuss strategies students use to solve the facts, emphasizing those that are more efficient than others. For example, to solve 7×6, students might double the answer to 7×3. Similarly, students may use doubling to solve facts for 4s. For example, to solve 4×6, students might double 6 to get 12 and then double 12 to get 24. Using break-apart facts is a possible strategy, but may not be efficient for some—$8 \times 7 = 8 \times 5 + 8 \times 2$ or $40 + 16 = 56$. Students may also say, "I just know it." Recall is obviously an efficient strategy.

Students should take home the *Triangle Flash Cards: The Last Six Facts* to study at home with a family member. Tell students when the quiz on this group of facts will be given. DPP Bit 19Q is Multiplication Quiz: The Last Six Facts.

19E Multiplication Table

Fill in the missing information on this multiplication table.

×	4	6	7	8
4				
6				
7				
8				

TIMS Bit

Discuss the strategies students used to complete the multiplication chart. Focus attention on how students solved the last six facts. (4 × 8, 4 × 7, 4 × 6, 7 × 6, 8 × 6, and 8 × 7)

19H Skip Counting

1. Skip count by 4s to 100. Say the numbers quietly to yourself. Write the numbers.

2. Skip count by 8s until you pass 100. Say the numbers quietly to yourself. Write the numbers.

3. Circle the numbers in your lists that are products of (answers to) the last six facts:

   4 × 6   4 × 7   4 × 8

   6 × 7   6 × 8   7 × 8

4. How could you use skip counting to find these facts?

5. Which of the last six facts is not circled? Why not?

TIMS Task

1–2. If your calculator has the constant feature, press
4 + 4 = = = = = = = =.
Each time = is pressed, the constant number (4) and the constant operation (addition) is repeated. Some students may find it helpful to count by twos, accentuating every other number: 2, 4, 6, 8, 10, 12, 14, 16, etc. Then, count by 8s.

Have students write down the numbers as they count. Discuss patterns in the two lists.

3. Students circle 24, 28, 32, 48, and 56 in both lists.

4. Answers will vary. To find 4 × 8, students can skip count by 4, eight times: 4, 8, 12, 16, 24, 28, (32.)

5. 6 × 7 = 42; 42 is not a multiple of 4.

Student Questions	Teacher Notes

19K **Double, Double Again**

Solve these problems.

1. $6 \times 2 =$ 2. $6 \times 4 =$

3. $8 \times 2 =$ 4. $8 \times 4 =$

5. $7 \times 2 =$ 6. $14 \times 2 =$

7. $7 \times 4 =$ 8. $14 \times 4 =$

9. $7 \times 8 =$

TIMS Bit Ⓝ $\frac{5}{\times 7}$

The first four are from students' multiplication tables. Discuss the patterns and answers before assigning Questions 5–9.

1. 12   2. 24
3. 16   4. 32
5. 14   6. 28
7. 28   8. 56
9. 56

19P **Rectangles and Products**

1. Using *Centimeter Grid Paper,* draw all the rectangles you can make with 32 tiles.

2. Draw all the rectangles you can make with 24 tiles.

TIMS Task ▧ Ⓝ $\frac{5}{\times 7}$

Distribute *Centimeter Grid Paper. Centimeter Grid Paper* is available in Lesson 1. Have students draw rectangles that can be formed using tiles.

1. 4 cm by 8 cm
    2 cm by 16 cm
    1 cm by 32 cm (will not fit on grid paper)

2. 6 cm by 4 cm
    8 cm by 3 cm
    12 cm by 2 cm
    24 cm by 1 cm (will not fit on grid paper)

19Q **Multiplication Quiz: The Last Six Facts**

A. $8 \times 6 =$ B. $6 \times 4 =$

C. $4 \times 7 =$ D. $7 \times 8 =$

E. $6 \times 7 =$ F. $8 \times 4 =$

TIMS Bit $\frac{5}{\times 7}$

This quiz is on the fifth and final group of multiplication facts, the last six facts. We recommend 1 minute for this quiz. Allow students to change pens or pencils after the time is up and complete the remaining problems in a different color.

After students take the test, have them update their *Multiplication Facts I Know* charts.

Section 5

Facts Distribution
Multiplication: All Facts Groups •
Weeks 35–36

Math Facts Groups	Weeks	Daily Practice and Problems	Home Practice	Flash Cards	Facts Quizzes and Tests
Multiplication: All Facts Groups	35–36	Unit 20: items 20E, 20J & 20K		*Triangle Flash Cards: 2s, 3s, 5s, 9s, 10s, Square Numbers & Last Six Facts*	DPP item 20K is an inventory test on all the multiplication facts. The *Multiplication Facts I Know* chart is updated.

Students may solve the items individually, in groups, or as a class. The items may also be assigned for homework. The DPPs are also available on the Teacher Resource CD.

Student Questions	Teacher Notes
20E **Multiplication Facts** 1. Which two multiplication facts were the hardest for you to learn? 2. Draw a picture and write a story for these facts. Label your picture with a number sentence. 3. Describe a strategy for each of these facts.	**TIMS Bit** $\boxed{\frac{5}{\times 7}}$ Discuss students' strategies. Remind students when you will give the test on all the facts. See DPP Bit 20K.
20J **Mathhopper** If the following mathhoppers start at 0: 1. How many hops would it take for a $+7$ mathhopper to reach 56? 2. How many hops would it take for a $+14$ mathhopper to reach 56? 3. How many hops would it take for a $+14$ mathhopper to reach 560?	**TIMS Task** $\boxed{N}$ $\boxed{\frac{5}{\times 7}}$ Discuss the variety of strategies students use to solve these problems. 1. 8 hops 2. 4; Since the hop is twice as big as the $+7$ hop, it will take half as many hops. Skip count by 14 on the calculator or with paper and pencil. 3. 40; In Problem 2 we discovered that $14 \times 4 = 56$. Therefore, $14 \times 40 = 560$.
20K **Multiplication Facts Inventory Test** Have two pens or pencils of different colors ready. Use the first color when you begin the test. Your teacher will tell you when to switch pens or pencils and complete the remaining items with the other color.	**TIMS Bit** $\boxed{\frac{5}{\times 7}}$ The test can be found at the end of this set of DPP items, following item P. The test includes all the basic multiplication facts. After the test, students should update their *Multiplication Facts I Know* charts. Students should discuss strategies for figuring out or remembering any facts that they do not know well. They can record these strategies in their journals.

Multiplication Facts
Inventory Test

Directions: You will need two pens or pencils of different colors. Use the first color when you begin the test. When your teacher tells you to switch pens or pencils, finish the test using the second color.

5 ×5	4 ×6	10 ×7	5 ×3	8 ×7
2 ×10	7 ×7	10 ×3	7 ×4	6 ×9
6 ×6	9 ×5	5 ×2	4 ×5	8 ×8
6 ×10	4 ×2	3 ×8	2 ×7	10 ×10
10 ×9	4 ×4	9 ×9	8 ×2	8 ×4
6 ×7	9 ×4	10 ×5	3 ×3	7 ×5
7 ×9	8 ×6	2 ×3	3 ×6	9 ×3
10 ×4	9 ×8	6 ×5	3 ×4	7 ×3
9 ×2	5 ×8	2 ×2	10 ×8	6 ×2

Copyright © Kendall/Hunt Publishing Company

This section contains games that provide practice with multiplication facts and concepts.

Name _____   Date _____

Floor Tiler

Players

This is a game for two to four players.

Materials

- $\frac{1}{2}$ sheet of *Centimeter Grid Paper* per player
- *Spinner 1–4*
- *Spinner 1–10*
- a crayon or marker for each player

Rules

I. The first player makes two spins so that he or she has two numbers. The player may either spin one spinner twice or spin each spinner once.

Copyright © Kendall/Hunt Publishing Company

Copyright © Kendall/Hunt Publishing Company

2. The player must then find the **product** of the two numbers he or she spun. For example, $3 \times 4 = \textbf{12}$.

3. After finding the product, the player colors in a rectangle that has the same number of grid squares on the grid paper. For example, he or she might color in 3 rows of 4 squares for a total of 12 squares. But the player could have colored in 2 rows of 6 squares or 1 row of 12 squares instead. (Remember, the squares colored in must connect so that they form a rectangle.)

4. Once the player has made his or her rectangle, the player draws an outline around it and writes its number sentence inside. For example, a player who colored in 3 rows of 4 squares would write "$3 \times 4 = 12$." A player who colored in 2 rows of 6 squares would write "$2 \times 6 = 12$."

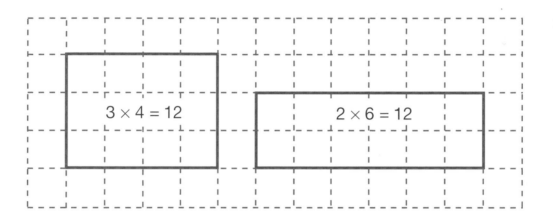

5. Players take turns spinning and filling in their grids.

6. If a player is unable to fill in a rectangle for his or her spin, he or she loses the turn, and the next player can play.

7. The first player to fill in his or her grid paper completely wins the game.

8. If no player is able to color in a rectangle in three rounds of spinning, the player with the fewest squares of the grid left is the winner.

Centimeter Grid Paper

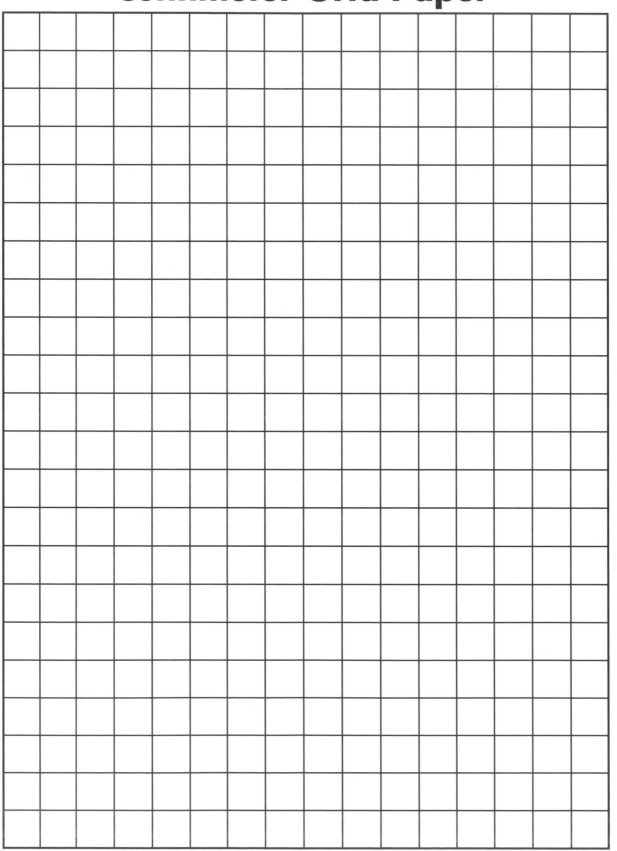

Copyright © Kendall/Hunt Publishing Company

Copyright © Kendall/Hunt Publishing Company

Name _____   Date _____

Spinners 1–4 and 1–10

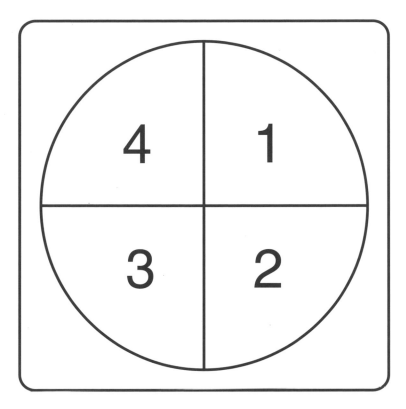

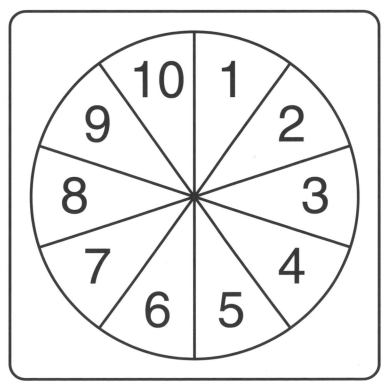

9 to 5 War

Players

This is a card game for two players.

Materials

- one pile per player of 9s and 5s cut from the two *9 to 5 War Cards* Activity Pages in the *Discovery Assignment Book*
- one pile per player of 20 other cards. This can be made from *Digit Cards (0–9)* or from a deck of playing cards with face cards removed (1–10, with aces representing 1s).

Copyright © Kendall/Hunt Publishing Company

Rules

1. Players place their two piles face down in front of them.

2. Each player turns over two cards, one from the 9s and 5s pile, and one from the other pile.

3. Each player should say a number sentence that tells the product of his or her two cards. Whoever has the greater product wins all four cards.

4. If there is a tie, then each player turns over two more cards. The player with the greater product of the second pairs wins all eight cards.

5. Play for ten minutes or until the players run out of cards. The player with more cards at the end is the winner.

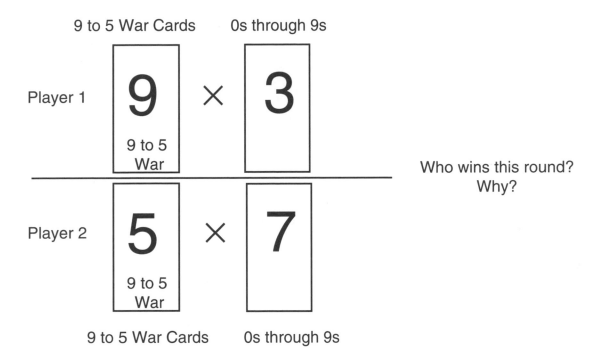

Who wins this round?
Why?

Copyright © Kendall/Hunt Publishing Company

Variations

1. Whoever has the *smaller* product takes the cards.

2. Play with more than two players.

3. Each player is given only one pile of cards (playing cards with face cards removed or *Digit Cards*). Each player takes the top two cards from his or her pile and multiplies the numbers. The player with the larger product wins all four cards. This game practices all the facts—it does not just focus on the 9s and 5s.

Copyright © Kendall/Hunt Publishing Company

Copyright © Kendall/Hunt Publishing Company

Name _____   Date _____

9 to 5 War Cards

9	9	9	9
9 to 5 War	9 to 5 War	9 to 5 War	9 to 5 War
9	5	5	5
9 to 5 War	9 to 5 War	9 to 5 War	9 to 5 War
5	5		
9 to 5 War	9 to 5 War		

Copyright © Kendall/Hunt Publishing Company

9 to 5 War Cards

Copyright © Kendall/Hunt Publishing Company

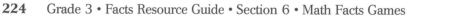

Copyright © Kendall/Hunt Publishing Company

4	9
3	8
2	7
1	6
0	5

Copyright © Kendall/Hunt Publishing Company

Copyright © Kendall/Hunt Publishing Company

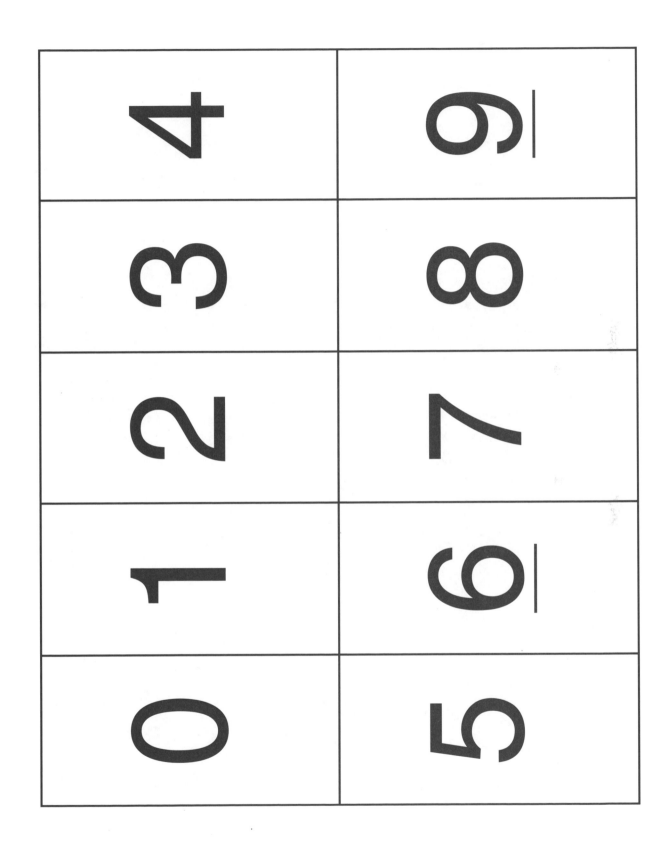

Copyright © Kendall/Hunt Publishing Company

Copyright © Kendall/Hunt Publishing Company

Section 7

Flash Cards
Subtraction and Multiplication

This section includes the subtraction flash cards for Groups 1–8 and the *Triangle Flash Cards* for the multiplication facts. See the Math Facts Calendar in Section 4 for when to use each group of flash cards.

To study the subtraction facts, one group of flash cards should be used at a time. Students hold up a flash card for their partners. As a student is quizzed, he or she places each flash card into one of three piles: those facts known and answered quickly, those that can be figured out with a strategy, and those that need to be learned. Discuss strategies for figuring out facts that students do not immediately recall. Some subtraction strategies that may be helpful are counting up, counting back, using a ten, making a ten, using doubles, and using related addition facts. Partners take turns quizzing each other on the subtraction facts. Students then circle the facts that they know on their *Subtraction Facts I Know* charts. This chart can be found in Section 5.

Using the Flash Cards to Study the Subtraction Facts and Update the *Subtraction Facts I Know* Chart

To use the flash cards to study the multiplication facts, one partner covers the corner containing the highest number (this number will be lightly shaded). This number is the answer to a multiplication problem, the product. The second person multiplies the two uncovered numbers, the factors. Partners take turns quizzing each other on the multiplication facts.

As a student is quizzed, he or she places each flash card into one of three piles: those facts known and answered quickly, those that can be figured out with a strategy, and those that need to be learned. Once students have sorted all their cards, they circle those facts that they know and can answer quickly on their *Multiplication Facts I Know* charts. A blackline master of this chart can be found in Section 5.

Using the *Triangle Flash Cards* to Study the Multiplication Facts and Update the *Multiplication Facts I Know* Chart

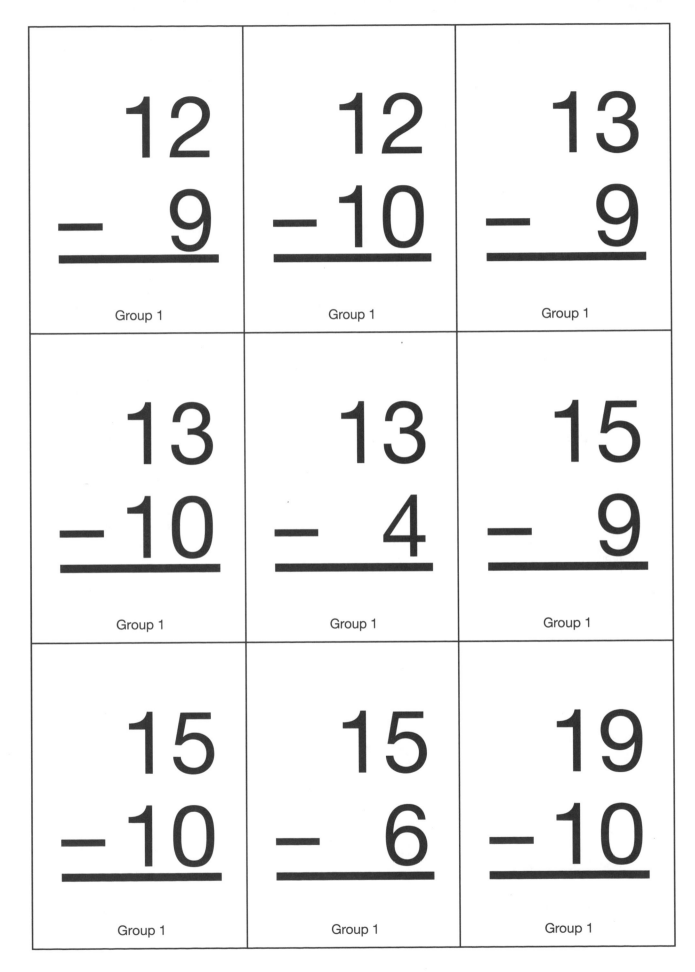

12 − 9	12 − 10	13 − 9
Group 1	Group 1	Group 1
13 − 10	13 − 4	15 − 9
Group 1	Group 1	Group 1
15 − 10	15 − 6	19 − 10
Group 1	Group 1	Group 1

Copyright © Kendall/Hunt Publishing Company

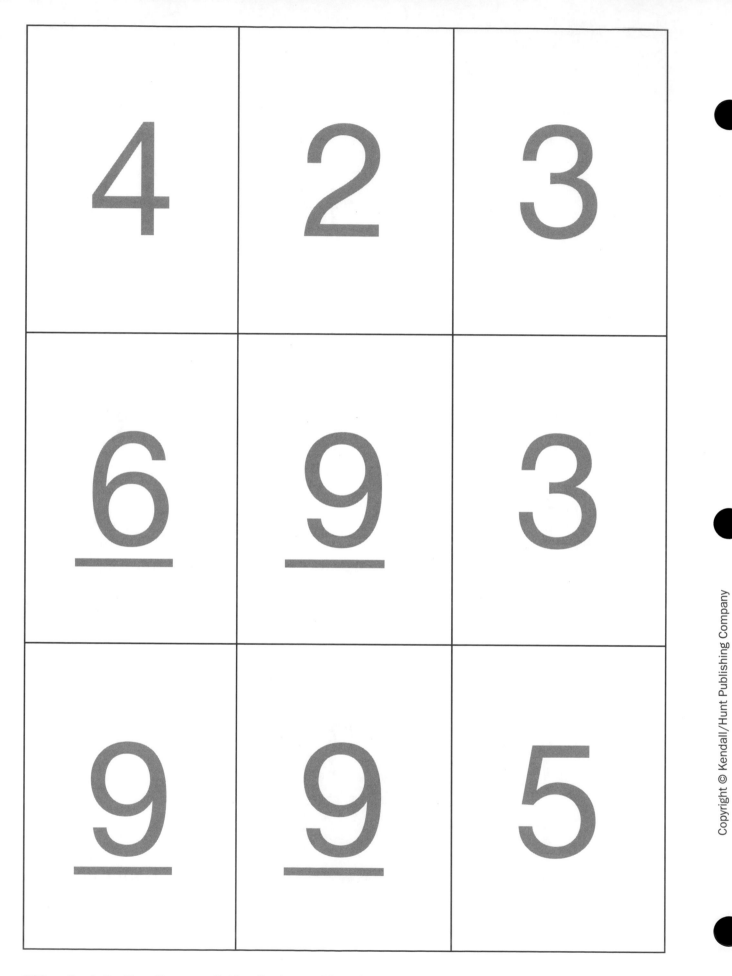

Copyright © Kendall/Hunt Publishing Company

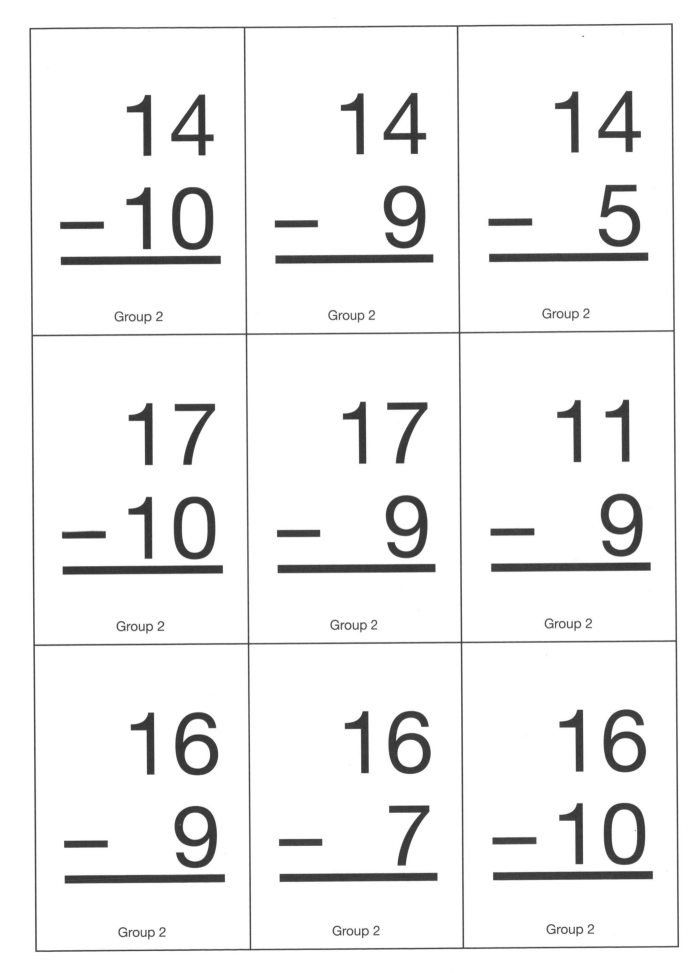

14 − 10 Group 2	14 − 9 Group 2	14 − 5 Group 2
17 − 10 Group 2	17 − 9 Group 2	11 − 9 Group 2
16 − 9 Group 2	16 − 7 Group 2	16 − 10 Group 2

Copyright © Kendall/Hunt Publishing Company

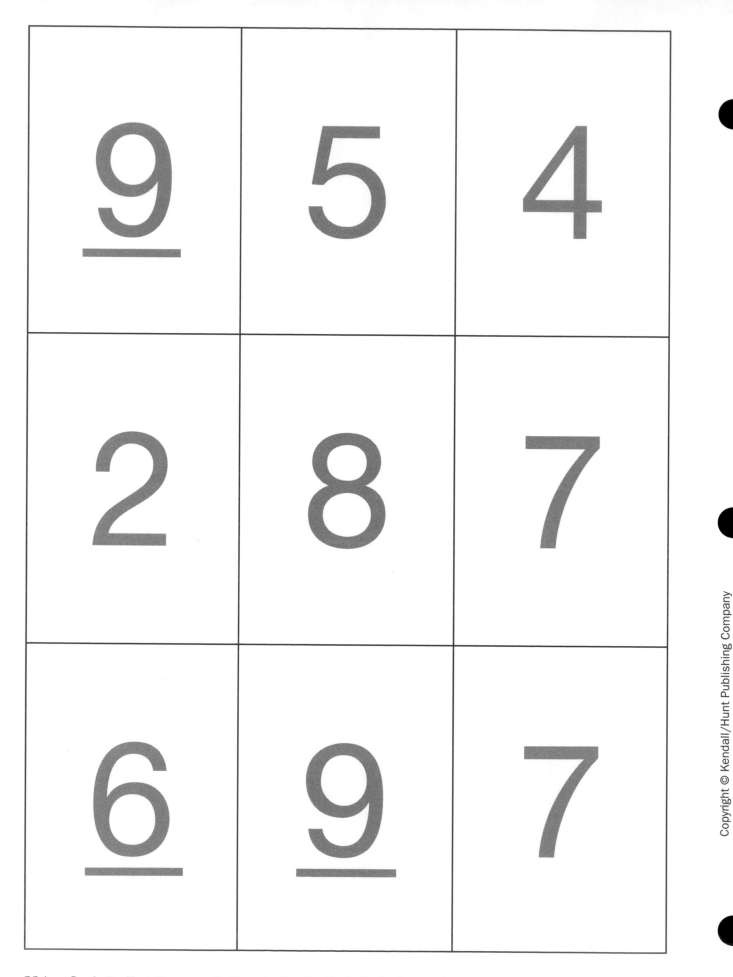

Copyright © Kendall/Hunt Publishing Company

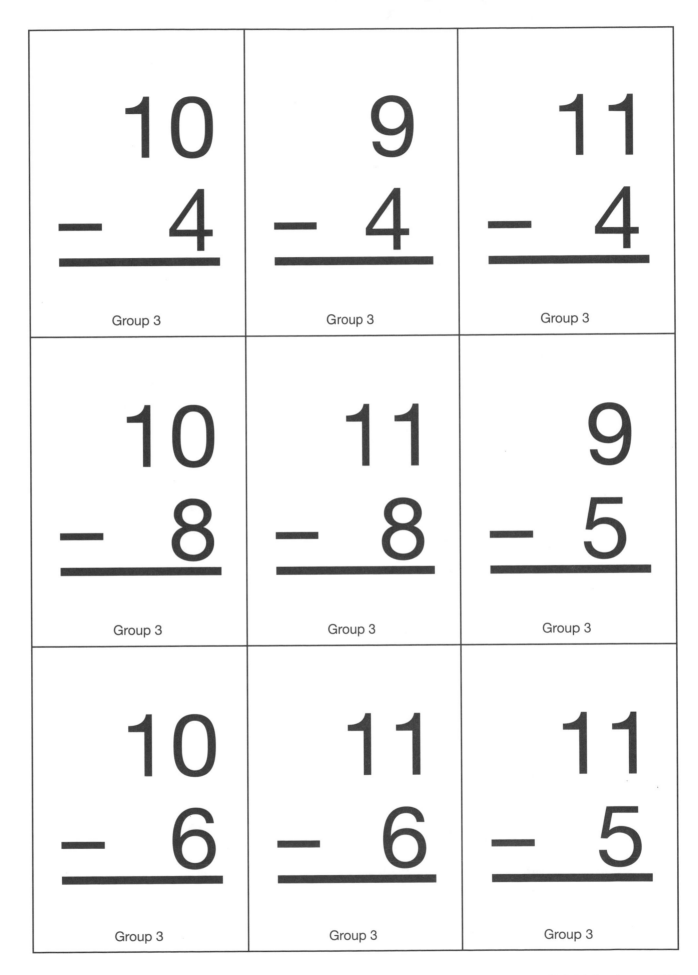

$\begin{array}{r} 10 \\ -\ 4 \\ \hline \end{array}$	$\begin{array}{r} 9 \\ -\ 4 \\ \hline \end{array}$	$\begin{array}{r} 11 \\ -\ 4 \\ \hline \end{array}$
Group 3	Group 3	Group 3
$\begin{array}{r} 10 \\ -\ 8 \\ \hline \end{array}$	$\begin{array}{r} 11 \\ -\ 8 \\ \hline \end{array}$	$\begin{array}{r} 9 \\ -\ 5 \\ \hline \end{array}$
Group 3	Group 3	Group 3
$\begin{array}{r} 10 \\ -\ 6 \\ \hline \end{array}$	$\begin{array}{r} 11 \\ -\ 6 \\ \hline \end{array}$	$\begin{array}{r} 11 \\ -\ 5 \\ \hline \end{array}$
Group 3	Group 3	Group 3

Copyright © Kendall/Hunt Publishing Company

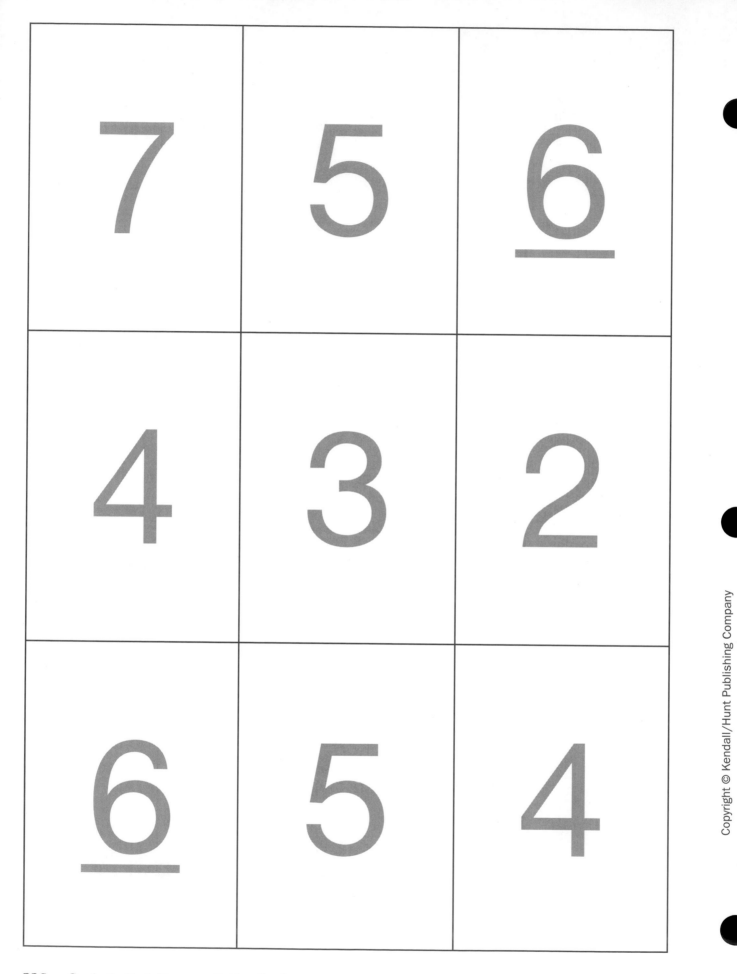

Copyright © Kendall/Hunt Publishing Company

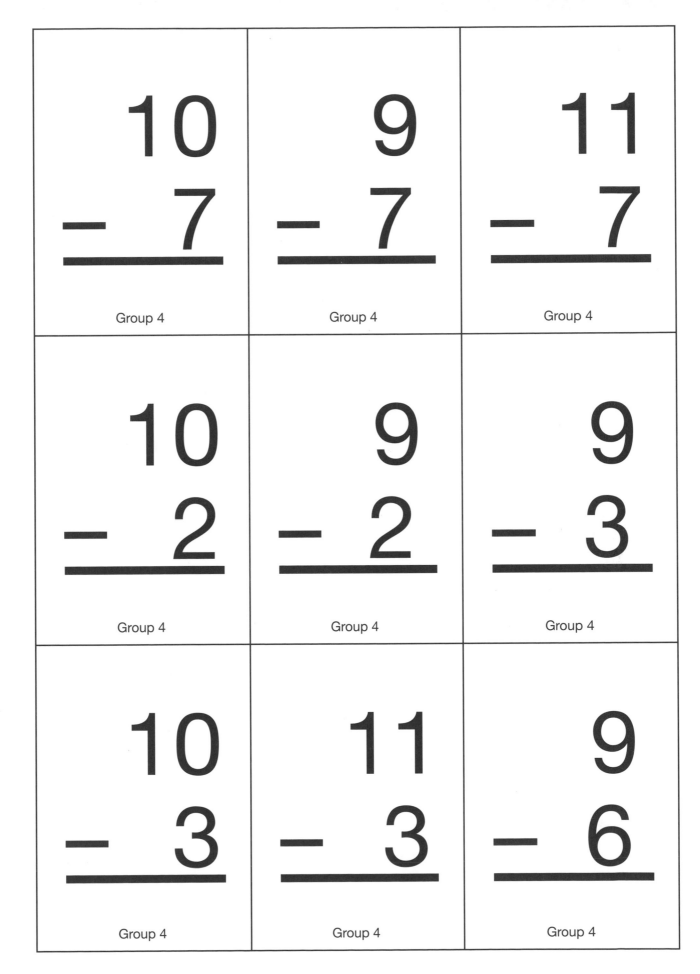

Copyright © Kendall/Hunt Publishing Company

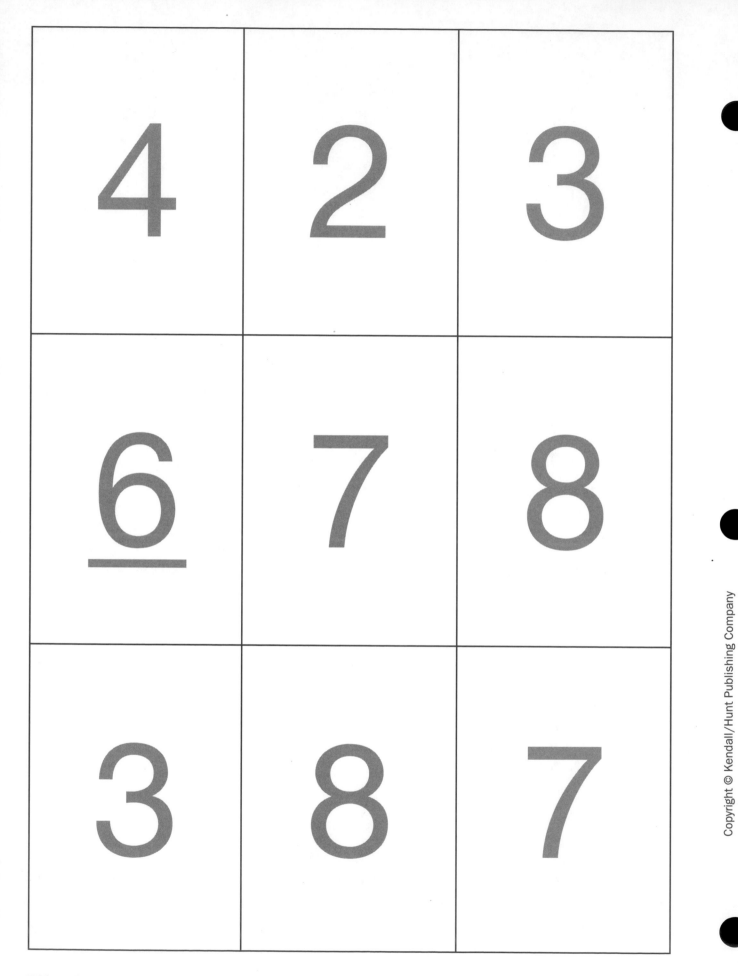

Copyright © Kendall/Hunt Publishing Company

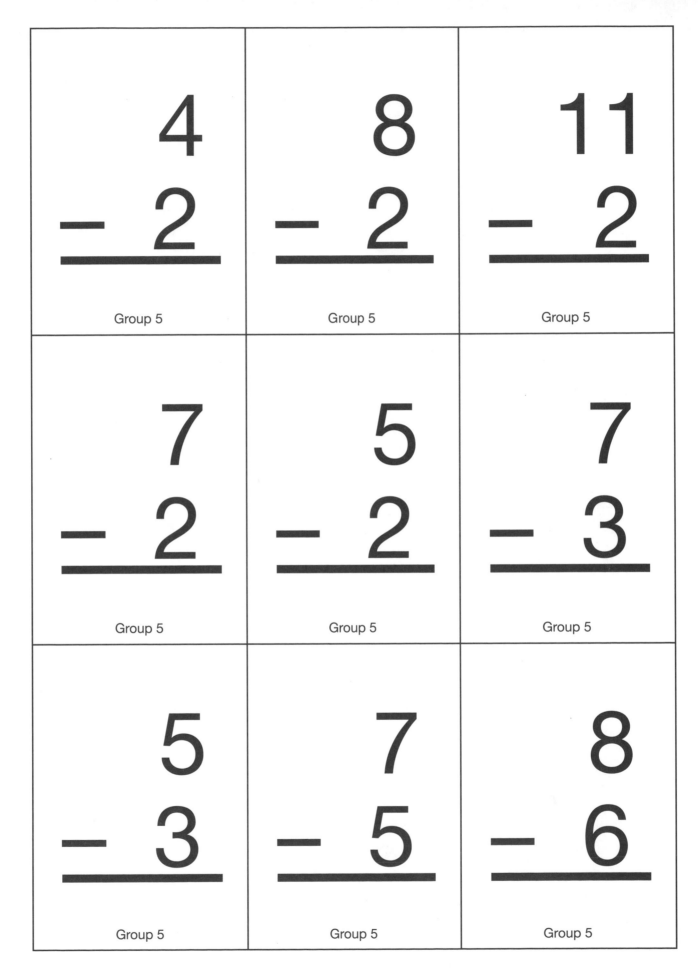

Copyright © Kendall/Hunt Publishing Company

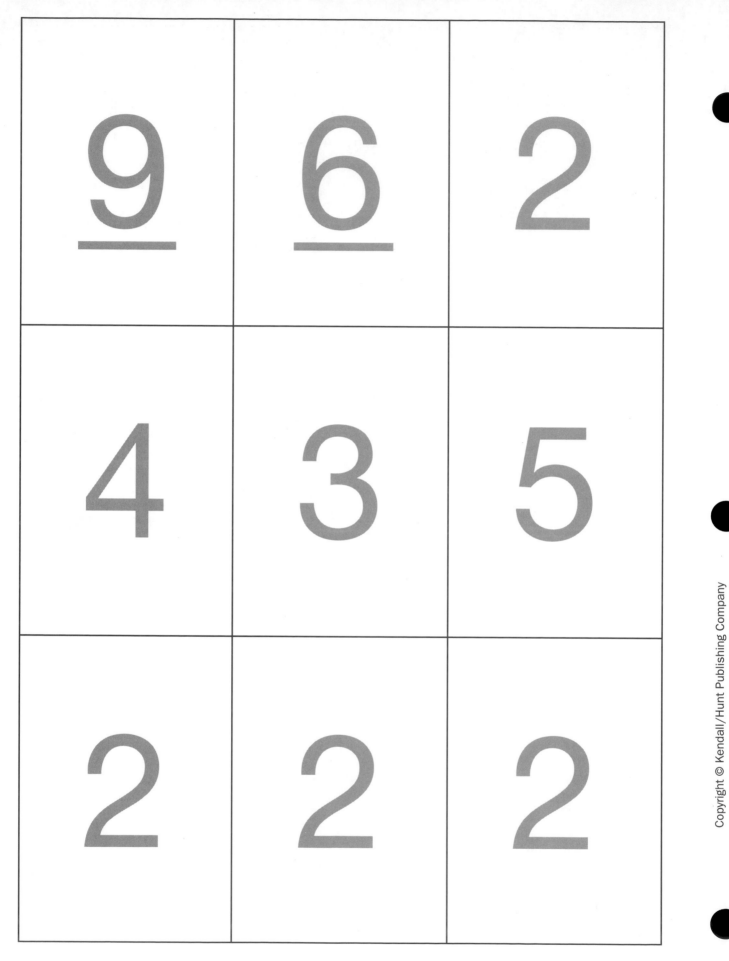

Copyright © Kendall/Hunt Publishing Company

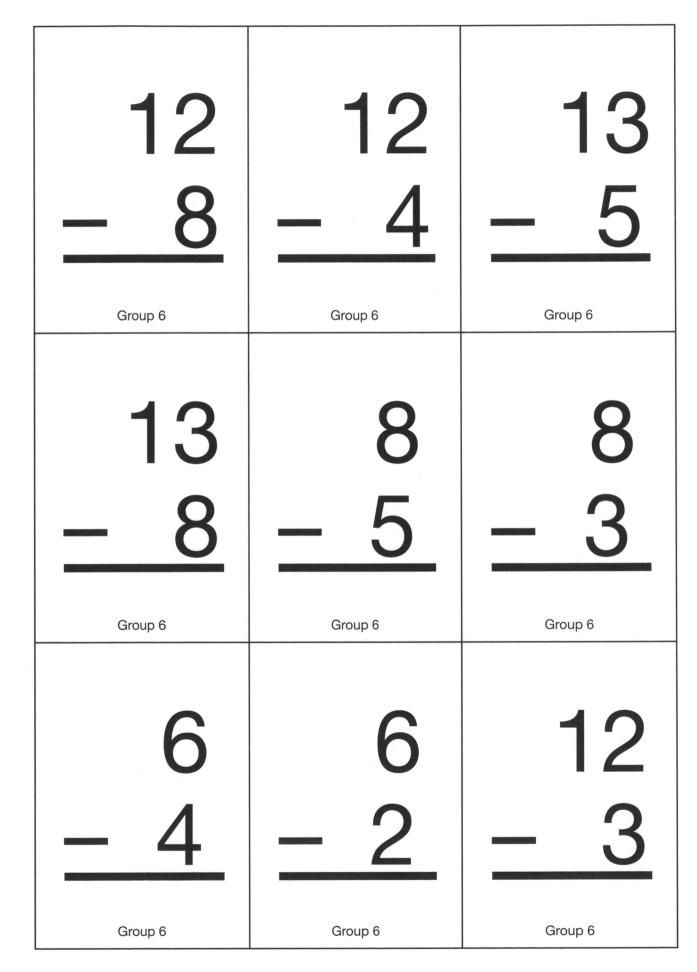

$\begin{array}{r} 12 \\ -\ 8 \\ \hline \end{array}$	$\begin{array}{r} 12 \\ -\ 4 \\ \hline \end{array}$	$\begin{array}{r} 13 \\ -\ 5 \\ \hline \end{array}$
Group 6	Group 6	Group 6
$\begin{array}{r} 13 \\ -\ 8 \\ \hline \end{array}$	$\begin{array}{r} 8 \\ -\ 5 \\ \hline \end{array}$	$\begin{array}{r} 8 \\ -\ 3 \\ \hline \end{array}$
Group 6	Group 6	Group 6
$\begin{array}{r} 6 \\ -\ 4 \\ \hline \end{array}$	$\begin{array}{r} 6 \\ -\ 2 \\ \hline \end{array}$	$\begin{array}{r} 12 \\ -\ 3 \\ \hline \end{array}$
Group 6	Group 6	Group 6

Copyright © Kendall/Hunt Publishing Company

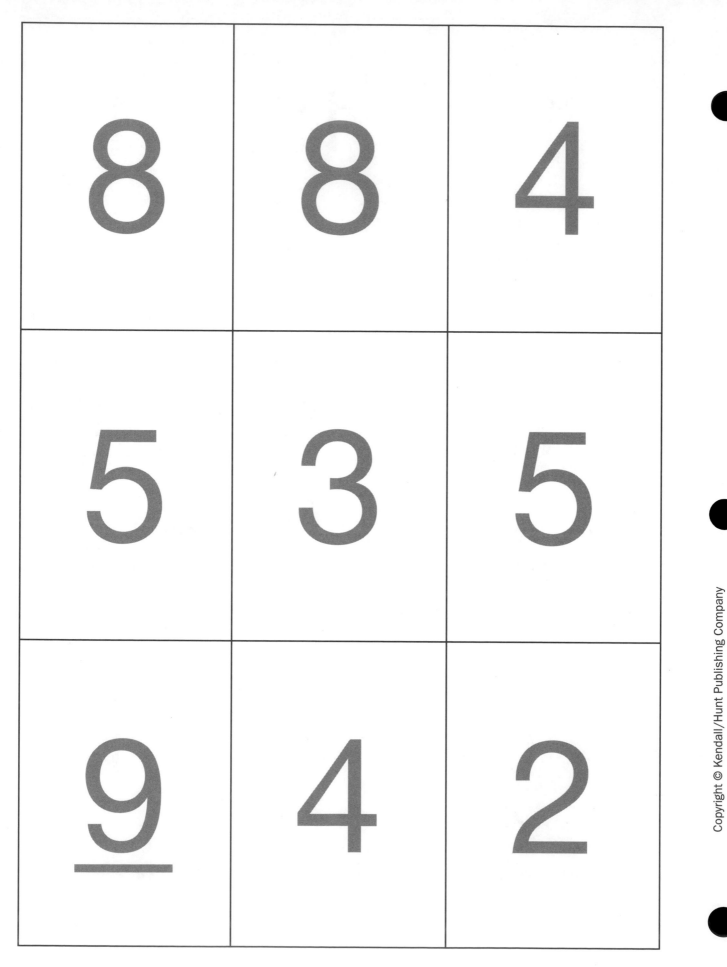

Copyright © Kendall/Hunt Publishing Company

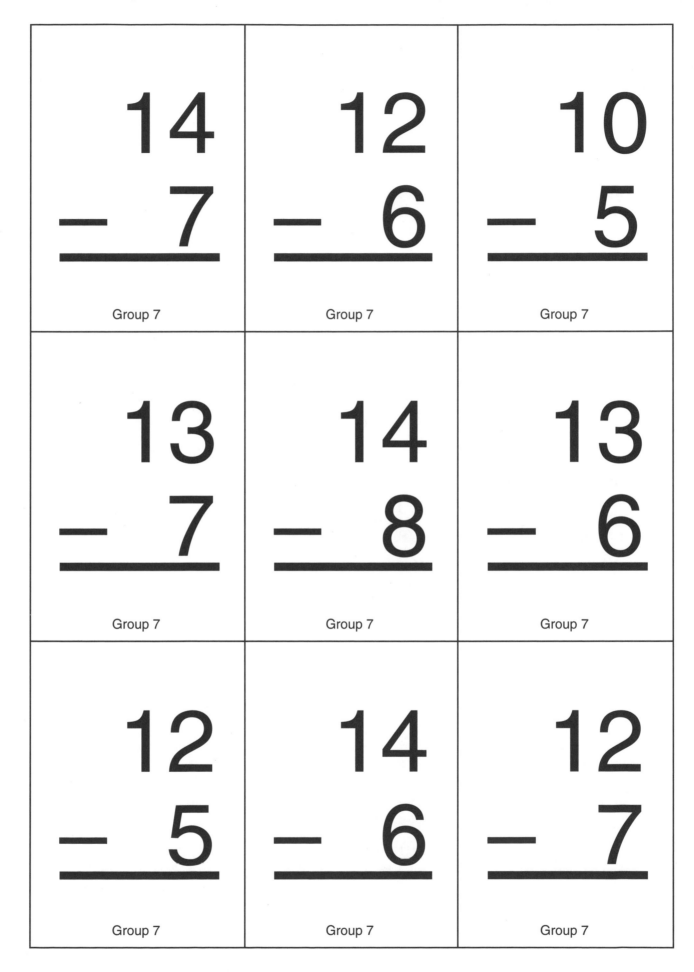

$$14$$
$$-\ 7$$

Group 7

$$12$$
$$-\ 6$$

Group 7

$$10$$
$$-\ 5$$

Group 7

$$13$$
$$-\ 7$$

Group 7

$$14$$
$$-\ 8$$

Group 7

$$13$$
$$-\ 6$$

Group 7

$$12$$
$$-\ 5$$

Group 7

$$14$$
$$-\ 6$$

Group 7

$$12$$
$$-\ 7$$

Group 7

Copyright © Kendall/Hunt Publishing Company

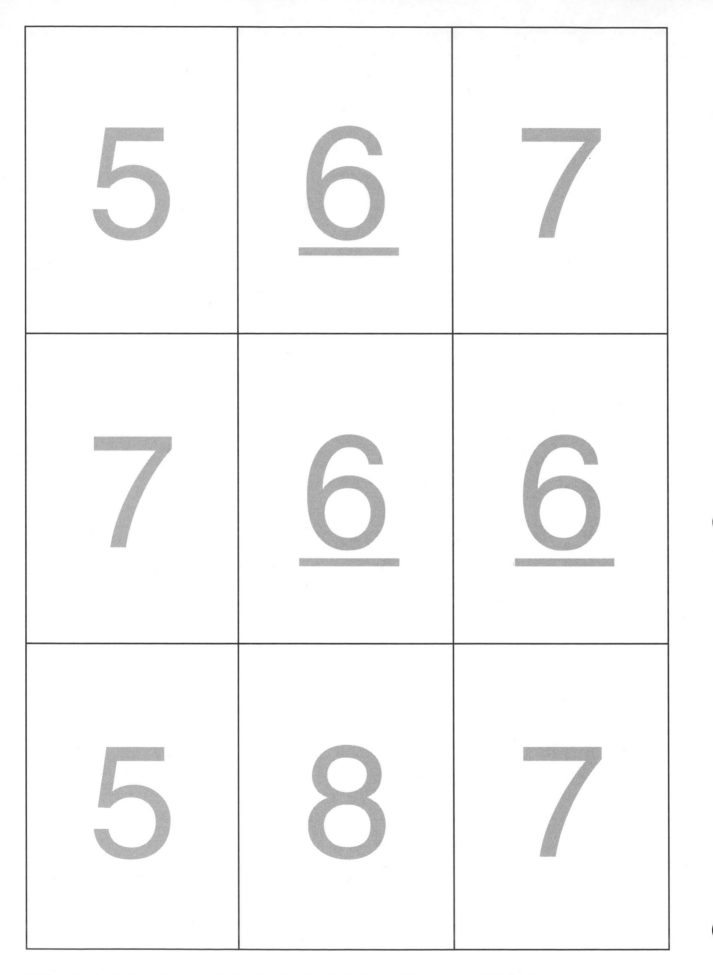

Copyright © Kendall/Hunt Publishing Company

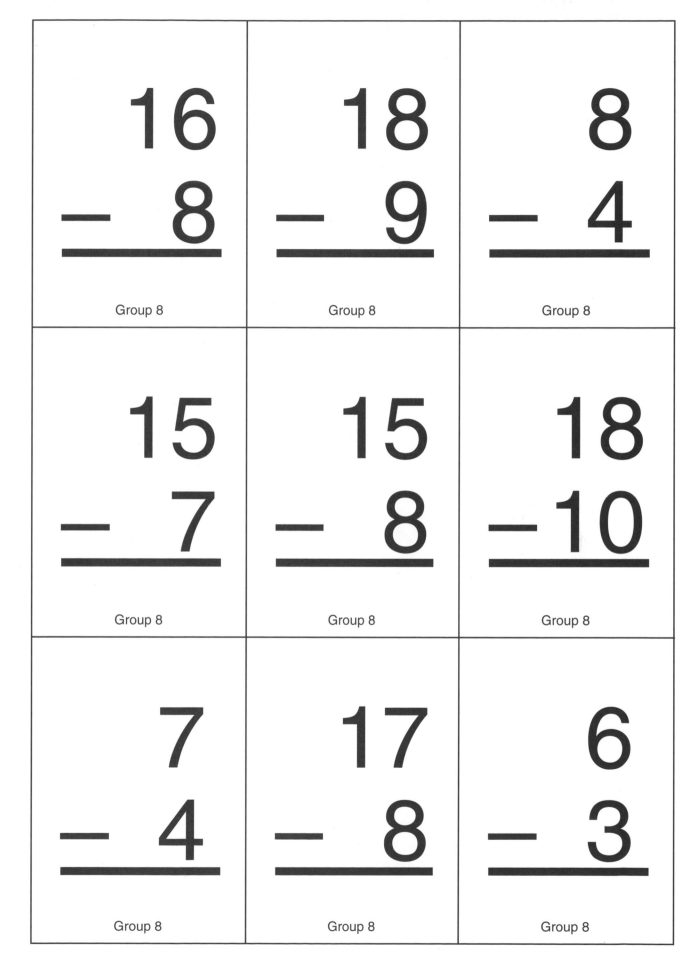

16
− 8
_____

Group 8

18
− 9
_____

Group 8

8
− 4
_____

Group 8

15
− 7
_____

Group 8

15
− 8
_____

Group 8

18
−10
_____

Group 8

7
− 4
_____

Group 8

17
− 8
_____

Group 8

6
− 3
_____

Group 8

Copyright © Kendall/Hunt Publishing Company

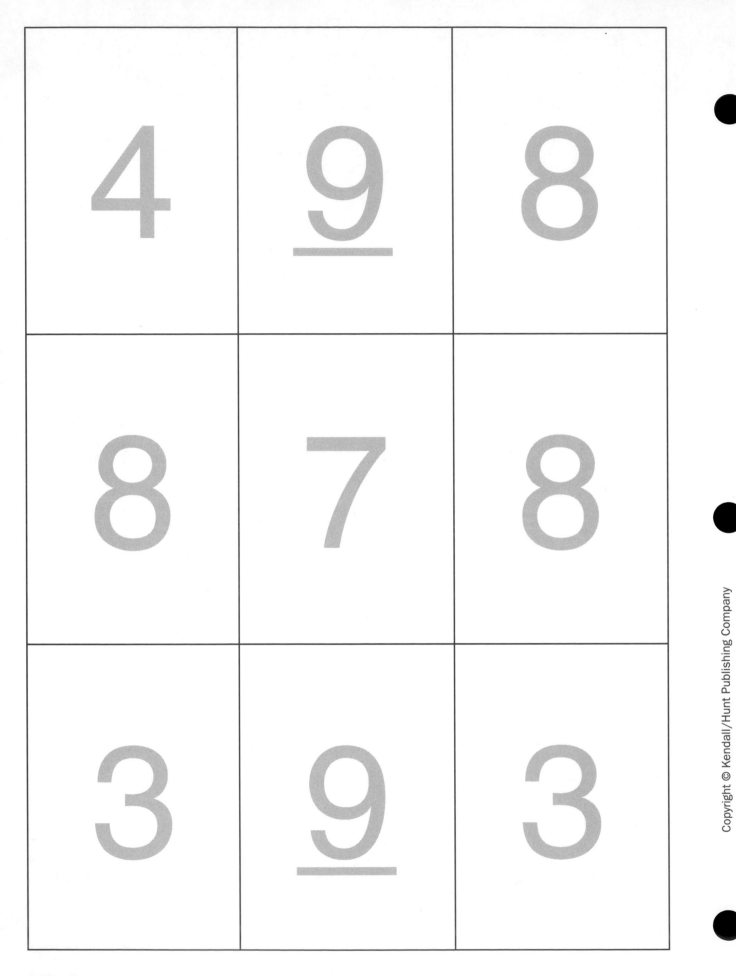

Copyright © Kendall/Hunt Publishing Company

Triangle Flash Cards: 2s

- Work with a partner. Each partner cuts out the flash cards below.

- Your partner chooses one card at a time and covers the shaded corner.

- Multiply the two uncovered numbers.

- Divide the used cards into three piles: those you know and can answer quickly, those you can figure out, and those you need to learn.

- Practice the last two piles again. Then make a list of the facts you need to practice at home.

- Repeat the directions for your partner.

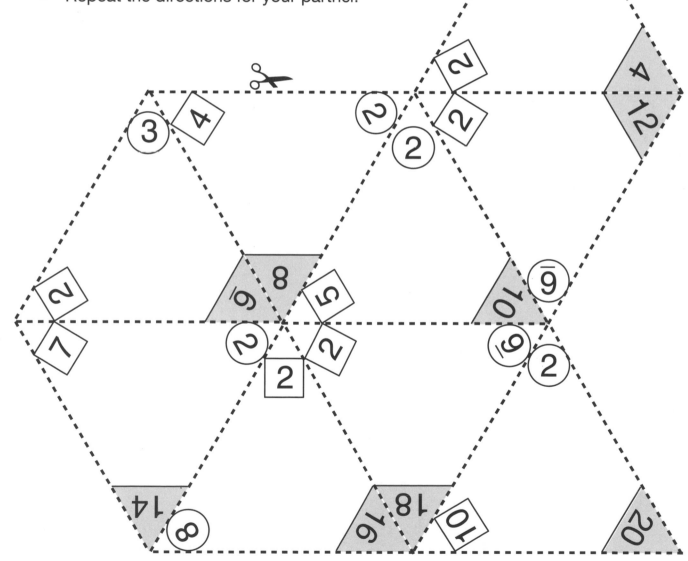

Copyright © Kendall/Hunt Publishing Company

Triangle Flash Cards: 3s

- Work with a partner. Each partner cuts out the flash cards below.

- Your partner chooses one card at a time and covers the shaded corner.

- Multiply the two uncovered numbers.

- Divide the used cards into three piles: those you know and can answer quickly, those you can figure out, and those you need to learn.

- Practice the last two piles again. Then make a list of the facts you need to practice at home.

- Repeat the directions for your partner.

Copyright © Kendall/Hunt Publishing Company

Triangle Flash Cards: 5s

- Work with a partner. Each partner cuts out the flash cards below.

- Your partner chooses one card at a time and covers the shaded corner.

- Multiply the two uncovered numbers.

- Divide the used cards into three piles: those you know and can answer quickly, those you can figure out, and those you need to learn.

- Practice the last two piles again. Then make a list of the facts you need to practice at home.

- Repeat the directions for your partner.

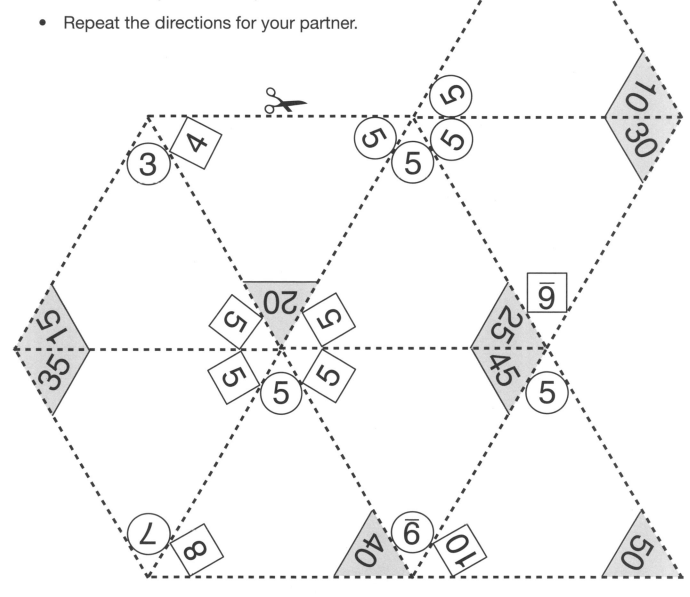

Copyright © Kendall/Hunt Publishing Company

Triangle Flash Cards: 9s

- Work with a partner. Each partner cuts out the 9 flash cards.

- Your partner chooses one card at a time and covers the shaded number.

- Multiply the two uncovered numbers.

- Divide the used cards into three piles: those you know and can answer quickly, those you can figure out, and those you need to learn.

- Practice the last two piles again. Then make a list of the facts you need to practice at home.

- Repeat the directions for your partner.

Copyright © Kendall/Hunt Publishing Company

Triangle Flash Cards: 10s

- Work with a partner. Each partner cuts out the 9 flash cards below.

- Your partner chooses one card at a time and covers the shaded corner.

- Multiply the two uncovered numbers.

- Divide the used cards into three piles: those you know and can answer quickly, those you can figure out, and those you need to learn.

- Practice the last two piles again. Then make a list of the facts you need to practice at home.

- Repeat the directions for your partner.

Copyright © Kendall/Hunt Publishing Company

Triangle Flash Cards: Square Numbers

- Work with a partner. Each partner cuts out the flash cards.

- Your partner chooses one card at a time and covers the shaded number.

- Multiply the two uncovered numbers.

- Divide the used cards into three piles: those you know and can answer quickly, those you can figure out, and those you need to learn.

- Practice the last two piles again. Then make a list of the facts you need to practice at home.

- Repeat the directions for your partner.

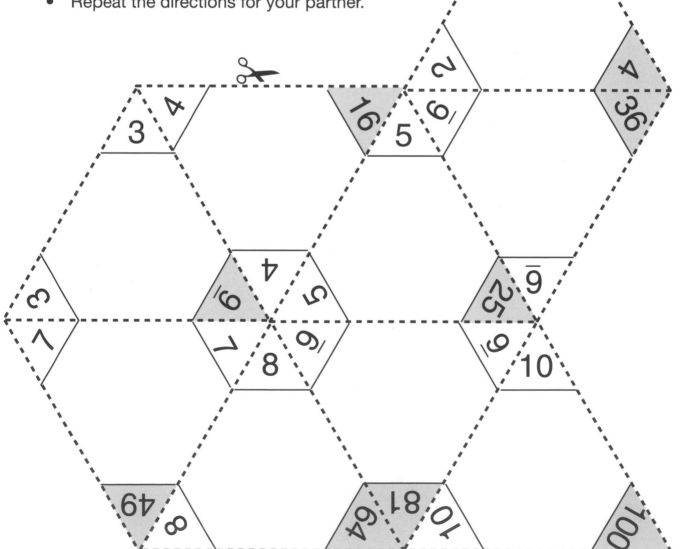

Copyright © Kendall/Hunt Publishing Company

Copyright © Kendall/Hunt Publishing Company

Triangle Flash Cards:
The Last Six Facts

- Work with a partner. Each partner cuts out the 6 flash cards.

- Your partner chooses one card at a time and covers the shaded number. Multiply the two uncovered numbers.

- Divide the used cards into three piles: those you know and can answer quickly, those you can figure out, and those you need to learn.

- Practice the last two piles again. Then make a list of the facts you need to practice at home.

- Repeat the directions for your partner.

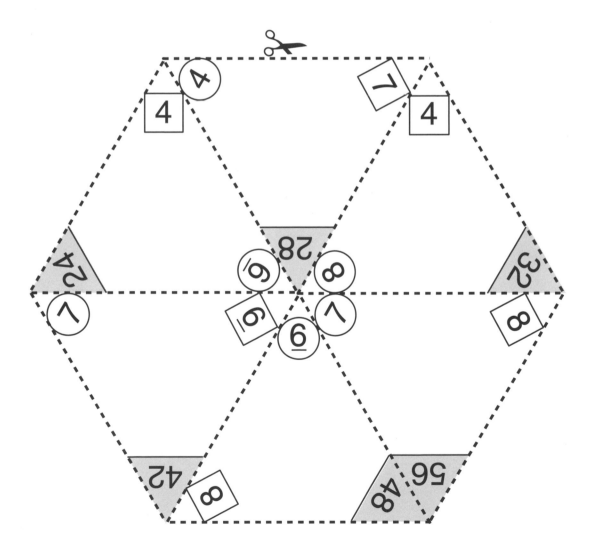

Triangle Flash Card Master

- Make a flash card for each fact that is not circled on your *Multiplication Facts I Know* chart. Write the largest number (the product) in the shaded corner of each triangle. Then cut out the flash cards.
- To quiz you on a multiplication fact, your partner covers the shaded number. Multiply the two uncovered numbers.
- Repeat the directions for your partner.

Copyright © Kendall/Hunt Publishing Company

The Addition Math Facts Review contains games and activities that can be used by those students who need extra practice with the addition facts. Some of the games and activities are from previous grades of the *Math Trailblazers* curriculum.

Items 1Q and 1S in the Daily Practice and Problems (DPP) in Section 5 provide addition facts inventory tests. Use these tests to see which of your students need additional work with the addition facts. Those who can find answers quickly and efficiently will continue to practice the addition facts throughout the year as they engage in labs, activities, and games, and as they solve problems in the DPP and Home Practice. However, for those students who need extra practice, we have developed games, activities, and flash cards, which can be found in this section.

Use DPP items 1Q and 1S as diagnostic tests to help you find out which facts individual students need to practice. The following table suggests which activities from this section you should assign to students who do not do well on specific diagnostic tests.

Diagnostic Test	Games and Flash Cards
Addition Test: Doubles, 2s, 3s	*Add 1, 2, 3* *Path to Glory* *Path to Glory: 100 Loses* *Path to Glory: Challenge* *Triangle Flash Cards for Groups A, B,* *C, D, E*
Addition Test: More Addition Facts	*Add 4, 5, 6* *Addition War!* *Triangle Flash Cards for Groups C, D,* *E, F, G* *Mixed-Up Addition Tables 1 and 2* *Line Math 1–3*

Students should gradually use the activities, games, and flash cards provided in the Addition Math Facts Review at home with family members. They should concentrate on one small group of facts at a time. Practicing small groups of facts often (for short periods of time) is more effective than practicing many facts less often (for long periods of time). While students practice the addition facts at home, in class they should be encouraged to use strategies, calculators, and printed addition tables. These tools allow students to continue to develop number sense and work on interesting problems and experiments while they are learning the facts. In this way, students who need extra practice are not prevented from learning more complex mathematics because they do not know all the math facts.

After students have been given the opportunity to use some of the items provided in the Addition Math Facts Review, you can administer the appropriate tests a second time to see students' progress. Alternate forms for each test are located at the end of this section. These tests should be administered over a period of time.

For more information about the distribution of the practice and assessment of the math facts in *Math Trailblazers,* see the TIMS Tutor: *Math Facts* in Section 3 and the Assessment section in the *Teacher Implementation Guide.*

Add 1, 2, 3

Players

This is a game for two players.

Rules

1. Player 1 (P1) adds 1, 2, or 3 to 0 and completes the number sentence:
   0 + _____ = _____.
2. Player 2 (P2) adds 1, 2, or 3 to Player 1's answer and records a number sentence.
3. Play continues. The player who reaches 10 exactly, wins. A game is started for you.

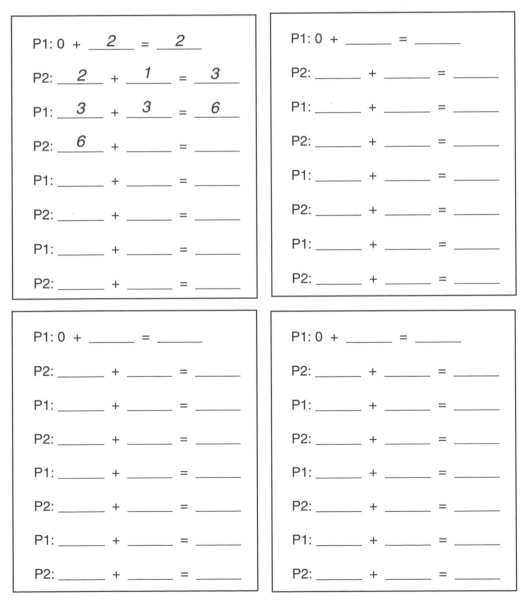

P1: 0 + __2__ = __2__

P2: __2__ + __1__ = __3__

P1: __3__ + __3__ = __6__

P2: __6__ + _____ = _____

P1: _____ + _____ = _____

P2: _____ + _____ = _____

P1: _____ + _____ = _____

P2: _____ + _____ = _____

P1: 0 + _____ = _____

P2: _____ + _____ = _____

P1: _____ + _____ = _____

P2: _____ + _____ = _____

P1: _____ + _____ = _____

P2: _____ + _____ = _____

P1: _____ + _____ = _____

P2: _____ + _____ = _____

P1: 0 + _____ = _____

P2: _____ + _____ = _____

P1: _____ + _____ = _____

P2: _____ + _____ = _____

P1: _____ + _____ = _____

P2: _____ + _____ = _____

P1: _____ + _____ = _____

P2: _____ + _____ = _____

P1: 0 + _____ = _____

P2: _____ + _____ = _____

P1: _____ + _____ = _____

P2: _____ + _____ = _____

P1: _____ + _____ = _____

P2: _____ + _____ = _____

P1: _____ + _____ = _____

P2: _____ + _____ = _____

Copyright © Kendall/Hunt Publishing Company

Path to Glory

Players

This is a game for two players.

Rules

Start at 0. Take turns adding 1, 2, 3, 10, 20, or 30. Write each number you add in a circle. Write the sums in the squares as you go. The player who reaches 100 exactly is the winner.

Here is the beginning of a game:

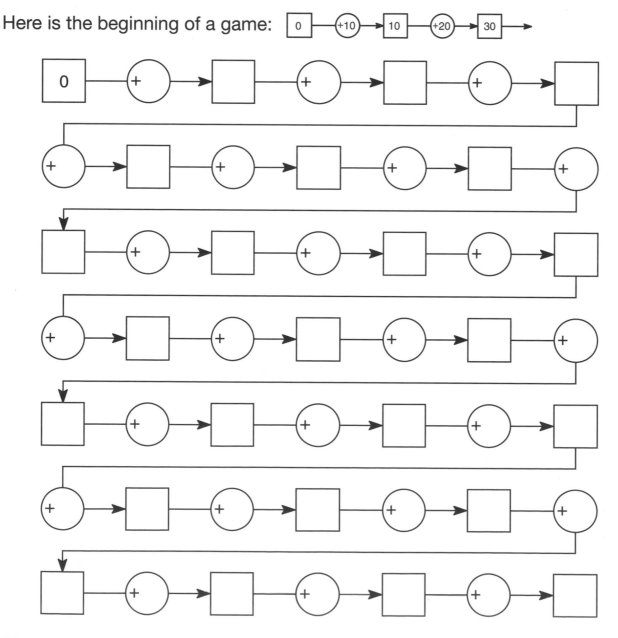

Play 2 or 3 games. Then, write about what happened. Tell how to win.

Copyright © Kendall/Hunt Publishing Company

Path to Glory: 100 Loses

Players

This game is for two players.

Rules

Start at 0. Take turns adding 1, 2, 3, 10, 20, or 30. Write each number you add in a circle. Write the sums in the squares as you go. The player who reaches 100 or more, loses.

Here is the beginning of a game: 0 → (+1) → 1 → (+30) → 31 →

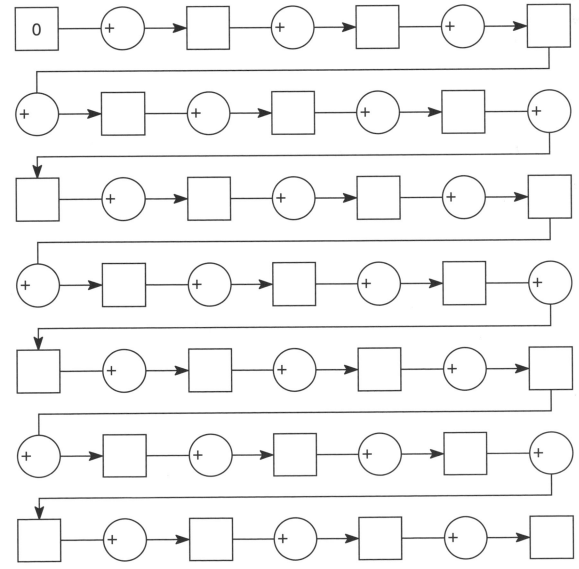

Play 2 or 3 games. Then, write about what happened. Tell how to win.

Copyright © Kendall/Hunt Publishing Company

Path to Glory: Challenge

Players

This is a game for two players.

Rules

Start at 0. Take turns adding 1, 2, 3, 10, 20, or 30. Write each number you add in a circle. Write the sums in the squares as you go. Can you reach 100 in exactly 11 steps?

Is there another way to reach 100 in exactly 11 steps? Write about what happened.

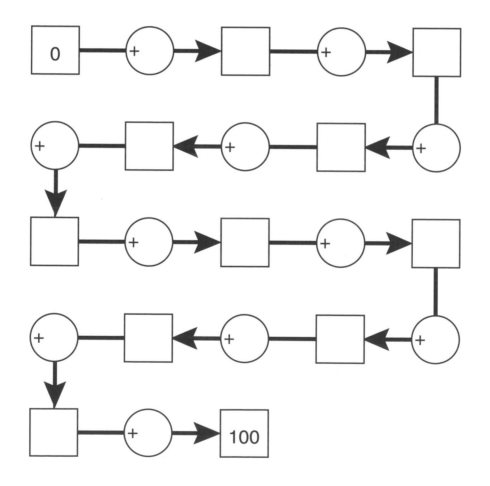

Copyright © Kendall/Hunt Publishing Company

Add 4, 5, 6

Players

This is a game for two players.

Rules

1. Player 1 (P1) adds 4, 5, or 6 to 0 and completes the number sentence: 0 + _____ = _____.
2. Player 2 (P2) adds 4, 5, or 6 to Player 1's answer and records a number sentence.
3. Play continues. The player who gets to 30 or more, wins. A game is started for you.

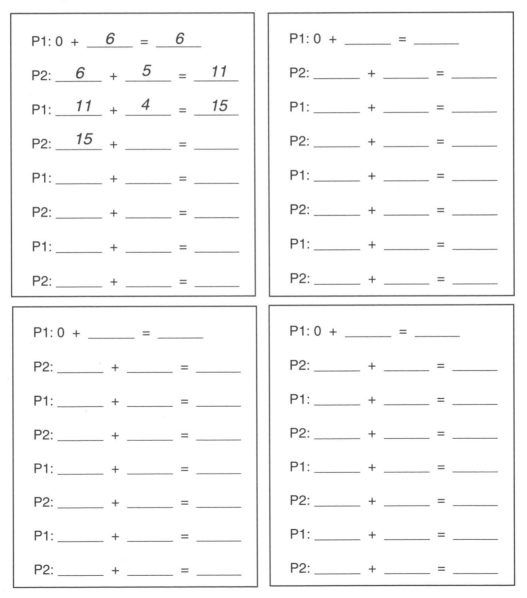

P1: 0 + __6__ = __6__

P2: __6__ + __5__ = __11__

P1: __11__ + __4__ = __15__

P2: __15__ + _____ = _____

P1: _____ + _____ = _____

P2: _____ + _____ = _____

P1: _____ + _____ = _____

P2: _____ + _____ = _____

P1: 0 + _____ = _____

P2: _____ + _____ = _____

P1: _____ + _____ = _____

P2: _____ + _____ = _____

P1: _____ + _____ = _____

P2: _____ + _____ = _____

P1: _____ + _____ = _____

P2: _____ + _____ = _____

P1: 0 + _____ = _____

P2: _____ + _____ = _____

P1: _____ + _____ = _____

P2: _____ + _____ = _____

P1: _____ + _____ = _____

P2: _____ + _____ = _____

P1: _____ + _____ = _____

P2: _____ + _____ = _____

P1: 0 + _____ = _____

P2: _____ + _____ = _____

P1: _____ + _____ = _____

P2: _____ + _____ = _____

P1: _____ + _____ = _____

P2: _____ + _____ = _____

P1: _____ + _____ = _____

P2: _____ + _____ = _____

Copyright © Kendall/Hunt Publishing Company

Addition War!

Players

This is a card game for two players.

Materials

You need *Digit Cards* with digits 0 to 9 on them.
You can use *Digit Cards* or regular playing cards. (Let the Ace = 1 and the Jack = 0. Remove the other face cards.)

Rules

1. Deal out all the cards.
2. Each player turns over two cards and says a number sentence that tells the sum of the numbers he or she turned up. Whoever has the larger sum wins all four cards.
3. If there is a tie, turn over two more cards. The larger of the second set takes all eight cards.
4. Play for ten minutes or until one player runs out of cards. The player with the most cards at the end wins.

Variations

- Remove 1s, 2s, and 3s for a harder game.
- Whoever has the *smaller* sum takes the cards.
- Play *Subtraction War!* Whoever has the largest difference wins the cards.
- Play with more than two players.

Copyright © Kendall/Hunt Publishing Company

Copyright © Kendall/Hunt Publishing Company

Name _____   Date _____

✂

9	**8**	**7**	**6**
Digit Cards	Digit Cards	Digit Cards	Digit Cards
5	**4**	**3**	**2**
Digit Cards	Digit Cards	Digit Cards	Digit Cards
1	**0**		
Digit Cards	Digit Cards		

Triangle Flash Cards: Addition

Addition Practice

With a partner, use your *Triangle Flash Cards* to practice the addition or subtraction facts. If you are practicing addition, one partner covers the corner containing the highest number. This number will be the answer to an addition problem. The second person adds the two uncovered numbers.

$9 + 4 = ?$

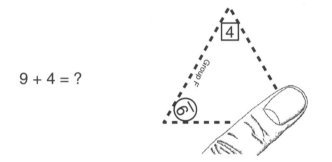

Sorting the Flash Cards

Separate the used cards into three piles: those facts you know and can answer quickly, those you can figure out with a strategy, and those you need to learn. Practice the last two piles again and then make a list of the facts you need to practice at home for homework.

Discuss how you can figure out facts you don't recall at once. Share your strategies with your partner.

Copyright © Kendall/Hunt Publishing Company

Triangle Flash Cards: Group A

1. Cut out the flash cards.
2. Work with a partner. To practice an addition fact, cover the corner with the highest number. (It is shaded.) Add the two uncovered numbers.
3. Divide the cards into three piles: those facts you know and can answer quickly, those you can figure out, and those you need to learn.
4. Practice the last two piles again. Then make a list of the facts you need to practice.

Copyright © Kendall/Hunt Publishing Company

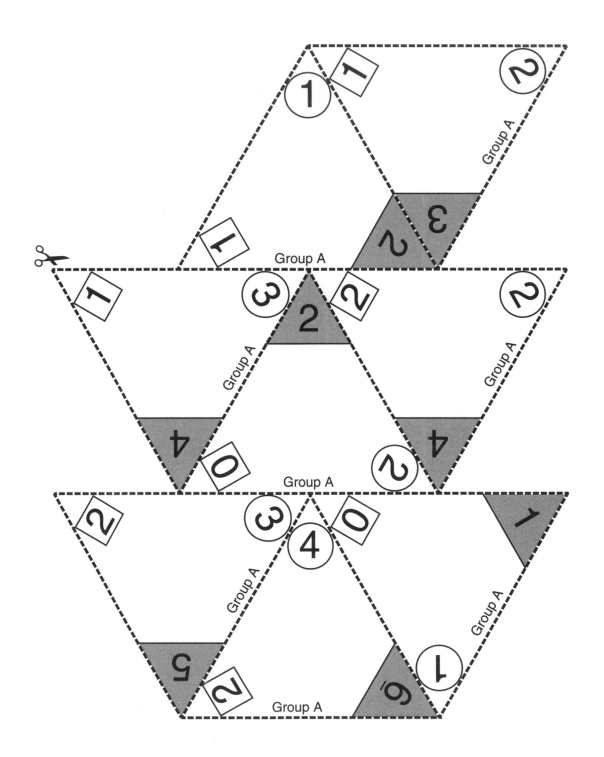

Copyright © Kendall/Hunt Publishing Company

Triangle Flash Cards: Group B

1. Cut out the flash cards.

2. Work with a partner. To practice an addition fact, cover the corner with the highest number. (It is shaded.) Add the two uncovered numbers.

3. Divide the cards into three piles: those facts you know and can answer quickly, those you can figure out, and those you need to learn.

4. Practice the last two piles again. Then make a list of the facts you need to practice.

Copyright © Kendall/Hunt Publishing Company

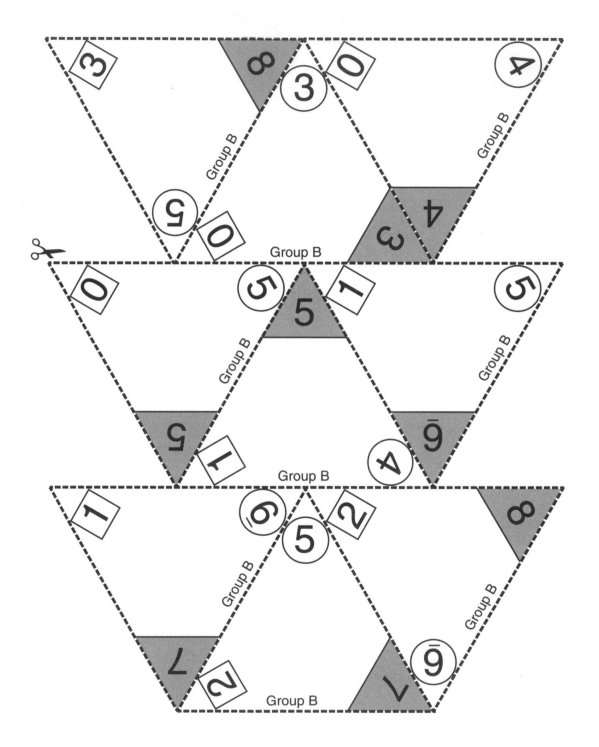

Copyright © Kendall/Hunt Publishing Company

Triangle Flash Cards:
Group C

1. Cut out the flash cards.

2. Work with a partner. To practice an addition fact, cover the corner with the highest number. (It is shaded.) Add the two uncovered numbers.

3. Divide the cards into three piles: those facts you know and can answer quickly, those you can figure out, and those you need to learn.

4. Practice the last two piles again. Then make a list of the facts you need to practice.

Copyright © Kendall/Hunt Publishing Company

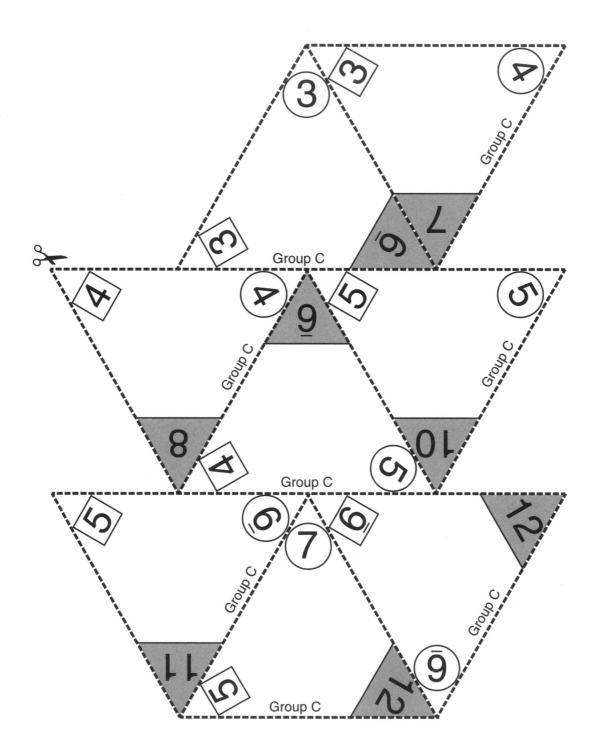

Copyright © Kendall/Hunt Publishing Company .

Triangle Flash Cards:
Group D

1. Cut out the flash cards.

2. Work with a partner. To practice an addition fact, cover the corner with the highest number. (It is shaded.) Add the two uncovered numbers.

3. Divide the cards into three piles: those facts you know and can answer quickly, those you can figure out, and those you need to learn.

4. Practice the last two piles again. Then make a list of the facts you need to practice.

Copyright © Kendall/Hunt Publishing Company

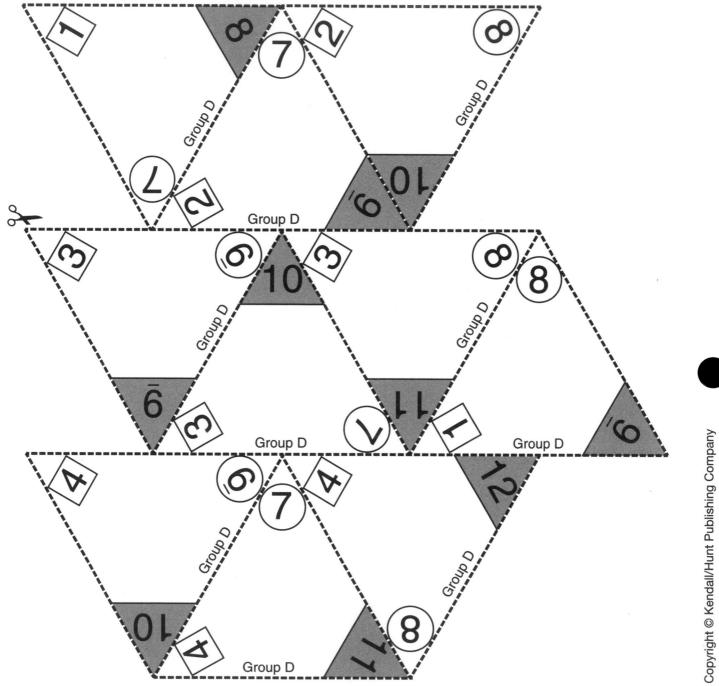

Copyright © Kendall/Hunt Publishing Company

Name _____   Date _____

Triangle Flash Cards:
Group E

1. Cut out the flash cards.

2. Work with a partner. To practice an addition fact, cover the corner with the highest number. (It is shaded.) Add the two uncovered numbers.

3. Divide the cards into three piles: those facts you know and can answer quickly, those you can figure out, and those you need to learn.

4. Practice the last two piles again. Then make a list of the facts you need to practice.

Copyright © Kendall/Hunt Publishing Company

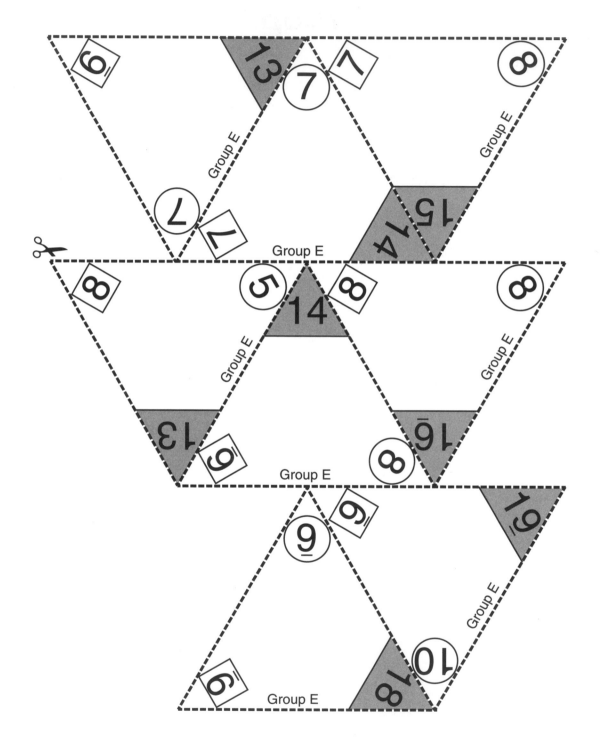

Group E

Copyright © Kendall/Hunt Publishing Company

Triangle Flash Cards:
Group F

1. Cut out the flash cards.
2. Work with a partner. To practice an addition fact, cover the corner with the highest number. (It is shaded.) Add the two uncovered numbers.
3. Divide the cards into three piles: those facts you know and can answer quickly, those you can figure out, and those you need to learn.
4. Practice the last two piles again. Then make a list of the facts you need to practice.

Copyright © Kendall/Hunt Publishing Company

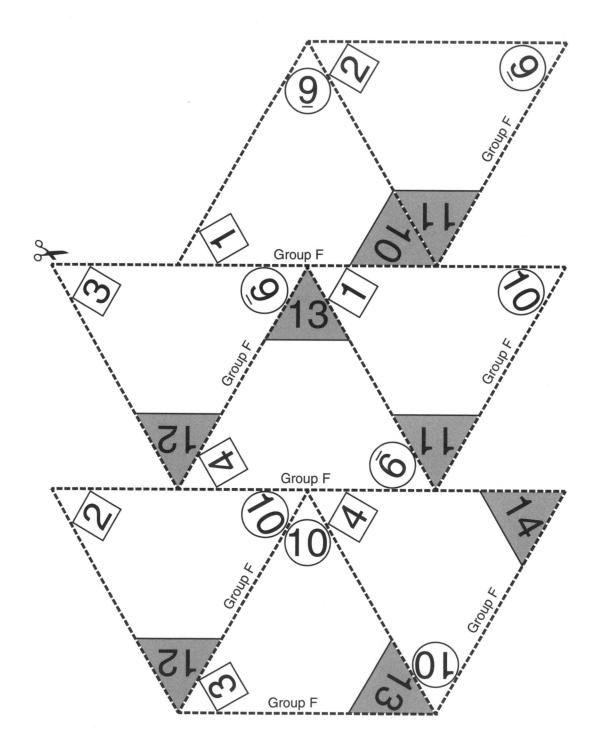

Copyright © Kendall/Hunt Publishing Company

Name _____   Date _____

Triangle Flash Cards:
Group G

1. Cut out the flash cards.

2. Work with a partner. To practice an addition fact, cover the corner with the highest number. (It is shaded.) Add the two uncovered numbers.

3. Divide the cards into three piles: those facts you know and can answer quickly, those you can figure out, and those you need to learn.

4. Practice the last two piles again. Then make a list of the facts you need to practice.

Copyright © Kendall/Hunt Publishing Company

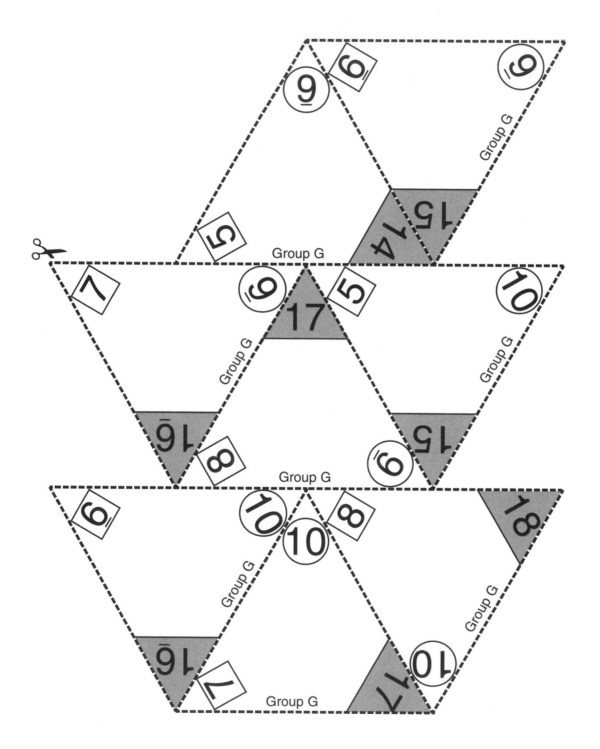

Copyright © Kendall/Hunt Publishing Company

Mixed-Up Addition Tables 1

Fill in the missing numbers in these tables.

+	3	6	9	5	7	0
4						
6						
5						
9				14		
8						
7						

+	5	7	8	2	9	6
7						
3						
5						
4						
8						
9						

Copyright © Kendall/Hunt Publishing Company

Mixed-Up Addition Tables 2

Fill in the missing numbers in this table.

+	4	6	2	1	8	7
5						
7						
1						
2		8				
9						
6						

Put your own numbers along the top and left side of this addition table. Ask a friend to complete the table. Check your friend's work.

+						

Copyright © Kendall/Hunt Publishing Company

Line Math 1

Put 1, 2, 3, 4, 5, and 6 in the boxes so that the sum on each line is 9. Cut out the digits in the dotted boxes to help.

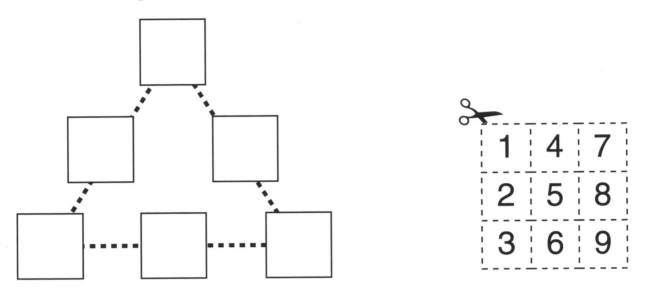

Put 4, 5, 6, 7, 8, and 9 in the boxes so that the sum on each line is 18.

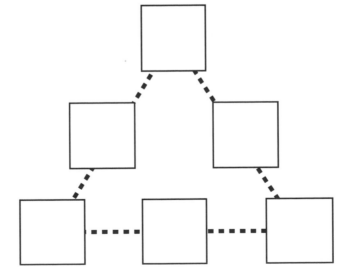

Copyright © Kendall/Hunt Publishing Company

Line Math 2

Put 1, 2, 3, 4, 5, 6, 7, 8, and 9 in the boxes so that the sum on each line is 15. Cut out the digits in the dotted boxes to help.

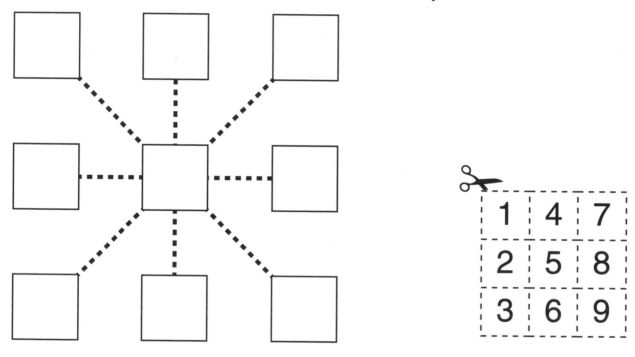

Put 1, 2, 3, 4, 5, 6, 7, 8, and 9 in the boxes so that the sum on each line is 17.

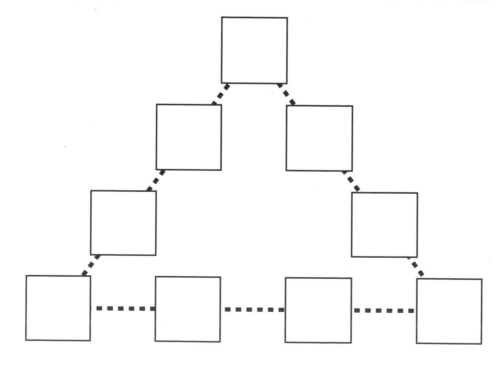

Copyright © Kendall/Hunt Publishing Company

Line Math 3

Put 1, 2, 3, 4, 5, 6, and 7 in the boxes so that the sum on each line is 12. Cut out the digits in the dotted boxes to help.

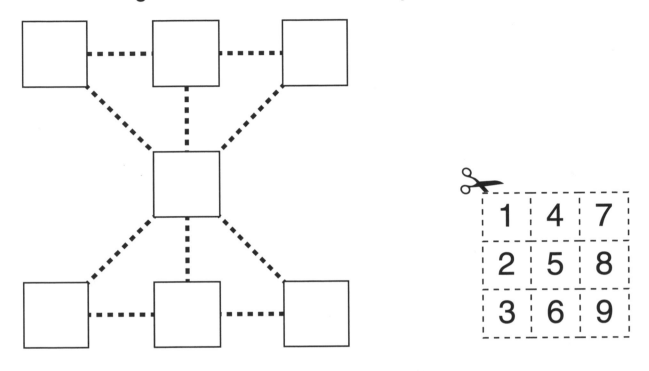

1	4	7
2	5	8
3	6	9

Put 1, 2, 3, 4, 5, 6, 7, 8, and 9 in the boxes so that the sum on each line is 23.

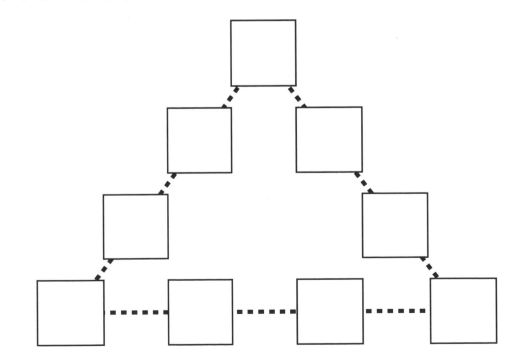

Copyright © Kendall/Hunt Publishing Company

Name _____   Date _____

Make N: + and –

Players

This is an activity for two players.

Materials

You need *Digit Cards* (0, 1, 2, 3, 4, 5, 6, 7, 8, and 9). You also need *Make N Cards* with the addition sign (+), the subtraction or minus sign (–), the equal sign (=), and the letter *N*.

Rules

1. Work with a partner. Use the cards to make a number sentence for each: $N = 1$, $N = 2$, $N = 3$, . . .

2. Use each digit only once in a number sentence. You can use + and – as often as you like.

   For example, for $N = 10$, one number sentence is $5 + 3 + 2 = N$.

   Another number sentence for $N = 10$ is $N = 6 + 3 + 2 - 1$.

3. Write down your number sentence in the space below. Work in order, starting with $N = 1$.

4. Both players should check that the number sentence is correct.

Use another sheet of paper if you need more room. An example for $N = 1$ is shown. Find another sentence for $N = 1$.

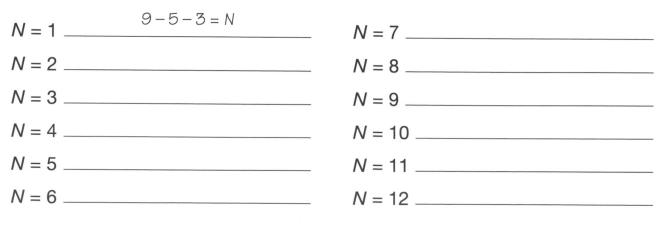

$N = 1$ $9 - 5 - 3 = N$ _____ $N = 7$ _____

$N = 2$ _____ $N = 8$ _____

$N = 3$ _____ $N = 9$ _____

$N = 4$ _____ $N = 10$ _____

$N = 5$ _____ $N = 11$ _____

$N = 6$ _____ $N = 12$ _____

Copyright © Kendall/Hunt Publishing Company

✂

9	**8**	**7**	**6**
Digit Cards	Digit Cards	Digit Cards	Digit Cards
5	**4**	**3**	**2**
Digit Cards	Digit Cards	Digit Cards	Digit Cards
1	**0**		
Digit Cards	Digit Cards		

Copyright © Kendall/Hunt Publishing Company

Name _____ Date _____

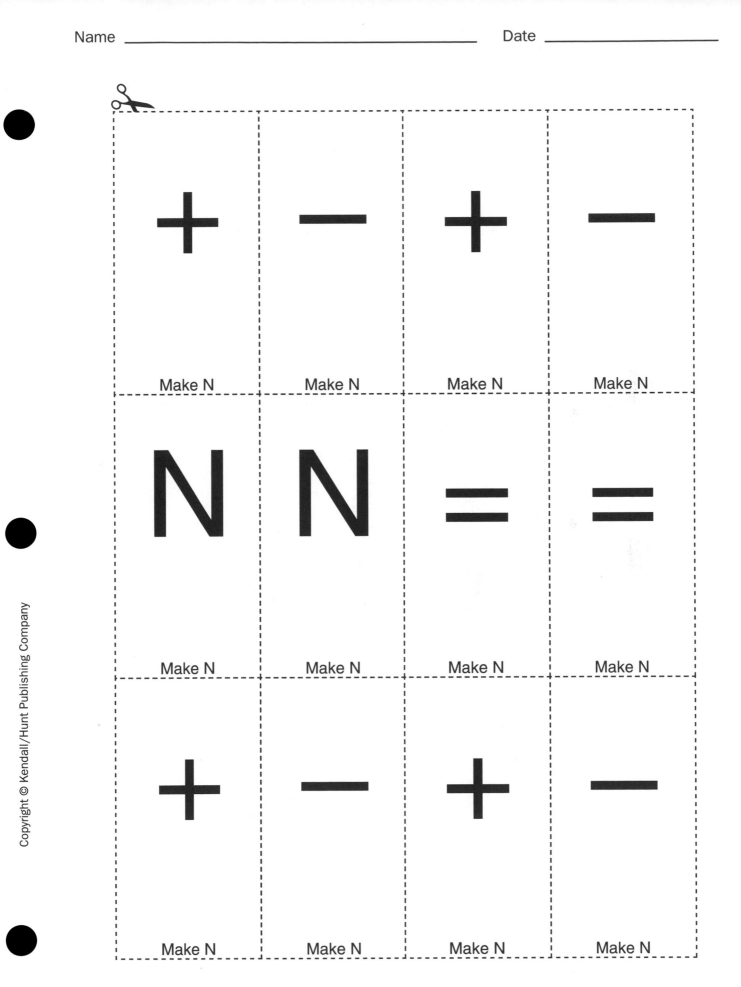

Copyright © Kendall/Hunt Publishing Company

Copyright © Kendall/Hunt Publishing Company

Make N: Challenge

Players

This is an activity for two players.

Materials

You need *Digit Cards* (0, 1, 2, 3, 4, 5, 6, 7, 8, and 9). You also need *Make N Cards* with the addition sign (+), the subtraction or minus sign (–), the equal sign (=), and cards with N on them.

Rules

Make N: Challenge is almost the same as *Make N: + and –*. But the goal of this game is to use as many digits as possible.

1. Work with a partner. Use the cards to make a number sentence for each: $N = 1$, $N = 2$, $N = 3$, . . .

2. Use each digit only once in a number sentence. Try to use as many digits as you can. Use + and – as often as you like.

   For example, for $N = 23$, one number sentence is $9 + 8 + 6 = N$.

   But the sentence $9 + 8 + 7 - 6 + 5 = N$ uses more digits, so in this game it's better.

3. Write down your number sentence in the space below. Work in order, starting with $N = 1$.

4. Both players should check that the number sentence is correct.

Use another sheet of paper if you need more room.

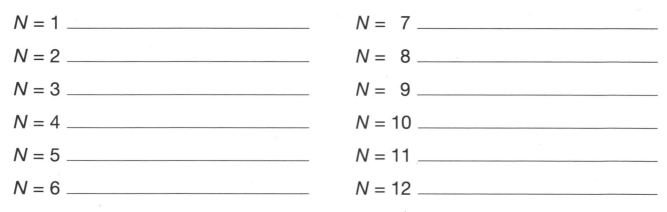

$N = 1$ _____ $N = 7$ _____

$N = 2$ _____ $N = 8$ _____

$N = 3$ _____ $N = 9$ _____

$N = 4$ _____ $N = 10$ _____

$N = 5$ _____ $N = 11$ _____

$N = 6$ _____ $N = 12$ _____

Copyright © Kendall/Hunt Publishing Company

Doubles, 2s, 3s

3 + 3 = _____

6 + 3 = _____

5 + 5 = _____

3 + 8 = _____

3 + 5 = _____

9 + 9 = _____

6 + 2 = _____

2 + 4 = _____

7 + 3 = _____

6 + 6 = _____

4 + 4 = _____

3 + 4 = _____

2 + 7 = _____

7 + 7 = _____

8 + 2 = _____

8 + 8 = _____

Copyright © Kendall/Hunt Publishing Company

More Addition Facts

5 + 4 = _____   9 + 5 = _____

6 + 7 = _____   4 + 6 = _____

7 + 4 = _____   6 + 8 = _____

8 + 4 = _____   4 + 9 = _____

9 + 6 = _____   7 + 8 = _____

7 + 9 = _____   5 + 6 = _____

5 + 7 = _____   8 + 9 = _____

8 + 5 = _____   9 + 3 = _____

4 + 10 = _____   10 + 9 = _____

Copyright © Kendall/Hunt Publishing Company